ACCESS YOUR ONLINE SUPPORT MATERIAL

I0875882

How to Teach Thinking is accompanied by a number of downloadable resources, designed to ensure this resource best supports your professional needs.

Go to https://resourcecentre.routledge.com/speechmark and click on the cover of this book

Answer the question prompt using your copy of the book to gain access to the online content.

HOW TO TEACH THINKING

How to Teach Thinking develops a range of tools for bringing together two essential components of effective learning: knowledge (what we know) and cognitive skills (how we learn). Mediation is the way in which these cognitive skills can be taught and promoted, ensuring successful learning for everyone and particularly for those with additional learning needs. This book blends theory and practice to embed thinking skills both in everyday classroom practice and for daily life activities.

The book is divided into two parts, the first of which offers an exploration of the conceptual foundations of cognitive skills, including executive functioning and metacognition, which can be applied to a range of problem-solving activities. The second part develops the infusion model of teaching, an inclusive approach which incorporates thinking skills within the day-to-day curriculum. A user-friendly framework is set out with step-by-step guidance for mediating cognitive thinking skills, together with a wealth of resources and strategies to support the process, including practical scripts.

With case examples to bring theory to life, *How to Teach Thinking* is an essential resource for Special Educational Needs Coordinators, teaching assistants, mainstream and specialist teachers, and educational psychologists, to enhance their practice. It will also be of use to speech and language therapists to incorporate a cognitive approach to enrich the development of reasoning skills.

Ruth M. Deutsch is a chartered educational psychologist. She consults to organisations and schools, also teaching on doctoral programmes for educational psychologists and on continuing professional development courses internationally. Ruth is the author of research articles and of the Cognitive Abilities Profile. She works with learners of all ages, specialising in cognitive assessment and development.

Jane Yeomans is an independent educational psychologist. She is an accredited practitioner for Feuerstein's Learning Propensity Assessment Device, Instrumental Enrichment and for the Bright Start programme. Jane has taught and tutored on doctoral programmes for educational psychologists. She has authored many papers for peer-reviewed journals and is the co-author of three books about aspects of educational psychology.

HOW TO TEACH THINKING

A Practitioner's Guide to Metacognition, Executive Function and Mediated Learning

Ruth M. Deutsch and Jane Yeomans

Routledge
Taylor & Francis Group
LONDON AND NEW YORK

Designed cover image: © Getty Images

First published 2027
by Routledge
4 Park Square, Milton Park, Abingdon, Oxon OX14 4RN

and by Routledge
605 Third Avenue, New York, NY 10158

Routledge is an imprint of the Taylor & Francis Group, an informa business

British Library Cataloguing-in-Publication Data
A catalogue record for this book is available from the British Library

ISBN: 9781041104988 (hbk)
ISBN: 9781041104896 (pbk)
ISBN: 9781003655329 (ebk)

DOI: 10.4324/9781003655329

Typeset in Interstate
by Deanta Global Publishing Services, Chennai, India

Access the Support Material: https://resourcecentre.routledge.com/speechmark

Contents

Acknowledgements

This book is more than just the collaborative effort of the authors. The case examples and other material draw on our many years of working with children and young people and on our work as trainers. We are indebted to numerous individuals and organisations with whom we have worked over the years.

We would like to acknowledge specific guidance and support from the following individuals:

Professor Alex Kozulin for clarification of concepts related to Feuerstein's work.

Catherine Hart for her lovely illustrations of mediation criteria, the Boat of Cognition and the House of Metacognition and the artwork for diagrams in Figures 1.1, 3.3 and 5.3. Also others noted in the text who have graciously allowed us to use their designs.

Debbie Smith for sharing her Games Matrix.

Clare Ashworth, commissioning editor, and Molly Kavanagh, editorial assistant at Routledge, for their support and feedback, together with their patience in dealing with our twentieth-century technical skills.

Finally, our heartfelt thanks goes out to our families, who have been a constant source of encouragement, coping patiently with the amount of time we have spent in joint discussions and in front of a computer screen.

Introduction

Our journey begins with us thinking about thinking, which is one of our fundamental human capacities. What is it that we want to reflect on and why?

There are many words that come to mind when defining thinking. A term that we will use to describe thinking is cognitive skills. In this book, we are going to analyse the cognitive skills used in the act of thinking and especially in the process of conscious thinking. We will discover, when we turn briefly to the history of investigations into these concepts, that in analysing thinking as a complex combination of cognitive processes, there is no universal agreement on what these components of thinking are, despite the fact that thinking itself is universal.

Thinking is done by everyone, so why do we, as psychologists, teachers, therapists and others, need to analyse and know more? One of the recurring concepts we want to address is how we human beings move, and need to move, from unconscious use of our faculties to conscious control. Together we will proceed step by step to explore *cognitive skills, executive function* and *metacognition*. These terms form major themes in this book and will be explored systematically in the chapters that follow.

One commonly held idea that we would like to set aside from the start is that there is a distinct category of people, whether children or adults, who should carry the label of Special Educational Needs and that this 'different' group are the ones on whom we focus as needing specialist interventions. We want to develop a more flexible and inclusive approach that applies to all of us. We all move up and down on the continuum of learning and growth at different times and in different places throughout our lives. Support and guidance are relevant to us all. As we delve into these topics, our perspective is that this is about all learners, whether mainstream typical neurodiverse, or those who have been placed in specialist environments because of a requirement for differentiation at a level or type which may not be easily deliverable in a mainstream setting. Therefore, this book addresses itself to all of us, educators in the broadest sense.

DOI: 10.4324/9781003655329-1

How objective are our views and actions?

As we explore these issues, can we say with confidence that our discussions are determined by objective criteria and that evidence-based actions will always follow?

The first step is to recognise, each and every one of us, that in claiming to be objective, we are deluding ourselves. Our basic positions derive from our beliefs and values. We do not use science and research to determine our actions or our judgements although we think we do. Quite the opposite (Kahneman, 2011). We selectively choose the evidence we want to notice and reject what we do not want to take note of to fit with our pre-existing beliefs. We can deconstruct our confidence in the soundness of our judgements even more by pointing to the far too many pieces of 'scientific' research which have been shown to contain misleading and even downright false information and statistics. If we can recognise this and not mislead ourselves or others that we follow science and research objectively, we may find ourselves in a more honest place, more reflective, more questioning, more humble and more willing to be open to change our minds.

Teaching thinking skills: revisiting an old debate

In the past, learning information and remembering it was critical. There was a great deal of emphasis on rote learning and testing memory. However, in a time of rapid technological change, such static information is simply not enough. It is interesting to reflect on how much of what we are teaching now will be obsolete ten years from now, or perhaps even five years. Therefore, our goal in education has to change in emphasis, which is to prepare learners for tomorrow's world, to teach them the skills for problem-solving and adaptation in a rapidly changing world. Content teaching is important; however, cognitive and metacognitive skills, flexibility and analytical thinking are equally, and possibly even more, important. This does not mean that facts and information are irrelevant, it means they are not enough! We need to teach the thinking and adaptive skills to be equipped for the future. We need to teach for adaptation and change. Therefore, from teaching the tools of a trade, we need to teach the tools of metacognition and flexible thinking.

From the 1980s onwards, as educators were becoming increasingly aware of the possibility of teaching processes of thinking in a way that had previously not been considered possible, a number of specific programmes were developed to create systematic structures towards these goals. Programmes such as Feuerstein's Instrumental Enrichment (Feuerstein et al., 1980; 2006), Somerset Thinking Skills (Blagg et al., 1988), Top Ten Thinking Tactics (Lake and Needham, 1997) and Habits of Mind (Costa and Kallick, 2000) were developed. Two examples aimed at young children were Tools of the Mind (Leong et al., 2024), a Vygotskyan-based programme which was developed for preschool settings; and the Bright Start Cognitive Curriculum for Young Children (Haywood et al., 2022), a cognitive developmental programme based on a combination of Piaget's, Vygotsky's and Feuerstein's concepts.

Many of these programmes have become available in translation. They were designed to be delivered as stand-alones; that is, they were delivered separately with individuals and small groups of learners outside of and in addition to the usual curriculum, which leads us to one important consideration for the model of support which will be introduced in this text. Approaches to support are examined in the next section, which will then lead to an outline of the purpose and structure of this book.

Skills programmes versus infusion approach

There have been discussions over many years about whether thinking skills apply to all domains of the school curriculum (domain-general) or whether they are specific to school subjects (domain-specific). If the thinking skills are general, it is important to consider whether they are best taught via discrete programmes or are fused into subject areas (Hamers et al., 1996). This discussion has resulted in two approaches, as noted by Maclure and Davies (1991):

- A general approach with separate courses for teaching thinking
- A specific approach with integrated courses, which means that the thinking skills are embedded in the school subjects.

In the first approach the basic assumption is that thinking skills can be taught explicitly and independently of the regular school curriculum. In this view, there are certain more or less universal thinking skills that can be generalised into school subjects. A prerequisite for the occurrence of a positive effect on, for instance, reading, writing and mathematics, is that, during the training, a 'bridge' is built between the thinking skills and the curriculum subjects. These general thinking skills are mostly trained with 'content poor' tasks.

The second approach assumes that thinking skills can best be taught embedded within school subjects (the 'infusion' or 'within-the-curriculum' approach). Thinking skills are being taught in specific or 'content-rich' domains such as reading, writing and science.

The comparison and impact of these two approaches has been widely researched and outcomes measured to examine changes in the learner's cognitive skills and academic achievements. Research varied, results varied and meta-analytical studies were equivocal. What worked, if, when and why and how impact was measured, is not something we will go into detail here. However, it would be mistaken to think that what emerged was a stark choice, in or out of the classroom or in or out of the curriculum; that is within subject teaching, or as a separate, stand-alone programme.

Fleetham (2003) outlines four approaches for bringing thinking skills to the classroom:

- *As a separate subject*. These are series of discrete activities which can be applied later in other curriculum areas. Examples in the UK included Top Ten Thinking Tactics (Lake and Needham, 1997) and Six Thinking Hats (de Bono, 1985);

- *As a series of skills for a specific subject.* An example of this approach is CASE, (Cognitive Acceleration in Science Education; Adey et al., 2003), a thinking skills programme designed to increase levels of knowledge and understanding in science;
- *Infused in a specific subject.* For example, Thinking through Geography (Chandler and Leat, 2001) is used to enhance what is already being taught;
- *Infused in all classroom activity.* This is often called the 'Thinking Classroom' approach, where thinking *percolates* through all aspects of the curriculum (Fleetham, 2003).

There are advantages and disadvantages for all of the above. A stand-alone programme will provide a high level of structure but has many organisational challenges where the curriculum is organised and delivered via subjects (as is the case with the National Curriculum in England and Wales). Infusion and subject-specific approaches risk being too specific and thus transfer to other contexts might not take place. The idea of percolation (the term used above by Fleetham), is not wrong, but it cannot be relied on. Often, perhaps very often, learning to become a good thinker, as separate from learning facts and information, just does not happen that way and we have learned that percolation (if you remember old coffee percolators which dripped the coffee into a jug) drip, drip, is not enough. Hoping that children will learn by osmosis is not sufficiently structured, direct or consistent and is simply not enough for many learners.

After more than 30 years of ongoing practice and research, the following has been confirmed in many settings:

- Infusing support through the curriculum was found to be more effective for most mainstream pupils;
- Low ability pupils benefited more from more intensive and systematic delivery through specific thinking skills programmes (Feuerstein et al., 2006).

For most mainstream learners, within subject and within curricula, teachers *trained in mediation and metacognitive teaching can be very effective* (Education Endowment Foundation, 2025). For learners with additional learning needs, there is a place for a systematic focused programme for 'learning how to learn'. This can be for individuals or small groups. There is a continuum: the more 'mainstream' the learner and the older they become, the more they benefit from within-subject metacognitive teaching. The more a learner has additional learning needs, the more they benefit from a so-called stand-alone structured developmental cognitive programme. Indeed, Feuerstein, one of the pioneers of teaching thinking (of whom more will be written in Chapter 2) had this target group in mind when developing Instrumental Enrichment (IE). Its goal was remediation of cognitive 'deficiencies', irrespective of the source or cause of these difficulties. IE is described as culture-free; however, nothing can be completely culture-free. Perhaps it would be more accurate to say that this and similar programmes are not designed for immersion in specific content or curricula, but can and should be actively linked to all relevant areas of the learner's experience.

Metacognition is a particular focus, reflected in the title of this book, because we have seen increasing use of this term in education, often in the context of promoting metacognitive approaches, or via use of terminology such as metacognitive teaching. However, when these various terms are unpicked, it is rarely clear what they might look like in practice. One of the drivers for writing this text was a deep sense of frustration that there is a great deal of rhetoric about metacognition which rarely moves beyond principles or very vague 'approaches'. We would argue that the reason for this is that many metacognitive approaches do not actually state clearly what thinking skills learners are expected to be aware of, use and evaluate. One of our important methods to support metacognition will be an exploration of *mediated learning*, which is how we deliberately facilitate the development of the skills of learning and thinking in others. This process starts by identifying the cognitive skills that the learner needs. Thus, mediated learning provides the missing link that moves metacognition from rhetoric to practice.

There are reasons why discussions about how to deliver thinking skills and metacognition were ongoing over many years. One is because such 'stand-alone' programmes did not fit easily in to the structure and time constraints of a National Curriculum, which was to be delivered and assessed mainly for acquisition of subject knowledge. Furthermore, it took time and training and cost, outside of one's regular duties, to learn how to use these materials effectively, not as worksheets, but as tools for the development of cognitive skills. These issues lead to considerations of whether the outcomes justify the investment in time and training, particularly in relation to taking time out of the learner's weekly timetable to have these additional sessions.

Ashman and Conway (1997) were amongst researchers who sought to compare the impact of individual versus classroom impact of metacognitive teaching. One of the consistently observed results of such training is that the first people to change are the teachers themselves. Training helps teachers become explicitly aware of their own thinking processes, that is, metacognitively aware of themselves and thus in a much better position to reflect and apply these insights for their pupils. This finding was echoed by the Education Endowment Foundation (EEF) over 20 years later. One of the first points made in the EEF publication (2025) is the need for teachers to be trained in mediation and metacognition.

Both of the present authors undertook extensive training and practice in Dynamic Assessment and Instrumental Enrichment and to say that it impacted us profoundly in our knowledge, awareness and professional practice is no exaggeration. However, we recognise that extensive training might not be readily available due to a range of factors, such as time, cost or requirements emanating from national and local legislation or policy, professional development priorities and development priorities for the organisation. One of the drivers for producing this text was to distil our many years of experience working in cognitive education in a way that provides a comprehensive guide for supporting implementation of thinking skills. The purpose is to fill gaps arising as a result of limited, or absence of, in-depth training, or of circumstances that challenge access to such training and its implementation. The final section of this introductory chapter outlines our rationale and the overall structure of this book.

Rationale

Our goal is for learners to be metacognitively aware. By this we mean learners who are independently able to:

- Select and use appropriate cognitive skills for the task or problem;
- Evaluate their thinking and adjust if needed;
- Apply their cognitive skills in a wide range of contexts beyond the immediate task/problem and the learning environment.

The discussion above about how to support and promote thinking skills does not offer any neat conclusions about the best way to do so. Whilst we reject reliance on percolation, there are arguments for and against infusion or stand-alone approaches. In this text we intend to emphasise an *embedded* approach that uses mediated learning to teach and support cognitive skills (thinking skills) in the context of the curriculum being delivered. It will provide methods for in-depth analysis and proactive, deliberately mediated metacognitive teaching. We will share both concepts and strategies of mediated learning and metacognitive teaching for practical immersion within schools and classrooms. This reflects the Education Endowment Foundation guidance (EEF, 2025), which emphasises sharing good practice across educational systems, rather than focusing on individual cognitive intervention.

Since thinking skills do not happen automatically, we cannot assume that these metacognitive skills will simply develop over time in learners. Our embedded approach uses the taught curriculum as the context for teaching thinking and uses structured, mediated learning in order to ensure that cognitive skills are used and applied widely, not just used in a specific context. In other words, our embedded approach aims to bring about *meaningful cognitive change*. In this book, we do not elaborate specific thinking skills programmes. We focus on an embedded model for one very practical reason: so that you can reach most learners, most of the time. We hope that this book will help you in your learning journey, because as you gain insights and strategies, you will carefully and sensitively share them with others.

In developing and writing this text, we considered how best to effect change in order to deliver support for thinking skills and to make the role of the processes of learning (rather than the products, or subjects) more prominent. We recognise that this can be challenging in an education system that is largely based on a subject-based model and where the curriculum is driven by standards and grades, whether these are related to the individual (such as national examinations, UK SATs or GCSEs) or the institution (such as inspection of standards and grading, for example, OFSTED in the UK). Consequently, we would argue that a high level of systemic change is needed in order to place more emphasis on the processes of learning. We would agree that this level of change is needed in order for cognitive thinking skills to be much more prominent, especially in a system that is largely subject-based. Whilst this level of change might be desirable, it is not our intention to address wholescale systems change or to suggest strategies and approaches that require substantial curriculum changes. In our experience, these kinds of changes are rarely implemented consistently or with any longevity because they are perceived as incompatible with the curriculum that is delivered. We are aware that this leaves us open to accusations of collusion with a flawed system. Our defence is that *some* change is better than *no* change. This pragmatic view led to our focus on an embedded approach.

Structure

This book is aimed at a broad readership: educational psychologists (including those in training), Special Educational Needs and Disabilities Coordinators (SENDCos), speech and language and other therapists, class teachers and specialist teachers. The material in this book can be used by practitioners working in educational settings and by practitioners who work as external consultants. Whatever your role or phase of education, this book will support your learning journey by using the following two-part structure:

- Part I, comprising three chapters, lays the theoretical foundations. It will explore theories of intelligence and cognition, examining static and flexible models and will include material about executive function and metacognition. We will argue for a flexible approach in preference to a static approach, because the former implies the possibility of cognitive change, whereas the latter does not. The final chapter in Part I introduces the tripartite learning partnership of the learner, task and mediator as the framework for the focus on practical applications of a flexible model of cognition.
- Part II, comprising five chapters, builds on Part I's theoretical foundations. It introduces a six-step mediation process that gives a structure for practical applications, and which is related to the content of the chapters. Chapters 4, 5 and 6 explore each of the three components of the tripartite partnership in detail, including worked examples. Chapter 7 looks specifically at transfer, which is a crucial part of mediated learning and metacognition, hence the decision to devote a separate chapter to this topic. Finally, Chapter 8 suggests a number of ways to draw together the various threads of mediated learning and metacognitive teaching covered in the previous chapters. It offers guidance for written and verbal feedback, consultation, and how to use lesson plans for whole class, individual and small group teaching in order to deliver the embedded model.

Your learning journey is also supported by a range of downloadable resources. These can be accessed via the Resource Centre.

We hope that our approach comprising a number of useful and flexible components really 'speaks to you'. Whether you work in the classroom, whether you are a therapist or psychologist, the content of this book will add to your range of choices and deepen your understanding and practice. At the time of going to press, the UK government published its policy document setting out reforms for the SEND system (Department for Education, 2026). Key issues even at this early discussion and consultation stage would seem to confirm the purpose and relevance of this book in addressing current and future practice.

References

Adey, P. and Shayer, M. (1994). *Really Raising Standards: Cognitive Intervention and Academic Achievement.* London: Routledge.

Adey, P., Shayer, M., & Yates, C. (2003). Thinking science: Professional edition. London: Nelson Thornes

Ashman, A.F. and Conway, N.F. (1997). *An Introduction to Cognitive Education.* London: Routledge.

Blagg, N., Ballinger, M. and Gardner, R. (1988). *Somerset Thinking Skills Course: Handbook.* Oxford: Basil Blackwell.

Chandler, S. and Leat, D. (2001). *Thinking Through Geography.* Cambridge: Chris Kington.

Costa, A. and Kallick, B. (2000). *Habits of Mind.* Alexandria: Association for Supervision and Curriculum Development.

De Bono, E. (1985). *Six Thinking Hats.* London: Penguin Books.

Department for Education (2026). *Every Child Achieving and Thriving.* Available at: www.gov.uk/government/publications/every-child-achieving-and-thriving. Accessed 24 February 2026.

Educational Endowment Foundation (EEF) (2025). *Metacognition and Self Regulated Learning: Guidance Report.* London: EEF.

Feuerstein, R., Rand, Y., Hoffman, M.B. and Miller, R. (1980). *Instrumental Enrichment: An Intervention Program for Cognitive Modifiability.* Baltimore: University Park Press.

Feuerstein, R., Feuerstein, R.S., Falik, L. and Rand, Y. (2006). *The Feuerstein Instrumental Enrichment Programme.* Jerusalem: ICELP Publications.

Fleetham, M. (2003). *How to Create and Develop a Thinking Classroom.* Cambridge: LDA.

Hamers, J.H.M., Van Luit, J.E.H. and Csapo, B. (Eds) (1996). *Teaching and Learning Thinking Skills.* Netherlands: Swetz and Zeitlinger.

Haywood, H.C., Brooks, P. and Burns, S. (2022). *Bright Start Cognitive Curriculum for Young Children,* rev. edn. Bright Start CCYC. Available at: www.brightstart-ccyc.com. Accessed 30 December 2025.

Kahneman, D. (2011). *Thinking, Fast and Slow.* New York: Farrar, Straus and Giroux.

Lake, M. and Needham, M. (1997). *Top Ten Thinking Tactics: A Practical Introduction to the Thinking Skills Revolution.* Birmingham: Imaginative Minds.

Leong, D. and Bodrova, E. (2024). *Tools of the Mind: The Vygotskian Approach to Early Childhood Education,* 3rd edn. New York: Routledge.

Maclure, S. and Davies, P. (1991). *Learning to Think. Thinking to Learn.* Leeds: Emerald Publishing.

Part I

Theoretical Foundations

1

What Is Thinking?

Introduction

A mantra we often use and teach when working with children and young people is '*description before analysis*'. For us to develop our conscious awareness and our skills we need to start with defining and then analysing the act of thinking so that we can select different methods and different levels of intervention to support the learning of others. The more we analyse, the more we become consciously aware and the more we can deliberately choose and refine our interventions to bring about the goals we want to achieve. You will decide the level of need, the quality and quantity of input, and how to deliver your knowledge and skills to match the needs of others, whether individuals or groups. We hope to share methods and strategies to achieve these goals. As we do so, we experience what has been shown in research many times, that the first people to change are ourselves. *Change* will be a major theme of our work as one of the main purposes of our interventions is to help people change.

We can describe thinking as a complex set of cognitive processes involving the manipulation of information through mental representation, reasoning, problem-solving and decision-making, leading to new ideas, judgements and actions. This highlights the active, process-oriented nature of thinking. It is a basis for analysing the complex interactions between different cognitive processes. It connects thinking to practical outcomes. Taking in information, problem-solving, weighing up alternatives, choosing, making decisions, are the business of all of us, whether at home, at school or at work.

Theory is not truth. Theories change over time. Although we often act as if what we understand to be true is *the* truth, we need to honestly examine our beliefs and not accept them as axiomatic. We need to recognise the extent to which our beliefs shape the way we interpret what we are doing in our role of working with others. This applies in all contexts, whether in formal learning or in our day-to-day environment.

Recognising that we are deeply products of the time and the culture (the zeitgeist) we live in, we see how major theorists inevitably reflect their era, their cultures and their communities. We can only do our best, indeed we must do our best, with what we know at a particular time, but always be open to new learning and the recognition that we may not be 'right'. For

DOI: 10.4324/9781003655329-3

millennia, the deeply held belief that the earth was flat was regarded as a central article of faith in some religions and those who dared argue otherwise were accused of heresy. Centuries of believing that disease was caused by the four humours determined 'medical' procedures until those theories were thrown out by discoveries made possible by the invention of the microscope. Psychology and education are no different.

Answering the question 'What is thinking?' leads us to pose more questions: What are these multiple processes and how do they develop? Should we, indeed, can we, help develop them in others? We can ask, as has been asked by many theorists, whether thinking is something that just happens in a timely fashion driven by our maturational biological systems, or whether it is facilitated by others and thus can be actively developed. If internally driven, then what is the role of the teacher? Is it to provide information and expose us to ideas and activities and the rest is managed by the child's own developmental clock? Are there differing perspectives on how our intelligence and thinking develops? The next section is our starting point: intelligence and cognition.

Intelligence and cognition

Intelligence and cognition are two terms that are frequently used in the context of discussions and debates about thinking. In order to address some of the questions posed in the Introduction and begin to 'unpick' cognition and intelligence, we will briefly visit some theories which involve sometimes complementary and sometimes opposing positions taken by different theoreticians over time, leading to the present, because prevailing concepts and beliefs drive our practice to a much greater extent than we often realise or acknowledge.

Intelligence: a little history

In the nineteenth century, the beginnings of psychology as its own discipline drew upon the kind of experimental work that was being undertaken in other branches of science, such as physics and chemistry. Psychology seemed to be trying to achieve a respectable place of its own next to its much more developed scientific siblings. Developments from the late nineteenth century onwards are where the waters of cognition and intelligence begin to be muddied. Francis Galton was a key figure in this early scientific movement, particularly in relation to ideas about intelligence. His view was that intelligence is inherited and that some individuals were genetically more likely to have higher intelligence than others. This, then, was the basis for the eugenics movement, which believed that it is acceptable to manipulate human reproduction in order to produce superior beings. This movement led to actions in the twentieth century such as forced sterilisation and was part of the belief system of National Socialism, particularly the Nazis, who believed that there should be a pure-bred Aryan race.

Galton's work was the 'touch paper' that lit investigations into the nature and measurement of intelligence from the late nineteenth century onwards. Table 1.1 gives a brief summary of

Table 1.1 Timeline of the development of intelligence concepts and testing

When?	***Who and where?***	***What?***
1883	Francis Galton, UK	*Inquiries into Human Faculty and its Development.* Founder of eugenics movement, used the term in the above publication.
1904	Charles Spearman, UK	The concept of '*g*': general intelligence. Founded the London School whose members included Cyril Burt, Raymond Cattell and Hans Eysenck. Member of the Eugenics Society. Due to his connections with this movement the British Psychological Society withdrew the Spearman Medal (awarded in his memory) in 2021.
1905	Alfred Binet and Theodore Simon, France	Developed the first intelligence test at the request of the French government first for recruiting to the army and later in order to identify pupils who could not be included in regular classrooms. Influenced by Galton but no specific eugenics connections.
1912	Wiliam Stern, Germany/USA	Introduced the concept of IQ and suggested a formula.
1916	Lewis Terman, USA.	Adapted the Binet-Simon test for use in the United States: the Stanford Binet. He also adapted Stern's IQ formula. Supporter of eugenics and forced sterilisation.
1917	Robert Yerkes, USA	Developed the Army Alpha and Beta tests, using the Stanford Binet as a starting point. Supporter of eugenics.
1920s	Louis Thurstone, USA	Suggested multiple abilities: the PMA (Primary Mental Abilities) model. No known links to eugenics.
1931	Cyril Burt, UK	Met Galton; the Galton and Burt families were acquainted. Studied under Spearman. Took over Spearman's chair at University College London in 1931. Member of the Eugenics Society.
1939	David Wechsler, USA	Administered the Alpha and Beta tests. Studied with Spearman in the UK. Adapted the Alpha and Beta tests to introduce his IQ test for adults (the Wechsler-Bellevue Test). A scale for children was first introduced in 1949 and for young children in 1981. Further updates and developments led to three current instruments: • Wechsler Pre School and Primary Scale of Intelligence (WPPSI, 2012) • Wechsler Intelligence Scale for Children (WISC-V, 2014) • Wechsler Adult Intelligence Scale (WAIS, 2024) Later versions of the above reflect elements of the Cattell-Horn-Carroll (CHC) model (see below). No known eugenics links.

(Continued)

Table 1.1 (Continued)

When?	***Who and where?***	***What?***
1943	Raymond Cattell, UK/USA	Suggested crystallised (*gc*) and fluid intelligence (*gf*). Supporter of eugenics. In 1997 the American Psychological Association withdrew their selection of Cattell to receive a Gold Medal Award for Life Achievement due to his links to eugenics and fascism.
1960s and 1970s	John Horn, USA	A student of Cattell. Proposed multiple abilities in addition to *gf* and *gc*. Horn's work led to the development of the Cattell-Horn model of intelligence. No known eugenics links; was involved in civil liberties movement.
1960s onwards	John Carroll, USA	Studied with Thurstone. *Human Cognitive Abilities* published in 1993. Suggested multiple abilities arranged in a three stratum model. Carroll's work led to the development of the CHC (Cattell-Horn-Carroll) model of intelligence, which is the basis for many current IQ tests. No known eugenics links.

the way in which ideas about intelligence and how it should be measured developed, including links to the eugenics movement. A more detailed overview is given by Yeomans (2025).

Issues arising from a fixed, heritable view

The testing movement summarised in Table 1.1, which drew on such early efforts at constructing intelligence tests and measurement procedures, developed rapidly and dominated the emerging profession of psychology and especially educational psychology for much of the twentieth century. According to this majority approach, although there were minority voices (Dearborn, 1921), if one could define the components of intelligence, these could be formally tested and the scores gained on such tests would describe a person's level of intelligence not only at the time of testing, but would enable prediction of future achievements: what you can and cannot do now determines what you will be able to do going forward. Such a view was possible because of a fundamental belief (notice our deliberate use of the word *belief* here) that intelligence is genetically determined and fixed. Therefore, if tasks could be developed that reflect what is considered to represent intelligence, then the use of such tests will capture not only current status but will also predict future skills and deficits. The idea of *change* in this view of intelligence and its determinants is a meaningless notion, unless you mean changing the amount of information or knowledge a person acquires over time. Gains in acquiring information can be tested and scored by using age-related norms which reflect expectations of performance as the learner's age increases. Of course, we continuously test throughout the education years. We rate and increase expectations of the increase of knowledge over time. We call it summative testing. It is expected that you will learn more information, facts and content knowledge, but your basic intelligence, according to this view, will not change.

Since it seemed obvious that one acquires different skills and knowledge at different ages, measurement of such scores was normed to different ages. In order to compare one child with another based on age, all tests must be administered in a standardised way, otherwise comparison with others, for example, same age peers, would be unreliable. Such measurement and normed comparison, as carried out with intelligence tests, resulted in the score called the individual's intelligence quotient (IQ).

Intelligence and culture

A concept which was not considered important to factor in was the notion of how intelligence manifests differently in different cultures. If one believes that the development of intelligence is largely determined by genetic, DNA and other inherited factors, then the environment around the individual is largely irrelevant. In other words, measurement of intelligence was based on the view that it is a within-child process. Tests are then held up to scrutiny for their validity in eliciting what they purport to test, and for their reliability, in the sense that if you cannot change over time, then aside from allowing for small margins of error, we should obtain more or less the same test results repeatedly.

Manifest intelligence being influenced and shaped by cultural factors and environmental differences was considered at best peripheral and mostly ignored. The expert in the white coat sat with the child, tested, scored and produced a report, and these numbers became a statement of unalterable facts. This might feel like exaggerated polemic; however, the assertion in this paragraph was reflected in educational policies, discussed in the next section.

Impact of fixed intelligence views on educational policy

Educational policy demonstrated this view, certainly in the UK, as determined by the 11+ examinations that dominated the UK education system for many years, based on the idea that testing everyone enabled separating the 'sheep from the goats'. If intelligent, invest in their education. If an individual scored below average or worse, it would be a waste of time and national resources to give them a higher level of education, as the individual was not considered capable of change and therefore unlikely to contribute to the economic wealth of the country. Therefore, a core purpose of such IQ type tests was to label and classify. Test, classify and adjust teaching to the scored level of the learner. Unsurprisingly the system was mostly self-fulfilling.

At a societal level, it confirmed in the minds of those who searched for such proof, that different classes in society or races were more or less intelligent based on their members' scores on standardised intelligence tests (Herrnstein and Murray, 1994). Even worse, a 'pure' society needed to be purged of these inferior beings, or at least, stop them reproducing (Gould, 1981). Psychology in the service of racism.

This type of intelligence testing was adopted as one of the core, indeed 'protected', tasks for the emerging profession of educational psychology (Farrell and Woods, 2007). That is not to say that measurement was not used in other areas of psychology, but for now we are focusing on widely held beliefs in the world of educational psychology about children's learning and development.

An example from one of the present authors' casework helps to illustrate some of the issues related to culture and static testing.

Hafsa, aged nine, arrived for an assessment session. Whilst we were working together, I noticed that she was shivering. When I looked closer, I saw that drops of water were dripping from under her hijab on to her shoulders. I stopped and asked her why her hair was wet. She explained that they had just had swimming and she could not dry her hair in front of the boys for reasons of modesty. She emerged from the swimming lesson wet, dripping and shivering. How could she possibly learn? 'Hafsa', I said, 'I am going to turn around and close my eyes. You take off your hijab, dry your hair until you feel comfortable and then when you tell me, "I'm ready" I will turn around again.'

Due to her culture, Hafsa could not dry her hair at that time. She therefore came to the assessment session in a state which was not conducive to learning and had this not been spotted and dealt with, the assessment results might have been affected by her discomfort and thus give a false picture of her cognition.

The above is a rapid and certainly over-simplistic view of standardised intelligence testing. The reason for presenting these ideas, knowing full well that what we have written above is neither nuanced nor balanced, is to make us think and challenge. Our purpose is not to dismiss and discard some of the important work in the field of standardised test batteries, but to constructively challenge the assumptions of these tests in order to select and use our professional tools in valid and appropriate ways to better understand our client's needs.

This historical reality in no way diminishes important work on factor analysis, including work by Spearman (1904), Thurstone (1947) and Cattell (1978), together with creative development of different activities and tasks designed to be valid representations of relevant aspects of what are considered factors of intelligence. In fact, one of the positions held by us as authors, alongside what we have just written, is that we are not trying to ask professionals to abandon such standardised tests as a matter of principle, nor to set up an either/or choice between such tests and other approaches to testing, which we regard as a false dichotomy. Our goal here is not to reject and dismiss, but rather to ask ourselves to be critical, to challenge, not to passively accept without questioning; not to use tools of the trade just because they are available on the market, look attractive and are easy to administer! As a way of addressing some of the issues related to the type of measurement instruments that are used, we will present material about blended assessment in Chapter

4, where we look at how to draw up a cognitive profile of a learner. This reflects that we can pose questions and try to answer them, using a combination of relevant resources to create a rich blended profile of the individual's needs as a basis for targeted intervention.

Cognition

The intensity of debates about intelligence and how to measure it has deflected attention from looking at cognition. Cognitive psychology is a specific discipline in psychology. This term was only used from the 1960s and was coined by Ulric Neisser (1967).

The idea of cognition relates to mental processes. There is no one definitive list of cognitive processes; however, the following are common areas in the range of definitions that have been proposed:

- Attention;
- Perception;
- Memory;
- Reasoning and problem-solving.

There is a lack of differentiation between cognition and intelligence. This might stem from the fact that cognition was considered the product of one's intelligence. As shown in Table 1.2, Haywood et al. (2022) distinguish between these two concepts, emphasising that intelligence can be seen as the biological substrata and is largely formed by genetic and DNA components. In this way, it is not easy to change. Cognition, on the other hand, is viewed as how we develop, use and manifest our skills, and this part of us is open to change, learning and modification. In considering recent analysis of DNA in animals and humans, it has been repeatedly shown that DNA accounts for little more than half of who we are, 40 to 60 per cent (Deary et al., 2022). In Haywood's words, there is a large percentage of us that is not pre-determined and is open to change.

Intelligence is strongly influenced by the environment. During a child's development, factors that contribute to intelligence include their home environment and parenting, education

Table 1.2 Comparison of intelligence and cognitive processes (adapted from Haywood et al., 2022)

Dimension	***Intelligence***	***Cognition***
Source	Genetic	Learned
Modifiability	Modest	High
Character	Global	Generalisable, specific
Assessment	Achievement	Process
Composition	Intellectual	Mix of aptitudes, native ability, motives, etc.
Parents' role	Genes, nutrition, health, safety	Mediated learning experience: active, directed, teaching

and availability of learning resources, healthcare and nutrition. If a person's level of intelligence is similar to that of their parents, is that similarity due to genetic factors passed down from parent to child, to shared environmental factors, or, more likely, a combination of both? It is clear that both environmental and genetic factors play a part in determining manifest intelligence.

Despite the wide acknowledgement that how we use our intelligence is a combination of nature and nurture, it should surprise us that so many tests of intelligence still focus on the child's performance as within child, internal, fixed and predictive. Genes and DNA are hard to change, but why test and score as if the environment in all aspects is also fixed?

Research indicates that both genetic inheritance and environmental experiences play significant, interwoven roles in determining intelligence. While a substantial portion of individual *differences* in intelligence within a population can be attributed to genetics, different studies varying from 10 per cent to approximately 50 per cent, this highlights the ample scope for environmental factors to influence an individual's cognitive potential (Deary et al., 2022). Table 1.2 compares cognition and intelligence.

Figure 1.1 illustrates the way in which intelligence is a combination of knowledge and cognitive processes, situated in overarching affective, social and cultural contexts.

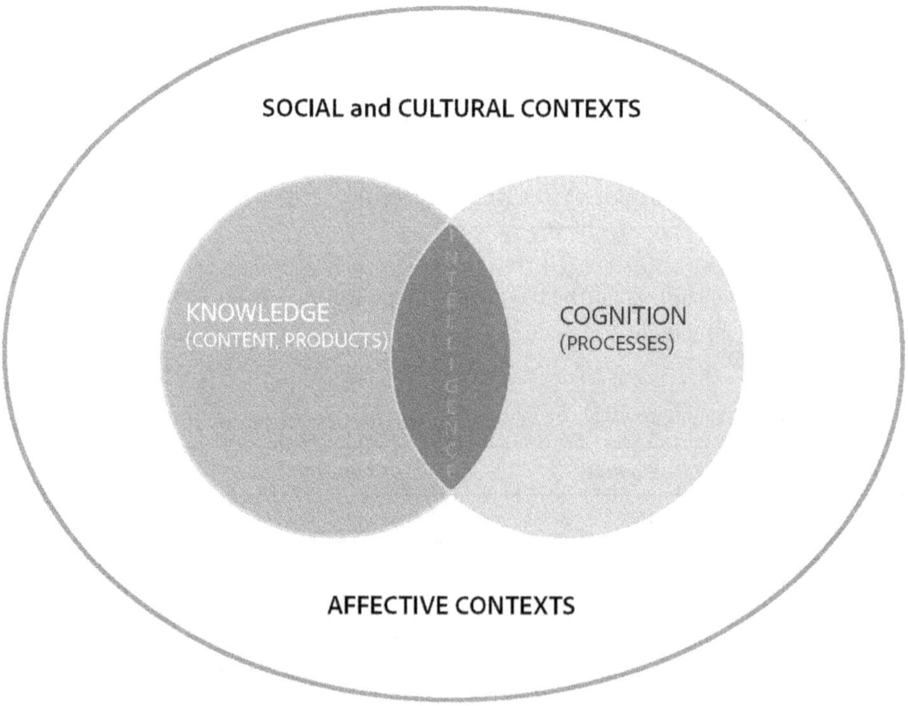

Figure 1.1 Cognition and intelligence

Having differentiated between cognition and intelligence, we will now move on to look at a related area, executive function (EF).

Executive function

EF has come to be an umbrella term used for a diversity of hypothesised cognitive processes, including planning, working memory, attention, inhibition, self-monitoring, self-regulation and initiation, associated with the prefrontal areas of the frontal lobes (see, for example, Goldstein et al., 2014).

What is executive function?

Although the concept of EF was first defined in the 1970s, the idea of a control mechanism was discussed as far back as the 1840s. By the 1950s, psychologists and neuroscientists became more interested in understanding the role of the prefrontal cortex in intelligent behaviour. British psychologist Broadbent (1953) described differences between automatic and controlled processes. This distinction was further elaborated by Schiffrin and Schneider (1977), who introduced the notion of selective attention, which is closely related to EF. In 1975, Posner and Snyder proposed that there is a separate executive branch of the attentional system responsible for focusing attention on selected aspects of the environment. He named this 'cognitive control'. Shallice (1988) also suggested that attention is regulated by a supervisory system which can override automatic responses in favour of scheduling behaviour on the basis of plans or intentions. Consensus slowly emerged that this control system is housed in the most anterior portion of the brain, the prefrontal cortex, which we discuss in more detail in Chapter 2 when describing Luria's concepts of brain structure and functions. Most of the studies on identifying processes of control, self-monitoring and planning were investigated as to their location in the working brain (Luria, 1966; 1973), as planning and inhibitory control were seen to be functions of the prefrontal cortex.

Pribram (1973) was one of the first to use the term 'executive' when discussing matters of prefrontal cortex functioning. Since then, at least 30 or more constructs have been included under the umbrella term, EF, making the concept hard to define. Many authors have made attempts to define the concept of EF using models that range from one to multiple components. Lezak (1995) suggested that EFs consisted of components related to volition, planning, purposeful action and effective performance. It has been hypothesised that each component involves a distinct set of related behaviours. The distinction is made that these levels of thinking are not about acquiring information. Reynolds and Horton (2008) suggested that EFs are distinct from general knowledge. They are not related to the quantity of knowledge that we possess. A person may have a great deal of subject knowledge, but have poor executive functioning and not be aware of their choices and processes.

Reynolds and Horton suggested that EF represents the capacity to plan, to do things and to perform adaptive actions, while general knowledge is related to the retention of an organised set of facts. They further hypothesised that EF involves decision-making, planning actions and generating novel motor outputs adapted to external demands, rather than the passive retention of information. Naglieri and Goldstein (2013) based their view of the behavioural aspects of EF on a large national study of children. They suggest that EF is best represented as a single phenomenon, conceptualised as the efficiency with which individuals go about acquiring knowledge as well as how well problems can be solved across nine areas: *attention, emotion regulation, flexibility, inhibitory control, initiation, organisation, planning, self-monitoring* and *working memory.*

Have we reached a consensus definition?

There is no formal, accepted definition of EF. We typically find general statements of EF, such as goal-directed action, cognitive control, top-down inhibition, effortful processing. Alternatively, a list of constructs is suggested, such as inhibition, working memory, planning, problem-solving, goal-directed activity, strategy development and execution, emotional self-regulation and self-motivation. The activities that require EF are those that involve planning, decision-making, error correction or troubleshooting. EF is required for situations when responses are not well rehearsed or contain novel sequences of actions, or for technically difficult situations and situations that require the overcoming of a strong habitual response or resisting temptation (Goldstein et al., 2014).

A key aspect is the capacity to self-regulate, both intellectually and emotionally. The following box highlights key points about self-regulation that are phrased positively as abilities (Goldstein et al., 2014)

Self-regulation

- The ability to inhibit;
- The ability to delay;
- The ability to separate thought from feeling;
- The ability to consider an experience, change perspective and consider an alternative response;
- The ability to change the response when confronted with new information.

With so many versions and definitions of EF, Goldstein and colleagues undertook a meta-analytic study of these multiple definitions. They found that planning was common to all of them (Goldstein et al., 2014). They asked another question: Executive functions or executive function? They used exploratory factor analyses when using parent (N = 1,400), teacher (N = 1,400) or self-ratings (N = 700), based on behaviours observed and reported for a nationally representative sample (N = 3,500) aged 5-18 years. Their conclusion was that the concept of EF is best defined as a unitary construct: how you do what you do. This is illustrated in Figure 1.2.

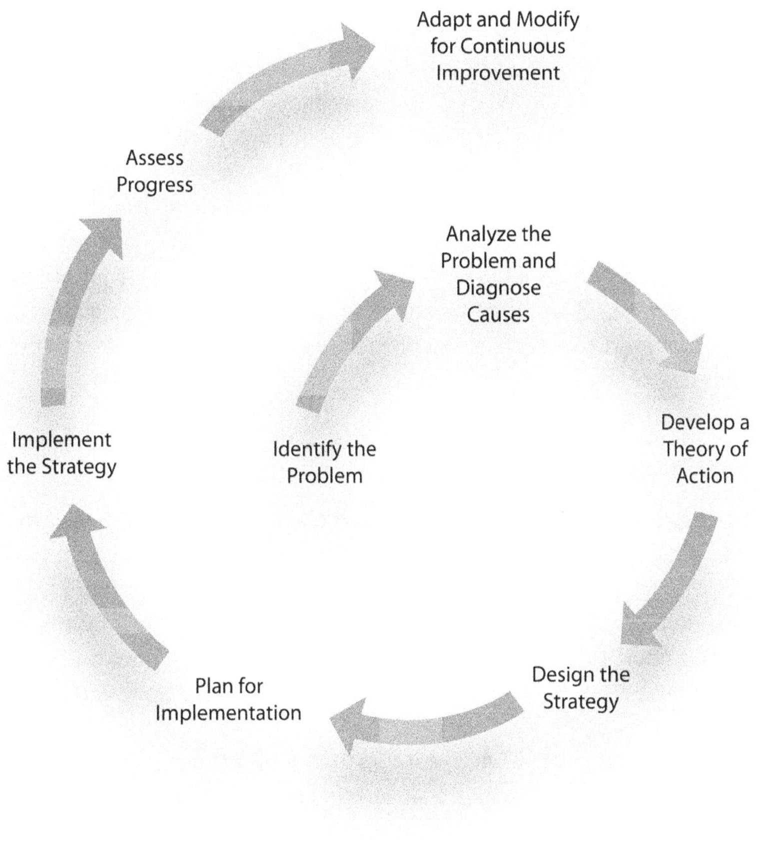

Figure 1.2 Executive function (Naglieri and Goldstein, 2012)

Most of us would say that we have difficulty with one or more aspect of EF and there are many reasons why EF is not easy to develop. Given our understanding that EF involves important control mechanisms leads us to ask whether we can teach EF. We would argue that, just as we can teach cognitive skills, we can also teach the control aspects of our thinking. The embedded approach to explicitly teaching and supporting cognitive skills that underpins this text will also cover aspects of EF that overlap with cognitive skills. Chapter 3 will set out these cognitive skills and EFs, which is then followed by the practical applications in Part II. In this chapter, we now move on to consider one final element of what constitutes thinking: metacognition.

Metacognition: the emperor's new clothes?

In the Hans Christian Andersen folktale, an emperor is conned into believing that he is wearing clothes made from materials that were only invisible to those who were stupid and because no one else wanted to look stupid they colluded with the idea. The notion of metacognition is a little like this. People do not want to appear ignorant or stupid by asking 'What actually is metacognition'? Or 'What does metacognition look like on a day-to-day basis? Is it just something to do with teaching in the classroom?' In fact, many users of the term cannot define it either! One of the present authors experienced this whilst attending a professional development course about mathematics intervention and support. The presenter said something along the lines of 'well of course we know that a metacognitive approach to maths is important', then moved on to talk about other approaches. That sentence was the sum total of what was said about metacognition! This experience - and many others - leads us to suggest that metacognition is one of those terms that everyone uses but which few understand or can define.

Defining metacognition

The term metacognition was first proposed in the 1970s by Flavell (1976), who described it as thinking about and monitoring one's thinking. A quick internet search of the term 'metacognition' is likely to produce the one-line definition of 'thinking about thinking', which is a very reductionist way of describing a complex concept. It is beyond the scope of this chapter, and this book, to critique the very large number of definitions and descriptions. In this book, we will use the Education Endowment Foundation (EEF)'s definition, which states:

> Metacognition is about the ways learners monitor and purposefully direct their learning. For example, having decided that a particular cognitive strategy for memorisation is likely to be successful, a pupil then monitors whether it has indeed been successful and then deliberately changes (or not) their memorisation method based on that evidence. By metacognitive strategies, we mean the strategies we use to monitor or control our cognition, such as checking that our memorisation technique was accurate or selecting the most appropriate cognitive strategy for the task we are undertaking.
> *(EEF, 2025: 8)*

This definition is useful in that it makes a link to cognitive strategies. In order to be 'metacognitive', it is necessary to start with cognitive strategies. However, the EEF does not separate out or define cognitive skills. Chapter 3 does exactly that, via our model of the Boat of Cognition. The learner needs not only to use, but more so, to *know* what cognitive skills they possess and which are required for the particular task in order to engage meaningfully in metacognition. Therefore, knowledge of a range of cognitive thinking skills is the starting point for becoming metacognitively aware. However, metacognitive awareness might not happen by some kind of process of osmosis. The journey from cognition to metacognition is developmental to some extent, but that does not mean that it will necessarily happen, or at a typical age.

Flavell (1976) suggested that metacognition should be developing around mid-primary or elementary school, approximately nine years upwards, and by the age of 11 learners are likely to need support for developing this awareness. Mediated learning is one important way in which that support is given. In the introductory chapter, we defined mediated learning as *how we deliberately facilitate the development of the skills of learning and thinking in others*. Mediation of cognitive thinking skills is the bridge that learners cross to move from cognition to metacognition: 'mediation helps children to learn to think, initially using fundamental and increasingly higher-level thinking' (Feuerstein and Lewin-Benham, 2012: 36). Chapter 3 will give an overview of mediated learning and Chapters 6 and 7 will cover mediated learning in more detail to support readers to use this approach.

Metacognition is a critical set of skills that can make a big difference to performance and motivation. It plays a very significant role in self-regulation, both cognitively and emotionally.

Here are some key words related to metacognition:

- Labelling;
- Creating awareness;
- Deliberate action (first by the mediator and then gradually by the learner);
- Conscious control;
- Choice: changing from being a passive recipient of information and strategies, to an active controller of one's own learning;
- Sense of mastery: I am the conductor of my own cognitive orchestra.

Metacognition: use and awareness

An important distinction can be made between a learner's *use* of metacognitive strategies and their *awareness* that this is what they are doing. We have often noticed in interactive assessment of learners that they use metacognitive strategies, but they do not know they are doing so. This is evident when we see and discuss how they solved a problem. However, because they are acting spontaneously, rather than deliberately, the conscious control is not there. It is still a 'hit or miss' way of working. It leaves the learner unsure how or why they solved a problem, even if successful. It has been quite a frequent experience in our work, that when we make the learner consciously aware of what they are doing, we label the strategy, we point it out, we have seen a lightbulb reaction: 'So that's what I have been doing and it worked!' Their subsequent performance jumps and so does their confidence.

Here we want to mention something that may seem obvious, but it was not always so. Why was it in the long history of studying thinking and learning, that the term metacognition was only used to describe these processes as late as the 1970s? We want to suggest that perhaps its identification relates to changes in the understanding of thinking. Why identify, why differentiate, if it is assumed that you either have these skills or you do not? If this type of 'higher' thinking is associated with people of greater intelligence, then so be it, summed up by the phrase, 'you've got it or you haven't'.

The change (we hope!) is the growing recognition that it does not have to be this way. That intelligent action (that is, cognitive and metacognitive skills) can be taught, and if they can be taught, perhaps there is a job that we need to do.

If this approach benefits everyone, it is not difficult to see how much more powerful it can be for those who experience some kind of learning disadvantage and do not readily achieve this type of thinking, for any number of reasons. Therefore, we need and can mediate metacognitive skills to less able learners. However, metacognition has implications for gifted learners too, which is explored in the next section.

Metacognition and the gifted learner

We come across children who seem to be gifted 'naturally' from early on. They grasp things rapidly, they retain and reuse information, they find learning easy and quite effortless. They may be very creative. We might assume that such children do not need our mediation. They certainly don't ask for it. They are often self-sufficient and, when they arrive in school, they may find it hard to work with peers and groups. They are fast and efficient and often feel impatient and frustrated by others. They prefer to work alone.

We also sometimes come across what we call the 'gifted underachiever', defined as a learner who is expected to achieve a lot better according to their innate or previously demonstrated abilities, but who fails to live up to expectations. This leads us to question how might we understand such a learner and how this relates to our selected interventions, and core methodology which is mediated learning experience, a central topic in this book. Tannenbaum (1991) explores this puzzling situation from the perspective of mediated learning experience theories, because mediation is viewed as an essential quality of interaction for the developing child. Let us take a closer look at what happens in the dance duet of the mediator and the child.

We imagine that we are the ones who initiate our mediation with the child, whether spontaneously or consciously. We are the givers; they are the receivers. However, this is not necessarily so. From early in life the healthy infant provokes mediation from us. They act; we react. We act; they react. We understand the importance of deliberate mediation for the child who, due to some developmental challenges, does not invite or provoke us to dance with them: see Mintzker's (1991) thought-provoking article, 'When the baby does not smile back'. The key message is to bring the world to the child as early as possible, if this child cannot reach out to the world around them.

Paradoxically, the same can be the case with a gifted child, because they do not need us! They do not reach out to us for mediation. They learn well and rapidly alone. However, there is a risk, because this is the child who has never consciously had to learn how to learn, how to correct errors and how to deal with lack of instant success. If they come across a task or a problem that they cannot do immediately they may easily give up, because they are used to being good at everything and not used to struggling or experiencing frustration. They may experience a great sense of failure. Ironically, this able child may not have a growth mindset. They see themselves as just doing things correctly. This does not imply that they are arrogant, it is just that learning has always been easy. There has been no need to reflect or to examine and check strategies. When suddenly faced with something they cannot do, the child may give up and crash emotionally.

Tannenbaum suggests that we owe it to the gifted child to mediate to them to understand their cognitive skills and become conscious and metacognitive about their own learning. In this way we may teach them to be aware and not be 'thrown' if they come across a difficulty. They can reach into their cognitive and metacognitive tool box and feel in control when things do not always go instantly right.

Here is an example of this from one of the present authors' casework.

Liz was a very able child and seemed to be blessed with being an all-rounder. At about the age of eight, she was asked if she wanted to have piano lessons, which at that time was an out-of-school activity. Liz was not interested. It was suggested to her to have a try, not because she had to become a concert pianist but because it was good for her to try learning something which did not come so quickly and easily (this can be seen as mediating the meaning of the suggested activity). Liz did try and worked on her piano lessons, despite not being particularly excited or motivated. After a while the lessons were discontinued.

Fast forward six years. At age 14+ in secondary school, the pupils were asked to take on some work experience. Liz chose to work in a geriatric hospital ward. She had a very difficult experience. She watched some of the elderly patients (who were clearly not well emotionally) physically attack each other. She was extremely shocked. The school told her that she could stop at once until they found her another placement. But Liz did not withdraw. She kept going back, determined to stick with the arrangement until an alternate placement was found.

After she began her second placement, Liz commented to her parents: 'You taught me this. When I was eight, you asked me to learn to play the piano which I had no interest in or talent for. You explained to me that it was important to persist and to learn to do things even when they are not easy. I thought about this all week. Keep going. Life isn't always about what comes easily. I made a commitment, and I was determined to see it through and not give up.'

This example illustrates how Liz showed insight into her learning, particularly the importance of persistence. Despite being very able, she was prepared to face a challenging situation and not give up.

Metacognition and self-regulated learning

Metacognition refers to the knowledge of and control over one's own cognition (Flavell, 1979) and is often perceived as a higher-order self-reflective cognitive process that monitors and regulates cognition. Garcia and Pintrich (1994) regarded metacognition as a set of common skills that is significantly associated with academic achievement. It is interesting to note that the recent EEF publication cover both metacognition and self-regulated learning (EEF, 2025), describing metacognition as one of 'the three essential components of self-regulated learning' (EEF, 2025: 8), the other two being cognition and motivation.

Three facets of metacognition have been identified and studied: metacognitive knowledge; metacognitive monitoring; and metacognitive control (Dunlosky and Metcalfe, 2008). Metacognitive knowledge refers to *people's knowledge about cognition*; metacognitive monitoring is the *evaluation of an ongoing cognitive process*; and metacognitive control refers to the *control and regulation of the cognitive activity*, usually based on the result of the monitoring. Multiple frameworks have been developed to portray how metacognition works, and how it impacts cognition. Among them, Nelson and Narens' (1990) framework suggests that people are capable of monitoring and managing thinking with higher-level representation and that effective monitoring is the prerequisite of effective control. Without accurate monitoring, it will be difficult to make proper judgements and effective control of the ongoing cognitive processes. For instance, if a learner underestimates how much they have learned, they may spend unnecessary time and effort on the learning materials that are already well learned. If a learner overestimates how much they have learned, they may end the learning process before the target learning materials are well learned and end up with lower learning outcomes. Accurate monitoring is the necessary step, enabling appropriate and efficient control actions (Nelson and Narens, 1990).

Metacognition has been found to be highly related to learning performance, including more specific learning outcomes and general academic achievement, such as reading (Van Kraayenoord and Schneider, 1999), chemistry (Rickey and Stacy, 2000), science (Topçu and Yılmaz-Tüzün, 2009) and learning abilities (Trainin and Swanson, 2005), and higher achievers presented more awareness of metacognitive knowledge and control than lower achievers (Van Kraayenoord and Schneider, 1999). Empirical research has repeatedly shown that the accuracy of metacognitive monitoring is highly associated with memory and learning performance across age and tasks (Zimmerman and Kitsantas, 1999; Maki, 1998; Roebers, 2017). It is not surprising that with much evidence that metacognition is associated with greater learning achievements, it has become an important goal for educators to work on. Thus, it is important for schools to focus on metacognition and self-regulated learning in order to:

- Increase attainment;
- Build learning autonomy and create independent learners;
- Prepare people for lifelong learning in the information age;
- Empower students to take responsibility for their own learning and personal development.

Metacognition is recommended by the EEF as an effective pedagogical strategy for disadvantaged students.

What is the difference between executive function and metacognition?

We propose a three-level hierarchy of thinking, where there is overlap and ongoing interaction between these three levels. The three levels are:

1. We start by learning to identify and use our cognitive skills.
2. We then learn to plan, self-regulate and control (EF).
3. We then learn how to select and evaluate our skills, our strategies and our methods (metacognition).

Figure 1.3 illustrates the hierarchy.

At all three levels these skills might develop without much deliberate help from others. However, as we emphasise throughout, we benefit greatly from the insight, support and direction of others in our development and awareness. This is the core of the concept of mediated learning: being mediated by others who stand between us and the world in order to shape, direct and facilitate our thinking and decision-making. Mediation is a unique human interaction that does not leave development to the vagaries of genetics, culture or environment.

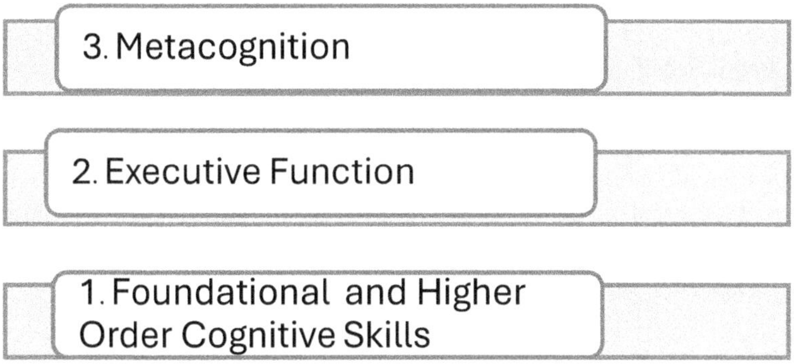

Figure 1.3 Thinking hierarchy

Executive function and metacognition: a dynamic relationship

Wu and Was (2023) investigated the relationship between EF and metacognition. They suggest the following, summarised on the next page.

Executive function (EF):

- *What it is*: The set of cognitive skills managing goal-directed behavior, controlling impulses, shifting attention, and holding information in mind;
- *Key components*: Working memory, inhibitory control (self-control), cognitive flexibility (shifting);
- *Role*: Helps you *do* the task - stay on track, ignore distractions, remember steps.

Metacognition

- *What it is*: Awareness, understanding, and control of one's own cognitive processes;
- *Key components*: Metacognitive knowledge (knowing *how* to learn), monitoring (checking understanding), and control (adjusting strategies);
- *Role*: Helps you *understand your learning* - planning your approach, evaluating your progress, and changing strategies if needed.

Despite many definitions and overlap, there is one important goal: to guide us in our interventions with learners. As we study the steps and components of creating a profile of a learner (developed in Chapter 4), we identify, we label and we may rate the quality of the strengths or challenges in their thinking. Only with this kind of analysis can we attempt to focus on where their needs are and to shape and monitor our interventions accordingly.

Summary

In this chapter, we have described key concepts which we need for our analysis of thinking: intelligence, cognition, EF and metacognition. We have drawn briefly on a large body of research, much of which has only taken place in the last 30 years. Despite many studies, some more neurological in their focus and others more focused on application to academic work and decision-making and not limited to school-age children, the complexity of these components of our thinking perhaps explains why none of these studies have resulted in a consensus of universally adopted definitions. Perhaps it also reminds us that the field is open and we are still learning.

Reflection and follow-up

- 'Study the past if you would define the future' (Confucius). Do you think this saying is relevant to psychology and education and, if so, in what ways?
- Reflect on any examples you have come across where culture has been a factor in the way a learner was assessed.
- In this first chapter we have begun to differentiate between intelligence, cognition, EF and metacognitive processes. Think about any of these challenges, shown by particular learners you know, that interfere with their learning processes.

References

Broadbent, D. (1953). Noise, paced performance and vigilance tasks. *British Journal of Psychology*, 44, 295-303.

Cattell, R. (1978). *The Scientific Use of Factor Analysis in Behavioral and Life Sciences*. New York: Plenum Press.

Dearborn, W.F. (1921). Intelligence and its measurement: a symposium - XII. *Journal of Educational Psychology*, 12(4), 210-212.

Deary, J., Cox, S.R. and Hill, W.D. (2022). Genetic variation, brain, and intelligence differences. *Molecular Psychiatry*, 27(1), 335-353

Dunlosky, J. and Metcalfe, J. (2008). *Metacognition*. Thousand Oaks: SAGE.

Education Endowment Foundation (EEF) (2025). *Metacognition and Self Regulated Learning*. London: Education Endowment Foundation.

Farrell, P. and Woods, K. (2007). The greatest contribution: Are we getting the best value from our educational psychologists? *Special*, 15-17.

Feuerstein, R. and Lewin-Benham, A. (2012). *What Learning Looks Like: Mediated Learning in Theory and Practice, K-6*. New York: Teachers College Press.

Flavell, J.H. (1976). Metacognitive aspects of problem solving. In L.B. Resnick (Ed.), *The Nature of Intelligence*. Hillsdale: Erlbaum.

Flavell, J.H. (1979). Metacognition and cognitive monitoring: a new area of cognitive-developmental inquiry. *American Psychologist*, 34, 906-911.

Garcia, T. and Pintrich, P.R. (1994). Regulating motivation and cognition in the classroom: the role of self-schemas and self-regulatory strategies. In D.H. Schunk and B.J. Zimmerman (Eds), *Self-Regulation of Learning and Performance: Issues and Educational Applications*. Hillsdale: Lawrence Erlbaum Associates.

Goldstein, S. and Naglieri, J.A. (Eds) (2013). *Handbook of Executive Function*. New York: Springer.

Goldstein, S., Naglieri, J.A., Princiotta, D. and Otero, T.M. (2014). A history of executive functioning as a theoretical and clinical construct. In S. Goldstein and J. Naglieri (Eds), *Handbook of Executive Functioning*. New York: Springer.

Gould, S.J. (1981). *The Mismeasure of Man*. New York: W.W. Norton and Company.

Haywood, H.C., Brooks, P. and Burns, M.S. (2022). Bright Start Cognitive Curriculum for Young Children, rev. edn. Bright Start CCYC. Available at: www.brightstart-ccyc.com.

Herrnstein, R.J. and Murray, C.A. (1994). *The Bell Curve: Intelligence and Class Structure in American Life*. New York: Free Press.

Lezak, M. (1995). *Neuropsychological Assessment*. Oxford: Oxford University Press

Luria, A.R. (1966). *Human Brain and Psychological Processes*. New York: Harper & Row.

Luria, A.R. (1973). *The Working Brain*. New York: Basic Books.

Maki, R. (1998). Metacognition of text: influence of absolute confidence, bias and accuracy. *Psychology of Learning and Motivation*, 38, 223-248.

Mintzker, Y. (1991). When the baby does not smile back. In R. Feuerstein, P. Klein and A. Tannenbaum (Eds), *Mediated Learning Experience*. London: Freund Publishing.

Naglieri, J. and Goldstein, S. (2013). *Comprehensive Executive Functioning Inventory Technical Manual*. Toronto: Multi-Health Systems.

Neisser, U. (1967). *Cognitive Psychology*. New York: Appleton-Century-Crofts.

Nelson, T.O. and Narens, L. (1990). Metamemory: a theoretical framework and new findings. In G. Bower (Ed.), *The Psychology of Learning and Motivation: Advances in Research and Theory*. New York: Academic Press.

Posner, M.I. and Snyder, C.R.R. (1975). Attention and cognitive control. In R. Solso (Ed.), *Information Processing and Cognition: The Loyola Symposium*. Hillsdale: Lawrence Erlbaum.

Pribram, K.H. (1973). The primate frontal cortex: executive of the brain. In K.H. Pribram and A.R. Luria, *Psychophysiology of the Frontal Lobes*. Cambridge, MA: Academic Press.

Reynolds, C.R. and Horton, A.M. (2008). Assessing executive functions: a life-span perspective. *Psychology in Schools*, 45, 875-892.

Rickey, D. and Stacy, A.M. (2000). The role of metacognition in learning chemistry. *Journal of Chemical Education*, 77, 915-920. doi:10.1021/ed077p915

Roebers, C.M. (2017). Executive function and metacognition: towards a unifying framework of cognitive self-regulation. *Developmental Review*, 45, 31–51.
Schiffrin, R.M. and Schneider, W. (1977). Controlled and automatic human information processing: perceptual learning, automatic attending and a general theory. *Psychological Review*, 84(2), 127–190.
Shallice, T. (1988). *From Neuropsychology to Mental Structure*. Cambridge: Cambridge University Press.
Spearman, C. (1904). General intelligence, objectively determined and measured. *The American Journal of Psychology*, 15, 201–292.
Tannenbaum, A.J. (1991). Unmasking and unmaking achievement among the gifted. In R. Feuerstein, P. Klein and A.J. Tannenbaum, *Mediated Leaning Experience (MLE) Theoretical, Psychosocial and Learning Implications*. London: Freund Publishing.
Thurstone, L.L. (1947). *Multiple Factor Analysis*. Chicago: University of Chicago Press.
Topçu, M.S. and Yılmaz-Tüzün, Ö. (2009). Elementary students' metacognition and epistemological beliefs considering science achievement, gender and socioeconomic status. *Ikö retim Online*, 8(3), 676–693.
Trainin, G. and Swanson, L. (2005). Cognition, metacognition, and achievement of college students with learning disabilities. *Learning Disability Quarterly*, 28, 261–272.
Van Kraayenoord, C.E. and Schneider, W.E. (1999). Reading achievement, metacognition, reading self-concept and interest: a study of German students in grades 3 and 4. *European Journal of Psychology of Education*, 14, 305–324.
Wu, M. and Was, C. (2023). The relationship between executive function and metacognition in college students. *Journal of Intelligence*, 11, Article 220. https://doi.org/ 10.3390/jintelligence11120220
Yeomans, J. (2025). Draining the swamp or shooting the alligators? Why theories of cognition and intelligence matter for practice. *PATOSS Bulletin*, winter.
Zimmerman, B.J. and Kitsantas, A. (1999). Acquiring writing revision skill: shifting from process to outcome self-regulatory goals. *Journal of Educational Psychology*, 91, 241–250.

2

Theoretical Foundations

East, West and Somewhere in Between

Introduction

The year 1896 is a significant date in the history of the development of approaches to understanding intelligence and learning, as both Jean Piaget in Switzerland and Lev Vygotsky in Russia were born in that year. Perhaps simplistically, we can speak about two paths in the development of psychological theories of intelligence in the past century as 'East and West'. The Eastern path was based in the Russian school of psychology. The Western path was developed by psychologists based in Western Europe and the United States. We will see that these paths, although partly parallel in time, were far from equal in their influence. This chapter looks at some theories about intelligence and intellectual development that emerged during the twentieth century and which form important foundations for this book.

This chapter will compare and contrast the work of Lev Vygotsky (1896–1934) with that of Jean Piaget (1896–1980), who was considered the most influential developmental psychologist of the twentieth century and was a contemporary of Lev Vygotsky. We then visit the contribution of a neuropsychological perspective in the work of Alexander Luria (1902–1977), who worked with Vygotsky. Finally, we will visit the work of Reuven Feuerstein (1921–2014), whose concepts relate to elements of both East and West.

The view from the East

Lev Vygotsky

Turning first to the East, we glimpse what was happening in the emerging field of child psychology in Russia during the period of the early twentieth century. Historically one might wonder why Vygotsky's work was little known in the West until the first translations into English in the 1960 and 1970s. This chapter will show that it was not because they lacked translators.

Lev Vygotsky, a young Russian psychologist, developed a very novel understanding about the development of learning and intelligence in children. Much has been published both in translation and in interpretation of his ideas (for example, Vygotsky, 1978). Here we seek to briefly summarise some key points and to show the contrast with Piaget's views on child

DOI: 10.4324/9781003655329-4

development, which are discussed in a later section of this chapter. Vygotsky began his own 'Russian Revolution', challenging the firm assumptions held at the time about intelligence, psychological testing, learning and teaching. These assumptions (as discussed in Chapter 1) were about the static nature of intelligence. Vygotsky proposed a sociocultural view of intelligence, which will be described in this section. We know that Vygotsky was writing to Piaget as early as 1929, as Vygotsky asked Piaget for permission to translate his book into Russian. Piaget agreed, and the translation was published in 1932 with a very long (50-page) introduction by Vygotsky in which he offered his own version of the relationship between thought and language, which was very different from that of Piaget. This introduction, in a revised form, appeared as chapter 2 in Vygotsky's *Thought and Language* (1986 [1934]).

Vygotsky had some major disagreements with Piaget, which were not so much about Piaget's meticulous description of cognitive functions, but more about how children develop their thinking and cognitive skills. Kozulin introduces his translation of *Thought and Language* (1986 [1934]), Vygotsky's most popular book, with the following remarks:

> Although Vygotsky's theory embraced all higher mental functions, Vygotsky himself was primarily interested in the development of language in its relation to thought. Language and speech occupy a special place in Vygotsky's psychological system because they play a double role. On the one hand they are a psychological tool, that helps form other mental functions; on the other hand, they are one of these functions, which means that they also undergo a cultural development.
>
> *(Kozulin, in Vygotsky, 1986 [1934]: xxx)*

For Vygotsky, parents, educators, the family and community were not just providers of information but were central to the development of cognition in the child. Vygotsky viewed society, family and community as the active and essential sources of the very tools of cognitive development. He did not deny biology, but biology was not the determining factor; rather, it was the quality and availability of direct engagement of the adult with the child that shaped and enhanced the development of the child's cognitive tools. Vygotsky's child was directed, shaped and formed by the active mediation and teaching of those adults who directly provided the psychological tools to become an active and independent thinker. This stance adopted by Vygotsky is the essence of sociocultural theory which underpinned his work. Together with his colleagues Luria and Leontiev, Vygotsky formed the 'troika' (a Russian vehicle pulled by three horses) due to their shared interest in sociocultural theory. They were already collaborating in 1924, shaping their radical social and cultural theories on the development of intelligence.

Already in the 1920s Vygotsky threw out a challenge to psychologists. Static testing on its own should not be the goal. He insisted that in nature we do not test children, we teach them. Famously, he asserted that what we see in a child's performance is not all there is. For each one of us (and not limited to childhood), there is a current level of performance which we can call the Zone of Actual Development (the ZOA), but that is only a baseline, a starting point. Vygotsky proposed that learning takes place in the Zone of Proximal (next) Development (the ZPD).

Vygotsky's ZPD

If we work with learners directly and teach them how to problem-solve, deliberately just ahead of what they have already grasped independently, we are both creating and working in their ZPD. We can identify what is in the process of formation, what is emerging, and hence estimate the individual's learning potential, not only capturing their current performance. According to Vygotsky and his colleagues, this is where we should be heading. This is what indicates the next steps of teaching. Following such intervention, the learner might be re-tested to measure the difference between what they could do unaided (their independent baseline performance) and what they can now do as a result of being provided with specific learning support. Psychological testing and learning should not be focused on what has already been acquired but rather to identify what will be the next steps of development. The difference between the learner's independent psychological measurement and what they can achieve as a result of supported learning, which he termed mediation, is captured by the notion of the ZPD. Vygotsky's use of the term *mediation* encompassed several methods; material tools, systems of symbols and in the behaviour of another human being (Kozulin, 1990). Later in this chapter we will see that when Feuerstein used the term mediation, or Mediated Learning Experience (MLE), he was referring specifically to human mediation. Linking to Vygotsky's concepts, Wood et al (1976) used the term *scaffolding* to describe how intentional mediation supports the learner's cognitive development.

Taking this a step further, Vygotsky asserted that all measurement and teaching should follow this model because exploring and mediating in the ZPD is fundamentally a much more valid form of psychological measurement. The teaching itself, using the tools of a specific culture, actively develops the next steps of learning. In contrast to Piaget (see later), for Vygotsky, *teaching leads development*.

Vygotsky had a further message, that the ZPD does not end with childhood. He must have been one of the first proponents of what we now call lifelong learning. He asserted that each of us, whatever our age, never functions at our maximum potential and that, throughout life, we can continue learning. Vygotsky also focused on the development of children with learning difficulties and was known as a 'defectologist', a term that feels quite negative to a contemporary audience, but which was a term used at the time to describe what now might be called special educational needs or additional needs support.

The iceberg model, shown in Figure 2.1, illustrates that according to Vygotsky, not all elements of intelligence or intellectual development are visible in a person's current independent performance but they are there potentially and it is up to us to bring out and develop these future skills.

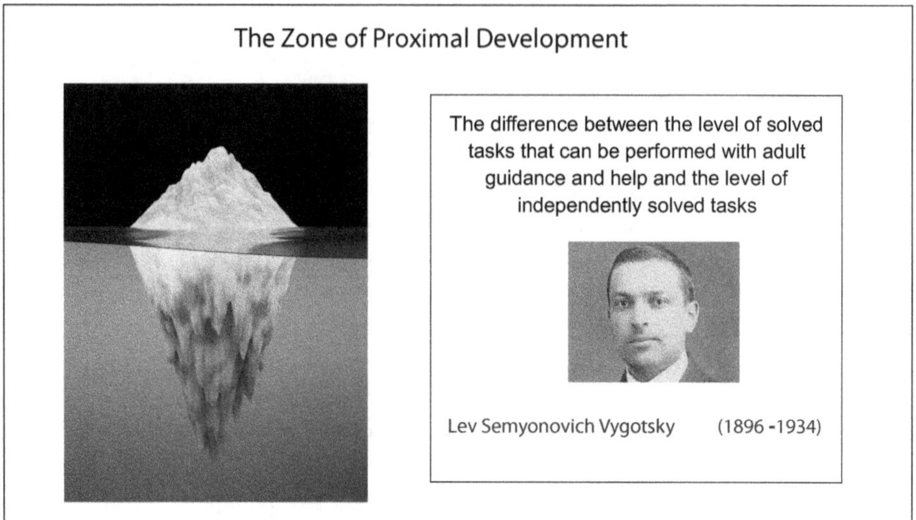

Source: Simon Lee via Unsplash

Figure 2.1 The Zone of Proximal Development (ZPD)

This has important implications. It suggests that cognitive plasticity, mental growth and change is not age limited. It is the opposite of a fixed model of intelligence. A key concept is that development can be continuous and is not limited to critical periods and can change the cognitive skills themselves. For Vygotsky, growing older did not mean inescapable cognitive decline. Dementia and Alzheimer's are not inevitable aspects of ageing. They are diseases of the brain.

Vygotsky's concepts would subsequently lead to the possibility of finding evidence of plasticity in the human brain, which was not possible to examine in living persons until many decades later. It also highlighted the essential and active role of others. From providers and bystanders, the parent, teacher and others take on a central mediation role in the development of the child. His was a universal model of learning, wherein what is taught, what is transmitted and what is mediated, including the very cognitive functions themselves, are differentially emphasised and will vary between different social and cultural settings.

In the early 1930s Vygotsky's sociocultural theory was condemned as anti-Marxist. Rival groups of psychologists were eager to denounce each other as Western or bourgeois, each group striving to prove that its work was the purest expression of anti-materialistic Marxism. A critical 'discussion' was meant to take place in 1933 or 1934. Vygotsky was prepared to rigorously defend his ideas, but it was suggested by Bluma Zeigarnik (Zeigarnik quoted in Yaroshevsky, 1988), one of the last survivors of that era, that the severe criticism of his work lead to anguish over being misunderstood by his contemporaries and may have contributed to his early death (Kozulin, 1990). His work was little known in Western psychology until translations of his writings began to appear in the 1970s. Ironically, when one of the present authors was invited to teach educational psychologists in training about Dynamic Assessment at the University of Vilnius, Lithuania, no one knew about Vygotsky's work as it had been banned in Lithuania following its declaration of independence from Russia, in 1990, because it was considered too Russian and too communist to be studied! However, as we will see shortly, when Vygotsky's work began to be available in the West, it contributed to some significant rethinking of models of thinking and learning and thus how intelligence should be measured.

Alexander Luria

The work of Alexander Luria is perhaps less widely known to educational psychologists, teachers and therapists. A number of the Russian psychologists of that period started their careers in the medical field. Alexander Luria was a neurologist by training and is considered one of the founding fathers of modern-day neuropsychology. He worked mainly with brain-injured adults. Nevertheless, in an unusual combination of neuropsychology and sociocultural psychology, he was a close follower and colleague of Vygotsky from 1924, when he first met Vygotsky, because he believed that irrespective of the nature of a brain injury, the use of cognitive skills is shaped by a person's social and cultural experiences.

Following the early death of Vygotsky in 1934, Vygotsky and Luria's work was condemned as being anti-Marxist (Kozulin, 1990). Luria is recorded as having published a 'confession' recanting of some of his ideas, but at the same time he carried on with publishing his work. Vygotsky's followers were placed in a defensive, apologetic position and his work was, so to speak, buried in the dusty archives of Moscow University Library. The political misrepresentation of what Vygotsky actually said is not explored here in detail but makes fascinating reading. Aleksei Nikolaevich Leontiev, the third member of the troika, developed Vygotsky's theory of psychological activity but later split off from Vygotsky still in the latter's lifetime, whilst Luria experimented in studies in the early 1930s, for example, comparing abstract reasoning in illiterate peasants, the Uzbeks, with sophisticated Moscow middle-class educated adults.

These ideas led to accusations against Vygotsky (as noted above), together with Luria, of being opposed to the prevailing psychological theories of the time and their work was not published for another 40 years (Luria, 1976). Vygotsky and Luria's theory was denounced as showing anti-materialist opposition to Marxism–Leninism. They were both condemned as 'bourgeois'. The historical and cultural aspects of their work were not revisited until the 1970s in the Soviet Union and through the efforts of Americans such as Michael Cole whose field of study was cross-cultural psychology (Cole and Scribner, 1974; Kozulin, 1990).

Alongside his collaboration with Vygotsky, Luria developed his concepts of brain functioning, which were inseparable from his conviction that brain functioning was to be understood within a social and cultural context. He researched language development in a study on speech and reasoning of urban, rural and homeless children (Luria, 1978 [1930]). He wrote: '[T]he social circumstances in which a child grows up will inevitably leave their mark on the mechanisms underlying complex psychological processes.' That is to say, different experiences will stimulate different types of mental processes, not just to supply different knowledge (Kozulin, 1990). Luria's data led him to the conclusion that an impoverished social environment affects the development of language and reasoning.

Luria's theory of functional units

Luria maintained that if two people who have experienced similar forms of brain injury do the same activity and even arrive at the same answer, the cognitive paths that they use would be different and shaped by their individual sociocultural experiences. Based on his clinical findings, Luria proposed a model of brain functions arranged in three interconnected functional units, each responsible for specific physiological and cognitive processes. In *The Working Brain* (1973) he expanded on earlier work and wrote extensively about his model of cerebral organisation. These units are:

- *Unit 1: Brainstem and regulating systems.* Responsible for the state of the brain: arousal, attention, and waking;
- *Unit 2: Posterior cortical regions.* Involved in receiving, analysing and storing sensory information (for example, vision, hearing, touch);
- *Unit 3: Frontal and prefrontal lobes.* Responsible for higher level executive functions such as planning, activating and checking results.

Luria stated that specific behaviours are the result of the dynamic interaction between these three systems. Although his was a vertically organised system, he maintained that multiple brain areas work together. No single area of functioning stands alone or should be examined in isolation from other functional areas. Evidence for the participation of numerous functional systems has been demonstrated using imaging technology such as Functional Magnetic Resonance Imaging (Lezak, 1992). Luria also emphasised the concept of neuroplasticity, where the brain can reorganise itself, especially after injury. He argued that higher level brain skills could compensate for the loss of lower level skills through adaptation and new learning, all within an individual's social and cultural context. Even though damage to one part of the adult brain may leave other areas intact, this has been challenged in the case of children in relation to neurodevelopmental difficulties (Bishop, 2010; Karmiloff-Smith et al. 2012). This view has important implications for our assessments and interventions with young children.

Luria's work emphasised a qualitative approach to neuropsychological assessment, where the focus is on how a patient performs a task, the types of errors they make and their overall behaviour, rather than quantitative scores. This approach influenced the development of clinical tools. However, American researchers did not know how to translate Luria's concepts into the kind of quantitative testing they were used to. Some researchers decided that the only way forward was to go and study directly with Luria in Moscow. Luria commented that he thought people would try to quantify his concepts, but quantitative scoring of performance was never a main focus of his work. At most, he conceded that a combination of quantitative and qualitative observations could be useful. The first attempt at standardisation of Luria's concepts was the Luria-Nebraska Neuropsychological Battery (Golden et al, 1979), published notably after Luria's death.

As with other models of thinking, there were subsequent challenges to Luria's formulations. One important point is that Luria's work was based on brain-injured adults, therefore his model was derived from neurological pathology, not a model of typical brain activity.

Key points for us are that the cognitive functions of each functional unit do not stand alone. They are interrelated. Luria's structure is not an accumulation or stack of processes to be added together, but are transactional, each aspect influencing others multi-directionally. This view of cognitive functioning was also expressed by Haywood (Haywood and Lidz, 1987), who proposed a transactional view of intelligence, such that cognitive functioning cannot be tested and judgements made in one area only.

The following section looks at applications of Luria's work that are relevant for understanding metacognition, executive function and for supporting the development of cognitive skills. Two applications are discussed that are relevant to this content of this book: applications to children and the development of the PASS theory of intelligence.

Applications of Luria's work

Applications to children

If we are working with children, we need to investigate whether Luria's concepts can be applied to children's development, as Luria's early formulations resulted from his work with work with brain-injured adults. In 1966, he proposed that higher cortical functions required interaction of normal neurological development and specific environmental stimuli of a cultural, historical and social nature of development. Thus, the result of the optimal interaction of neurological development and environmental stimuli would result in more efficient cortical functioning related to abilities such as language, attention, memory and intelligence.

Luria set out a number of stages by which neuropsychological functions critical for intelligence are developed. These stages were thought to interact with environmental stimuli based on Vygotsky's cultural and historical theory (Van der Veer and Valsiner, 1994). Luria connected his concepts to Vygotsky's theory related to language and thought processes. He emphasised that environmental and/or cultural influences were important in understanding the development of neurological structures responsible for higher-level mental abilities, such as abstraction, memory and attention. In this way, Luria expanded Vygotsky's original theories. Luria suggested that various stages of mental development, encountered as children mature, provide a unique opportunity to study how executive function develops (see Chapter 1 for an overview of executive function).

Luria proposed five stages of human development:

- *Stage One*: This stage begins in the first year of life and involves development of the brain stem structures such as the reticular activating system;
- *Stage Two*: This stage involves the activation of the primary sensory areas for vision, hearing, and tactile perception and the primary motor areas of gross motor movement during the second year of life. This is consistent with Piaget's stage of sensorimotor operations;
- *Stage Three*: This stage involves development of single modalities in the secondary association areas of the brain as children enter their preschool years. The child's mind recognises and reproduces various symbolic materials and develops the ability to model physical movement. This stage is consistent with Piaget's description of preoperational functioning;
- *Stage Four*: This stage begins as the child enters the early stage of primary/elementary school (7–8 years of age), as the tertiary areas of the parietal lobes are activated. The tertiary parietal lobes, the temporal parietal and occipital lobes join anatomically and involve coordination of the three major sensory input channels. During this stage, the child's mind begins to make sense of sensory input and environmental stimulation. It is particularly important for the development of complex mental abilities. This stage fits that of Piaget's concrete operations;
- *Stage Five*: During this stage, the brain becomes activated, beginning at approximately eight years of age, through adolescence and adulthood. This operation involves the frontal lobes; the area anterior to the central sulcus is crucial to the development of complex mental abilities involving abstract thinking, intentional memory, as well as the execution monitoring and evaluating for complex learning (Stuss and Benson, 1984). This stage spans the period between Piaget's concrete operations leading to the formal mental operations of adolescence.

In adapting some of Luria's neurologically based ideas to educational psychology, tests such as the Developmental Neuropsychological Assessment (NEPSY; Korkman et al. 1998), the Cognitive Assessment System test (CAS2, Naglieri et al, 2014) and parts of Kaufman's Assessment Battery for Children (K-ABC; Kaufman and Kaufman, 2004 [1983]) are based on his concepts. These tests of cognitive functioning in children are not related to testing for IQ scores, but with utility for children's learning. Lidz (1987) adapted Luria's neurologically based structure in carrying out Dynamic Assessment of school-age children. Deutsch (2020) adapted Luria's concepts into six interrelated domains of cognitive processes for use as an observation and consultation framework in the Cognitive Abilities Profile (CAP). (The seventh domain of the CAP does not derive from Luria's work). The CAP (Deutsch, 2020) emphasises that no cognitive domain should be observed and rated on its own.

PASS theory

Luria's (1973; 1980) research on the functional aspects of brain structures forms the basis for the development of PASS (planning, attention, simultaneous and successive processing) theory (Das et al. 1994). This was operationalised by Naglieri et al. (2014) in the Cognitive Assessment System (CAS2) test. The four PASS areas of processing are derived from Luria's functional units as follows:

- Unit One: equivalent to Attention Processing;
- Unit Two: equivalent to Simultaneous and Successive Processing;
- Unit Three: equivalent to Planning Processing.

Luria's third functional unit provides the most complex aspects of human behaviour, including personality and consciousness (Das, 1980). The connection between units also links the psychological processes that are routed in each of the functional units. Luria believed no part of the brain works by itself; thus, no cognitive task solely requires simultaneous, successive planning or attention processing, or any other processes, but rather it is a matter of emphasis. Luria stated that 'perception of memorizing, speech and thinking, writing, reading and arithmetic cannot be regarded as isolated or even indivisible faculties' (Luria, 1973: 29). Thus, an attempt to identify a fixed cortical location for any complex behaviour would be considered a mistaken endeavour.

For PASS theory this means that the psychological processes of attention and planning are necessarily strongly related because planning involves conscious control of attention. In other words, one's limited attentional resources are dictated by the plan for one's behaviour. The combination of attention and planning offers a functional description of *executive function*. However, attention and other PASS processes are influenced by many variables beyond planning. One of the influences is the environment. Novel encounters within daily life demand that individuals act in one way or another. The interaction of knowledge and several PASS processes are involved as individuals make judgements about similarities and differences between past situations and present demands, while estimating possible outcomes of action, even as acting. Humans are able to think one thing while saying and/or doing something else and are uniquely the only species capable of simultaneously thinking, evaluating and acting.

The view from the West

Historically, the concept of fixed intelligence and the tests derived thereof occupied the front row of belief and practice for psychologists and teachers for many decades from the late nineteenth century to the 1960s at least (see the historical timeline in Chapter 1).

Jean Piaget

Jean Piaget, the most famous developmental psychologist of the twentieth century, might turn in his grave to be assigned to the group of fixed intelligence theorists. His was a theoretical search to explain the structure of thinking or epistemology. He spent more than 50 years devising the most creative experiments to describe children's thinking and its progression through different ages and stages. He was one of the first psychologists who examined the development of children's thinking as a field in its own right, instead of regarding children as just immature versions of what they will become when they grow up. We owe an enormous debt to Piaget for his detailed descriptions of cognitive functions and the structure of mental operations (his terminology) over the span of birth to adulthood.

However, we also need to acknowledge that some of his positions have been subsequently challenged. For example, one of his central tenets, the hierarchical nature of cognitive development linked to fairly rigid ages and stages, has been challenged by many researchers including Donaldson (1987) and Goswami (1998). The internalised, largely non- social view of learning has also been challenged by post-Piagetian researchers. Piaget's age-related stages were, in his view, biologically driven and maturational. We will briefly explore how he explained the way in which development proceeds from stage to stage.

In Piaget's model (see, for example, Piaget, 1926; 1958), it is the child, and the child alone, doing the developmental work, by noticing and interacting with objects and stimuli in the environment. Piaget proposed a within-child model. He wanted to develop a structural model of typical thinking. Thus, he asserted that development will be organised hierarchically in ages and stages because he maintained that the developmental journey is determined by orderly biological maturation.

Piaget was much more interested in producing a general model of the structure of intelligence and did not particularly concern himself with children with learning difficulties. He saw children's stages of development much as one would describe growth in the plant world. In fact, in some of his writing, he referred to children as organisms.

Piaget's structural framework

Piaget suggested a structural framework from birth leading to the highest stages of thinking to be achieved during adolescence. It was a trajectory of cognitive skills driven by the goal of achieving Western higher education goals of abstract formal reasoning, linguistic and mathematical intelligence, as seen within his own cultural framework, which was more or less aligned with the ages and stages in the school systems of Europe. His explanation of why the learning journey had to be the child's own efforts was also influenced by his own experiences as a parent. He devised many of his theoretical constructs from observing his own children.

For Piaget, parents (and indeed all adults) were figures of authority. Due to this powerful unequal relationship, he did not believe they could directly interact with the child. They were providers of nurturing (the family) and learning stimuli (the school), but this did not include any direct involvement with the child's cognitive development. He had more to say about peers learning together, which he considered both possible and desirable. He was deeply influenced by his own time and culture in the way he theorised about children's path from infancy to adulthood.

Piaget and his team at the University of Geneva spent more than 50 years devising fascinating experiments along the lines of his theories. Piaget believed that he had found the answers to child development. It has been reported by those who worked in Piaget's department in his later years that he did not welcome researchers who challenged his constructs (Karmiloff-Smith, 2003). His elaboration of each stage of development, consisting of a number of cognitive processes which developed and matured in four age-related stages, fitted well with the emerging field of intelligence testing. If intelligence develops in a hierarchical way, with one stage building on another, testing a child on the cognitive processes of that age and stage and using age-related norm referencing sat well with his theories. Indeed a 'good' Piagetian psychologist would not even look for higher functions in a child of a certain age, if the child's age was below the next age or stage of development.

As part of his theory, Piaget had to address how this maturational development took place. He described a process by which children would be exposed to a stimulus sufficiently frequently to internalise a certain cognitive process and to develop the skills needed to activate that cognitive skill. In the very early years (birth to 18/24 months) infants use sensory and perceptual means to access the world around them, gradually proceeding to learning via concrete experiences during the preschool years (approximately 2–6 years old). Then follows the gradual development of mental representation during the childhood years, roughly equivalent to primary or elementary school education (age 7–11 years), eventually leading to abstract reasoning, which Piaget termed formal reasoning, in adolescence (12 years old and above) to achieve mature adult modes of thinking. This would be assimilated within and then added into their existing cognitive structures (schema). This process might be pictured as a cupboard full of shelves and coat hangers. As a stimulus is presented and noticed by the child and repeated enough times, it would enter the mental cupboard and be stored on a hanger. Ideas and repeated stimuli will be assimilated on the same hanger, the beginning of association into a group, or accommodated on a different hanger, if it is a new concept, demanding a new skill, new language or a new process. As the cognitive cupboard is filled, at a certain point the child is developmentally ready to move on to the next stage.

However, according to Piaget, who is doing the work? What is the role of the teacher, parent and the child him or herself? This is where Piaget maintained that it is the child who is doing the work, whom he referred to as 'the little lone scientist'. In this, he contradicted the prevailing view that children were empty vessels waiting to be filled. He saw them as active constructors of their own learning. This was achieved through the child's own attention, absorption and maturational processes. The parents' role is to provide love and nurture. The teacher's role is to provide stimuli for the child to discover and engage with but to stand back. It is the child observing, working on and internalising the processes. Three generations of teachers were trained in what was called *discovery learning*. Piaget had more to say on the role of peers, suggesting that children of a similar developmental stage can and should work together. They can be challenged to discover and solve problems together. They can interact with each other in a way that parents and teachers cannot because peers are at a similar stage of development, but parents and teachers, as authority figures, cannot be directly involved in the child's learning.

Implications for teaching and learning

Piaget's ideas were widely disseminated and very influential, and partly because of the condemnation of Vygotsky's work in Stalinist Russia, he had little competition in more than three decades (the 1930s to 1960s) in the emerging field of child development.

There were important implications of his theory for teachers. For each child at a certain age or stage, the role of the teacher was to provide them with objects, tasks and activities (that is, stimuli), appropriate to the cognitive skills of that stage. The teacher was not expected to provide any activities which would be ahead of development for that age or stage as this was not considered possible. Thus, a teacher would provide activities matched to the *already acquired* and observed cognitive skills. First the teacher sees evidence of the skill and then provides stimuli to what has already developed. That is, *teaching follows development*. Note the contrast to Vygotsky who maintained that *teaching leads development*.

In briefly summarising these few points, without any pretensions of attempting to do justice to Piaget's deeply influential work, our goal is to compare some of these ideas with the contrasting perspective, coming from the East, and note how these different streams of thought underpinned and influenced many concepts in our current practices. The next section looks at the impact of Vygotsky's theories when they began to reach the West in the 1970s.

Where East and West meet: the influence of Russian psychologists

Vygotsky's work started to become available in translation in the Western world from the 1970s (see, for example, Cole and Wertsch, 1996). The influence of his ideas grew rapidly amongst psychologists and educators, leading to a growing awareness of the role of environmental and cultural influences on children's development. In the UK, for example, changing demographics led to psychologists starting to give more consideration to social, linguistic, environmental and cultural influences on the development of thinking and on intelligence and its measurement. This was partly driven by increasing immigration of families from former British colonies, whose children were entering the school system in increasing numbers. Voices in the psychology community started to question the validity of standardised intelligence tests for migrants, asylum seekers and refugees from different cultures. The strictly within-child genetic view of intelligence began to be challenged, gradually being modified towards a broader ecological view of the child developing and responding, even in core psychological processes, within family, community, school and other environmental influences. Subsequently with increasing numbers of migrants, refugees and asylum seekers across Europe, the issues became even more acute, leading to questioning about how to assess and understand these children.

Vygotsky's ideas in translation, such as *Thought and Language* (Vygotsky, 1986 [1934]), were taking hold amongst some psychologists and researchers in the United States, linked to the growing movements towards social equality in the face of the long history of racism which had dominated American life and legislation. With voices such as Martin Luther King and the struggle for equal rights in the United States, some psychologists began to challenge the prevailing and dominant mode of IQ type testing and started asking whether these tests were culturally unfair to minority population groups. It had been noted for many years that children from African American and Hispanic homes found themselves excluded from mainstream education and assigned to special schools in numbers far in excess of their proportions in the wider population. For those who supported the Civil Rights Movement, together with emerging sociocultural theories such as those of Vygotsky, questions were being asked about the validity of the measurement of intelligence adopted by normed intelligence tests. These tests largely reflected knowledge within one specific culture and its educational structures and were increasingly challenged as lacking validity for minority and culturally different groups who did not share the same mainstream educational experiences and expectations, upon which these tests were based and normed. Thus, we see the emergence of one avenue of research such as Budoff and Pagel's (1968) learning potential procedure; Feuerstein et al. (1979) Learning Potential Assessment Device (LPAD); and Campione et al. (1984) starting to experiment with various dynamic (interactive) assessment models, where the assessor actively intervenes in the assessment process. In the United States and subsequently in other countries, Vygotsky's concept of the ZPD became a conceptual basis for comparing differences in test performance between different social and cultural groups. Standardised traditional test results appeared to distinguish different ethnic minority groups at baseline (that is, at the initial, unaided phase of testing), but such differences were seen to significantly diminish when all the children, following baseline unassisted testing, were offered a supported learning experience such as teaching them methods and strategies needed for problem-solving of the presented tasks. Following such an intervention stage, the post-test scores of the minority cultural groups were in line with general population norms.

Increasing evidence supported the view that differences in performance on static intelligence tests, thought of as resulting from differences in innate intelligence, were due to the impact of different cultural experiences to a much greater extent than was previously believed. A key finding was the difference between current unaided performance and potential changes supported by a mediated learning experience, as proposed by Vygotsky's notion of potential changes in the ZPD. Similar research was conducted for example, by Carlson and Wiedl (1980), Guthke and Beckmann (2000), Hessels-Schlatter (2002), Resing (2000; 2006) and Femke et al. (2018), all of whom were addressing issues of demographic changes and the needs of minority groups within their own countries. Exploring possible uses of dynamic assessment procedures with adolescents and adults with psychiatric conditions was carried out by (Wiedl et al. 2001). The issue of culture-fair testing became increasingly acknowledged and led to interest and development of alternate and complementary forms of testing, such as Dynamic or Interactive Testing (Haywood and Tzuriel, 1992; Lidz and Elliott, 2000). In the field of language assessment, similar research was being undertaken by psychologists and language specialists, for example, Peña et al. (2001) and Lidz and Peña's (2009) work with Hispanic children in the United States. Research was also starting to provide evidence in relation to children who were tested and categorised as mildly, moderately or severely 'mentally retarded' (the labels used at the time), Although changes in learning potential before and after intervention were more modest than pre- to post-tests changes in the scores of minority children, change was evident, albeit smaller and requiring more intensive intervention.

The impact of this growing body of research challenged not only those who routinely used IQ tests in their work, but went hand in hand with a widening view of the relevance of ecological factors, the environment around the child and the need to consider the real-world context both in and out of school more holistically, in understanding how a child learns and performs.

Somewhere in between: Feuerstein's contribution

Feuerstein's early professional life

We now turn to another historical source of change in perspective of what is thinking and what is intelligence, as seen in the work of Reuven Feuerstein, which began in the late 1940s. A little history will show us the synergy between his work and that of Piaget. At the same time, some of Feuerstein's concepts were remarkably similar to Vygotsky's, despite the fact that Feuerstein, like most other European psychologists of that time, had no access to Vygotsky's writings (Kozulin, 1998).

Given that Piaget and Vygotsky were corresponding in the late 1920s, questions have been raised as to why the psychologists around Piaget knew little or nothing of Vygotsky's work. It has been suggested that because Piaget was convinced that his theories were *the* correct view of child development, other perspectives were dismissed or not even discussed in his department in Geneva (Karmiloff-Smith, 2003).

A Romanian by birth, a teacher and later a psychologist by profession, Feuerstein escaped from his native country in 1942, after its invasion by Nazi Germany. Following the end of the Second World War, he was sent to Displaced Persons (DP) camps in Europe where survivors of the Holocaust were held, whilst organisations such as the Red Cross searched for relatives and, in the case of child survivors, for any family who could take these children.

For those youngsters for whom no surviving relatives could be found, an organisation named Youth Aliyah was set up to bring these youngsters to Israel to begin a new life. It was this organisation that hired Feuerstein to assess adolescents to determine where in the education system of their new country these youngsters should be placed.

Feuerstein arrived to do his job, bringing with him well known psychological tests of that period, such as the Wechsler Intelligence Scale for Children (WISC) and Stanford Binet. His target group was adolescents. As he began to test these child survivors using the standardised tests of his profession, child after child scored in what was known at the time as the 'mentally retarded' range. These children, having lost their families, their homes and their education, were suffering trauma and were simply unable to perform adequately on these tests. In addition, they came from varying cultural backgrounds, some of which were not reflected in the standardised tests that Feuerstein was using. This was another reason for their poor test performance. Feuerstein knew he had a problem. The tools he had brought with him were clearly not appropriate to do the job he was sent to do. He went to Geneva, where he was at the same time studying under Piaget and particularly with one of the departmental assistant professors, Andre Rey. He had to find another way to find out what these children were able to do.

Andre Rey, a prolific and creative test developer, was a rich source of materials which Feuerstein borrowed as he searched for activities which were as culturally neutral as possible. Sitting down with the adolescents again, he used these materials to engage them in learning and problem-solving. In fact, in some of his earliest writings in his work with Andre Rey in the 1950s, he started by just making some 'adjustments' to standard tests. Rey and Feuerstein did not set out to 'break the rules' but made some 'additions' and 'adjustments'. It was not a revolution, but rather an evolution. Feuerstein told this story himself; one can see the history of these 'adjustments' in the report written by Richelle and Feuerstein (1957) under the direction of Professor Andre Rey.

Feuerstein made two very puzzling discoveries. First, he already knew that when he gave the children an activity in a standardised way, they performed very poorly. However, following structured intervention in which he taught them methods and strategies for how to solve these tasks and then gave them parallel items to solve alone, he was surprised to discover that their post-intervention performance was much better than their first unaided responses.

Second, having no published norms to compare their performances with same-age peers, Feuerstein made his own detailed clinical notes and individual lists of the cognitive processes he observed. Comparing many of these sets of notes, he noticed something very puzzling. The same poorly executed cognitive processes, which he termed *deficient cognitive functions*, were appearing again and again, despite the fact that these children had nothing in common in terms of their backgrounds, education and languages. This led him to question the reason for these strangely consistent deficiencies, resulting in a radical reconceptualisation of intelligence and learning.

Feuerstein on how intelligence develops

Back with his colleagues in Geneva, Feuerstein started examining what were then current theories of learning, in particular stimulus-response theory developed by Pavlov and Skinner, psychodynamic theories, associated with the work of Freud, Jung and Adler, and cognitive accounts of development, of which he was most familiar with the work of the man he called 'my master', Jean Piaget. Using this research to help him make sense of his perplexing findings, Feuerstein developed two theoretical proposals.

First, he asserted that manifest intelligence is not all there is and all there will be, as suggested by dominant psychological theory at the time, and as scored in static tests, but that cognitive functioning can be changed through intervention by an adult or more knowledgeable peers, modifying performance in the direction of greater learning potential than is first evident.

Second, he sought to explain the strange commonality of the deficient cognitive functions he noted in the adolescents he had tested and his answer to this question was *loss*. Loss of home, loss of family and community. Loss of the very foundations of interpersonal interaction which are essential to the development of every human being's cognitive development. This critical relationship he termed Mediated Learning Experience. Feuerstein maintained that this is nothing new. By observing our parents and grandparents, we see the human mediated interactions which occur naturally within families and from generation to generation. This is not only essential to the development of the individual child's cognitive tools, but is the vehicle for the transmission of culture, knowledge and beliefs, making us uniquely different from the animal world. Animals do not leave us cave paintings or hand us down books and music. Our history, our memories, our very understanding of who we are, are essentially formed by mediation intergenerationally as well as interpersonally.

In formulating his observations in this way, Feuerstein was much closer to Vygotsky's concepts than to Piaget's, although at the time, as a student of Piaget, as we mentioned, he did not know about Vygotsky's work. However, he did not disagree with Piaget altogether, in fact his list of deficient cognitive functions was heavily influenced by Piaget's description of the fourth stage of thinking, that of formal operational reasoning. This was the yardstick and reference for Feuerstein in determining the deficient cognitive processes of the adolescents he was assessing. The notion of 'deficiency' was defined in relation to the fourth stage of Piaget's list of mental operations, formal operational reasoning, to be expected of young people in their adolescent years.

Feuerstein's theories

Feuerstein developed his theory of Structural Cognitive Modifiability (SCM), publishing his first major text in 1979 (Feuerstein et al. 1979). Simply put, intelligent behaviours and cognitive skills can be modified through a specific type of human intervention, facilitating higher structures of thinking than may be evident in a person's unaided, independent functioning. Feuerstein maintained that age, causality and severity should not be considered immovable barriers which, a priori, determine and limit cognitive development.

His concepts grew from his clinical work with children. Feuerstein was not aiming to develop an overarching theory of intelligence and learning as was Piaget, but rather, he sought to explain the poor cognitive functioning he observed, the capacity to bring about change not limited by traditional barriers to learning, which were widely accepted at the time. His was a model of the potential for change and was grounded in his approach to remediation built on his own experiences. He was greatly influenced by Piagetian theory and his use of the term cognitive structures and his descriptions of mental operations was the terminology used by Piaget.

Nevertheless, he departed significantly from Piaget's account of the maturational process of development. He stated that Piaget was right, but only up to a point. He agreed with Piaget that there is constant incidental learning from repeated exposure to stimuli in the environment and, indeed, this may be our main way of gaining information and cognitive skills. This he termed Direct Learning Experience (DLE). However, he suggested that Piaget had underestimated a second essential source of development, the universal role of the human mediator in the development of a child, which he termed Mediation or Mediated Learning Experience (MLE). In Feuerstein's view, we need both. As in our brief accounts of other important players in the field, we will not elaborate further here. There are many published accounts of Feuerstein's theories and the practical tools he developed to apply his ideas in practice (see, for example, Feuerstein et al. 2002).

Additionally, in at least three aspects, common ground can be shown between Feuerstein's approach and that of Luria. First, both were primarily clinicians placing relatively little importance on the use of standardised tests. Their clinical observations were of prime importance. Second, they shared the view that cognition develops within a person's social and cultural context, even taking account of genetic and medical history. Third, both were addressing the impact of atypical conditions or disorders in their patients, whether environmental, developmental or in adult functioning. Feuerstein's ideas also shared some important similarities with those of Vygotsky (Kozulin, 1998), sharing Vygotsky's belief that humans can potentially change and grow their cognitive skills in vital mediational interaction with others and that neither their circumstances nor their genes need to have the last word. To that end, his first departure from standardised psychological testing became the basis for developing tests of learning potential, as Vygotsky had theorised but never lived to develop or publish.

Feuerstein's Dynamic Assessment battery, which he called the LPAD (Learning Potential Assessment Device [Feuerstein et al. 1979; 2002]) was one of the first, if not the very first, attempt to construct an alternate or complementary way of assessing children's learning (and not only children) for whom standardised tests were not appropriate or sufficient. Feuerstein's first major text (Feuerstein et al. 1979) distinguished between manifest performance and potential ability. He suggested that we may test people who perform in a 'retarded' way but this does not mean that they themselves are retarded. In referring to some of these early writings, the term 'retarded' is used because it was the term in use at the time. Today this is not an acceptable descriptor. It was only from the 1970s onwards in the UK, following the Warnock report and legislative changes, that the use of this diagnostic label ceased.

Regarding neurological and genetic foundations of intelligence, Feuerstein did not deny biology but placed much more emphasis on mediational intervention as the proximal determinant of cognitive change. Nevertheless, he thought that changes in the neurological structures of the brain itself may be possible through intensive cognitive intervention. He stated that he only whispered these ideas, because non-invasive technology, such as CAT (Computerised Axial Tomography) and PET (Positron Emission Tomography) scans, had not yet been developed to test for such neurological evidence and he was afraid he would be considered a crank.

Feuerstein's challenge to the determinism of static testing was not well accepted in traditional psychology circles. He was considered an ideologue whose proposals were not evidence-based. His concepts were not intended as an epistemological theory of learning as Piaget proposed, but rather an approach to the remediation of cognitive difficulties in children and adults. Whereas Piaget was intent on developing a model of typical cognitive development, Feuerstein, as a result of his professional experiences, was concerned about those who for any number of reasons were atypical in their development. He stated that 'atypical development is like a piece of Swiss cheese – full of holes'.

From his beginnings with traumatised adolescent survivors, Feuerstein gradually widened his approach to those who, for reasons of developmental, genetic, medical conditions, chromosomal disorders or brain injury, showed 'deficient cognitive functions' not associated with social and cultural deprivation. We sampled above some of the research which, from the start, broadened the possible applications of Dynamic Assessment. His main goal was to develop intervention methods of mediation and change. Thus, following the LPAD, Feuerstein and colleagues brought out the Instrumental Enrichment programme (Feuerstein et al. 1980) to place MLE methods at the core of a systematic approach to facilitate cognitive change in the hands of teachers and therapists.

Feuerstein's legacy in relation to reconceptualising intelligence and the development of tools to both assess and support cognitive skills cannot be overemphasised. His work in the 1950s onwards identified the profound impact of trauma and cultural differences on an individual's thinking and problem-solving long before the rise of culturally aware and trauma-informed practice in the West. These are now key drivers for psychologists, therapists and educators in understanding many of the challenges experienced by children and young people. Dynamic Assessment (DA) is used increasingly by educational psychologists and speech and language therapists as an alternative to static tests that are not always fit for purpose when working with traumatised learners and for work in linguistically and ethnically diverse communities. DA is now included in the curriculum for educational psychology training courses in the UK, and in some speech and language therapy training courses. DA will be explored further in Chapter 4, in the context of drawing up a cognitive profile for a learner, where the assessor has some background and training in this approach, as it is outside the scope of this text to provide comprehensive training.

Summary

In this chapter, we have outlined some of the important theoretical contributions which influenced and challenged the historical trajectory of our understanding of children's cognitive development and intelligence. We have briefly traced some of the different contributions from the East, which led to challenges to the predominantly (Western) view of fixed intelligence and the widespread reliance on standardised intelligence testing, opening up a way of understanding development and functioning as significantly context and culturally driven, which takes into account social and demographic changes. We saw that a more holistic view of development might lead to a more ecologically valid range of assessment tools and models for understanding the learning profile of an individual. These changes reflect educators' growing awareness of the importance of the world around the child.

Reflection and follow-up

- Are we there yet? Do our practices in psychology and teaching really reflect what we have learned?
- How do we address the need to balance curriculum and content learning with the need to teach our children to learn how to learn in a rapidly changing technological world?
- How do we apply what we have learnt to whole classes and yet be able to address individual needs?
- How has the content of this chapter built on the material in Chapter 1 about the idea of fixed intelligence? What insights into the concept of 'intelligence' have you gained from ideas about flexible intelligence discussed in this chapter?

In the chapters that follow, the above questions will be addressed, systematically setting out methods and strategies. These will provide a framework and tools to help implement and achieve goals of supporting children's healthy and successful development.

References

Bishop, D. (2010). *What's in a Name?* Available at: bishoptechbits.blogspot.com. Accessed 28 December 2025.

Budoff, M. and Pagel, W. (1968). Learning potential and rigidity in the adolescent mentally retarded. *Journal of Abnormal Psychology*, 73(5), 479–486.

Campione, J.C., Brown, A.L., Ferrara, R.A. and Bryant, N.R. (1984). The zone of proximal development: implications for individual difference and learning. In B. Rogoff and J.V. Wertsch (Eds), *Children's Learning in the Zone of Proximal Development*. San Francisco: Jossey-Bass.

Carlson, J.S. and Wiedl, K.H. (1980). Applications of a dynamic testing approach in intelligence assessment: empirical results and theoretical formulations. *Zeitschrift für Differentielle und Diagnostische Psychologie*, 1, 303–318.

Cole, M. and Scribner, S. (1974). *Culture & Thought: A Psychological Introduction*. New York: John Wiley & Sons.

Cole, M. and Wertsch, J. (1996). Beyond the individual-social antinomy in discussions of Piaget and Vygotsky. *Human Development*, 39(5), 250–256.

Das, J.P. (1980). Planning: theoretical considerations and empirical evidence. *Psychological Research*, 41(2-3), 141–151.

Das, J.P., Naglieri, J.A. and Kirby, J.R. (1994). *Assessment of Cognitive Processes: The PASS Theory of Intelligence*. Boston: Allyn & Bacon.

Deutsch, R. (2020). *The Cognitive Abilities Profile*, rev. edn. Canterbury: Real Group.
Donaldson, M. (1987). *Children's Minds.* London: Fontana Press.
Femke, E.S., Wiedl, K.H., Vogelaar, B., Bakker, M. and Resing, W. (2018). The role of cognitive flexibility in young children's potential for learning under dynamic testing conditions. *European Journal of Psychology of Education*, 34, 123–146.
Feuerstein, R., Rand, Y. and Hoffman, M. (1979). *The Dynamic Assessment of Retarded Performers.* Baltimore: Scott Foresman.
Feuerstein, R., Rand, Y., Hoffman, M.B., Hoffman, M. and Miller, R. (1980). *Instrumental Enrichment: An Intervention Program for Cognitive Modifiability.* Baltimore: University Park Press.
Feuerstein, R., Feuerstein, R.S., Falik, L.H. and Rand, Y. (2002). *The Dynamic Assessment of Cognitive Modifiability: The Learning Propensity Assessment Device: Theory, Instruments and Techniques*, rev. and expanded edn. Jerusalem: ICELP Publications.
Golden, C.J., Purisch, A.D. and Hammeke, T.A. (1979). *Manual of the Luria-Nebraska Neuropsychological Battery.* Nebraska: University of Nebraska Press.
Goswami, U. (1998). *Cognition in Children.* Hove: Psychology Press.
Guthke, J. and Beckmann, J.F. (2000). The learning test concept: Application in practice. In C.S. Lidz and J. Elliott (Eds), *Dynamic Assessment: Prevailing Models and Applications.* London: Elsevier.
Haywood, H.C. and Lidz, C.S. (1987). *Dynamic Assessment in Practice.* Cambridge: Cambridge University Press.
Haywood, H.C. and Tzuriel, D. (Eds) (1992). *Interactive Assessment.* New York: Springer-Verlag Publishing/Springer Nature.
Hessels-Schlatter, C. (2002). A dynamic test to assess learning capacity in people with severe impairments. *American Journal on Mental Retardation*, 107(5), 340-351.
Karmiloff-Smith, A. (2003). Personal communication.
Karmiloff-Smith, A., D'Souza, D., Dekerra T., Van Herwegenb, J., Xuc, F., Rodica, M. and Ansar, D. (2012). Genetic and environmental vulnerabilities in children with neurodevelopmental disorders. *Proceedings of National Academy of Sciences*, 109(Supplement 2), 17261-17265. Available at: www.pnas.org. Accessed 28 December 2025.
Kaufman, A.S. and Kaufman, N.L. (2004 [1983]). *Kaufman Assessment Battery for Children K-ABC*, 2nd edn. Circle Pines: American Guidance Service.
Korkman, M., Kirk, U. and Kemp, S. (1998). *NEPSY: A Developmental Neuropsychological Assessment.* San Antonio: Psychological Corporation.
Kozulin, A. (1990). *Vygotsky's Psychology: A Biography of Ideas.* Hertfordshire: Harvester Wheatsheaf.
Kozulin, A. (1998). *Psychological Tools: A Sociocultural Approach to Education.* Cambridge, MA: Harvard University Press.
Lezak, M. (1992). *Neuropsychological Assessment.* Oxford: Oxford University Press.
Lidz, C.S. (Ed.) (1987). *Dynamic Assessment: An Interactional Approach to Evaluating Learning Potential.* New York: Guilford.
Lidz, C.S. and Elliott, J.G. (Eds) (2000) *Dynamic Assessment: Prevailing Models and Applications.* New York: Elsevier Science.
Lidz, C.S. and Peña, E.D. (2009). Response to intervention and dynamic assessment: do we just appear to be speaking the same language? *Seminars in Speech and Language*, 30(2), 121–133.
Luria, A.R. (1973). *The Working Brain: An Introduction to Neuropsychology.* London: Penguin Books.
Luria, A.R. (1976). *Cognitive Development: Its Cultural and Social Foundations.* Cambridge, MA: Harvard University Press.
Luria, A.R. (1978 [1930]). Speech and intellect of rural, urban and homeless children. In *Selected Writings.* New York: Sharpe.
Luria, A. (1980). *Higher Cortical Functions in Man.* New York: Springer.
Naglieri, J.A., Das, J.P. and Goldstein, S. (2014). *Cognitive Assessment System: Second Edition (CAS2).* Austin: Pro-Ed.
Peña, E.D., Iglesias, A. and Lidz, C.S. (2001). Dynamic assessment of children's word learning ability. *Journal of Speech, Language and Hearing Research*, 44(6), 1323–1339.
Piaget, J. (1926). *The Language and Thought of the Child.* London: Routledge and Kegan Paul.
Piaget, J. (1958). *The Child's Construction of Reality.* London: Routledge and Kegan Paul.

Resing, W.C.M. (2000). Assessing the learning potential for inductive reasoning (LIR) in young children. In C. Lidz and J.G. Elliott (Eds), *Dynamic Assessment: Prevailing Models and Applications* (pp. 229-262). New York: Elsevier Science.
Resing, W.C.M. (2006). Using children's 'ability to learn' in diagnosis and assessment. *Educational and Child Psychology*, 23(3), 6-11.
Richelle, M. and Feuerstein, R. (under direction of Prof. Andre Rey, and in collaboration with M. Jeannet) (1957). *Enfants Juifs Nord-Africans: Essai Psycho-Pedagogique a l'Intention des Educateurs*. Tel Aviv: Youth Aliyah.
Stuss, D.T. and Benson, D.F. (1984). Neuropsychological studies of the frontal lobes. *Psychological Bulletin*, 95(1), 3-28.
Van der Veer, R. and Valsiner, J. (1994). *The Vygotsky Reader*. Cambridge: Blackwell.
Vygotsky, L.S. (1978). *Mind in Society: The Development of Higher Mental Process*. Cambridge, MA: Harvard University Press.
Vygotsky, L.S. (1986 [1934]). *Thought and Language*. Edited and translated by A. Kozulin. Cambridge, MA: MIT Press. Edited and translated by A. Kozulin.
Wiedl, K.H., Schöttke, H. and Garcia, M.D.C. (2001). Dynamic assessment of cognitive rehabilitation potential in schizophrenic persons and in elderly persons with and without dementia. *European Journal of Psychological Assessment*, 17(2), 112-119.
Wood, D.J., Bruner, J.S. and Ross, G. (1976). The role of tutoring in problem solving. *Journal of Child Psychiatry and Psychology*, 17(2), 89-100.
Yaroshevsky, M. (1988). V shkole Kurta Lewina [In the school of Kurt Lewin: conversation with B. Zeigarnik]. *Voprosy Psikhlogii*, 3, 179.

3

A Framework for Mediated Learning

Introduction

The central focus of this book is to provide theoretical and practical foundations for supporting individuals to become metacognitively aware and to provide practical strategies to foster such awareness, enabling its use in and out of school or other settings. The purpose of this final chapter of Part I is to draw together the various strands of theory related to intelligence, the development of cognitive skills and executive function which will lead onto metacognitive competence. This chapter will provide a framework for mediated learning, providing essential tools for the practical applications covered in Part II.

Chapter 2 introduced Feuerstein's theory of Structural Cognitive Modifiability (SCM). One important element of this theory was his suggestion that learning consists of a three-way relationship between the mediator, the learner and the stimulus or task (Feuerstein, 1986; 1990). This is one of the ways in which he distinguishes direct learning from mediated learning. Feuerstein argues that exposure to information, whether formal or incidental, is not enough; what is needed is the mediator to deliberately stand between the learner and stimulus in order to shape, filter and interpret the stimulus for the learner. This three-way relationship is illustrated in Figure 3.1 (see, for example, Deutsch, 2017; 2020).

The tripartite learning partnership provides a structure for this chapter, and for the practical applications in Part II. It provides a framework for linking together the various parts of our thinking processes that combine to form the foundations upon which our higher order choices can be made. It illustrates the relationship between three elements necessary for cognitive and metacognitive awareness: the learner, the mediator and the task. The three elements are not only related but are mutually dependent. Metacognitive awareness is the outcome of successful integration of all three elements of the partnership. The next three sections of this chapter will examine each element of the partnership. Although we will explain these three parts in the order of learner, the task and the mediator, this is not a given order. We can start anywhere as long as our investigations include consideration of all three elements.

DOI: 10.4324/9781003655329-5

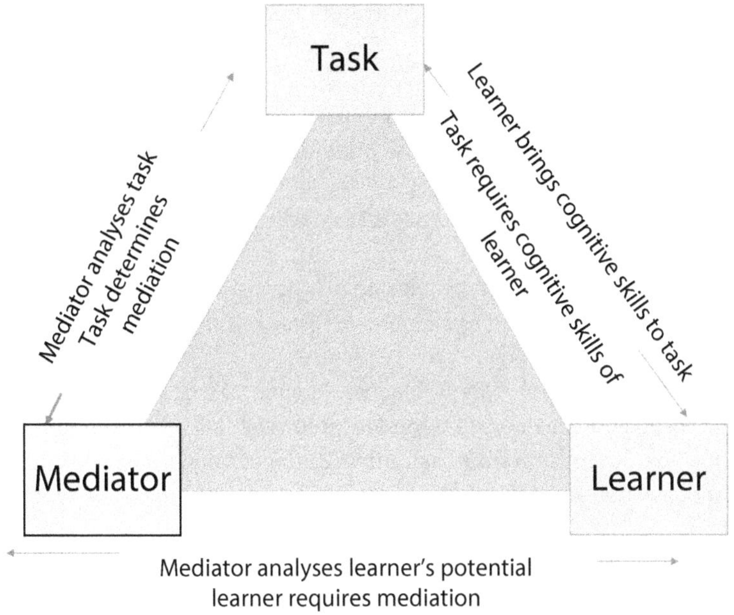

Figure 3.1 A tripartite learning partnership

Defining terms

A clear definition of each element of the tripartite model will be given before looking at the elements in detail.

Learner. The *Oxford English Dictionary* defines a learner as 'a person who is finding out about a subject or how to do something'. The subject matter of this book mean that our focus will be on the *how* aspect, via identification of the learner's cognitive skills. There are two important points to make in defining a 'learner':

- Being a learner is lifelong. Cognitive skills are not limited to school age learners or to childhood more broadly; they are applicable across the entire lifespan;
- In this text, 'learner' means all learners. The cognitive skills and emotional states that we will propose in this chapter apply to any learner. The profile of strengths and needs will vary, since all learners are individuals. This means that although there may clusters and patterns which are associated with some conditions and diagnostic labels, this is not a checklist approach. We are not trying to fit individual learners into specific cognitive profiles that 'match' learners with particular diagnostic labels such as PMLD (profound and multiple learning difficulties) or various neurodiverse labels such as autistic spectrum condition, attention deficit hyperactivity disorder (ADHD), dyslexia, dyscalculia or dyspraxia, to name just a few. We recognise there might be some frequently occurring aspects of cognition that are more challenging for certain learners.

However, the starting point is the learner, not the label. In this way our detailed analysis of a learner's cognitive profile may contribute to a diagnosis, but is not designed as a primary diagnostic tool.

Task. A task can be any activity, formal or informal, a problem to be solved, or a job to be done in any context. It is important to know what task demands are because they help to:

- Identify what skills, relevant processes and knowledge are needed for a task;
- Plan and sequence mediated learning;
- See which parts of a task might be causing a difficulty or be a strength for that learner;
- Identify what can be adjusted or changed in order to support learning.

Mediator. A mediator (such as a parent, teacher, teaching assistant, therapist or peer) who intervenes in purposeful ways to help the learner make links and develop thinking skills which can then be used in different situations. We cannot take progress for granted and so we have to actively intervene to help learners make sense of their experience and be able to learn from it.

The learner

The focus of this part of the partnership is on the cognitive skills of the learner. A brief internet search using terms such as 'cognitive skills' or 'thinking skills' yields numerous lists of these skills, which can be bewildering when trying to decide what should (or should not) be included in a list of cognitive skills. McGuinness (1999) reports Resnick's (1987) comment about thinking skills: 'although high quality thinking was difficult to define, it was easy to recognise' (McGuinness, 1999: 5). That said, some kind of list of cognitive skills is needed in order to make the tripartite partnership meaningful and useful; if we do not define what cognitive skills are involved in learning then it is very challenging to identify, support and promote them.

Feuerstein's contribution

Reuven Feuerstein's theories on psychology and educational practice were discussed in Chapter 2. This chapter acknowledges and builds on his contribution and legacy in relation to describing cognitive skills.

Feuerstein's list of deficient cognitive functions was never intended to explain thinking as a whole or to be a stand-alone list, that is separate from other aspects of his theory of SCM. Haywood et al. (2022) comment: 'There is no "official" or complete list of cognitive functions. Feuerstein offered his own list, derived from clinical experience and logically derived from essentially Piagetian theories of cognitive development' (Haywood et al., 2022).

Feuerstein later referred to 'developed' cognitive functions (Feuerstein Institute, 2018) when dealing with the developmental difficulties of younger learners, rather than using the original list which was developed in relation to the adolescents with whom he first worked. Feuerstein organised his list of cognitive functions into three phases of the mental act: input, elaboration and output. Assigning deficient cognitive functions to phases was intended to indicate where to mediate (intervene). He also added a list of what he called non-intellective factors, that is, the affective, emotional and behavioural factors of a person's approach to learning, emphasising the interrelationship between cognition and the affective elements of learning 'as two sides of a transparent coin' (Feuerstein et al., 2002: 33). Recognition of the significant and sometimes central impact that emotion can have on an individual's thinking and reasoning skills is in contrast with static tests of intelligence, where all the examiner does do is to comment on the possible impact of affective factors on the test results. Other authors draw on this conceptualisation of the role of affective factors (for example, Greenberg, 2000; Deutsch, 2020; Haywood and Lidz, 2007; Haywood et al., 2022).

A new starting point: the Boat of Cognition model

Theory and research are not static. Advances in knowledge and understanding make further contributions, resulting in evolution, adaptation and changes. The changes do not remove what has gone previously; rather, they build on it, where successive developments in knowledge and understanding add more insights to the bigger picture. We can understand and use the new in the context of what has gone before.

The Boat of Cognition, illustrated in Figure 3.2, is our conceptualisation of the learner's cognitive and affective factors. In addition to reflecting aspects of Feuerstein's work and legacy, it also draws on a domain model, based on Luria's functional units (Luria, 1976), discussed in detail in Chapter 2, as used by Haywood and Lidz (2007) and Deutsch (2020).

Luria's functional units model and the domains give an overall structure but they do not 'drill down' to identify specific cognitive skills. Identifying these specific cognitive skills is a necessary first step in order to identify and mediate these skills. Feuerstein describes these as 'prerequisites of thinking' (Feuerstein et al., 2002: 522), which further emphasises the need for establishing and consolidating cognitive skills before metacognition is possible. The linkage of cognitive and affective skills is afforded equal emphasis in our model, in contrast to their role in psychometric assessment, where the affective presentation of the individual is only the subject of comment even if it is clear that the results of testing are significantly skewed by these factors. As in Feuerstein's concepts, the Boat of Cognition emphasises this linkage. The term '*emotional states*' is used to describe the affective elements of the Boat of Cognition.

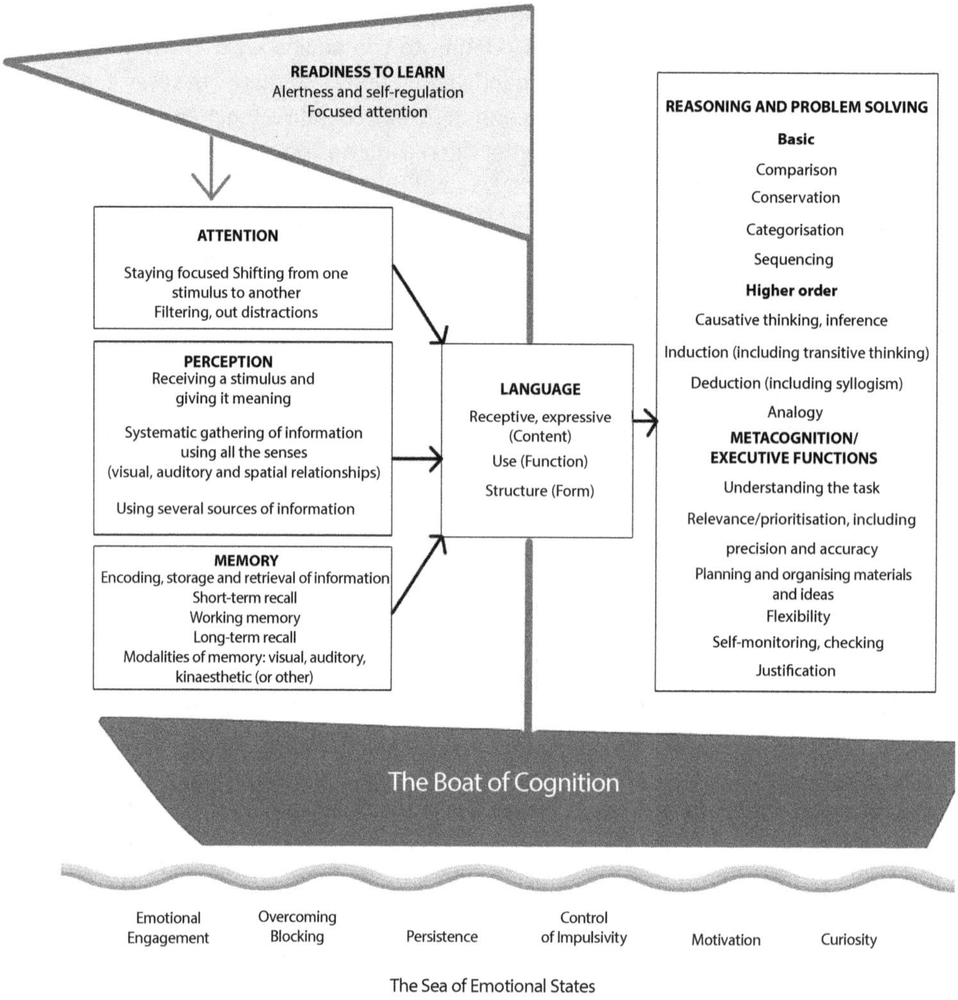

Figure 3.2 The Boat of Cognition

Characteristics of the Boat of Cognition

One principle aim in developing our model is for it to have three basic, generic characteristics:

- Clarity of language;
- A manageable number of elements;
- A list that can be used across a range of ages and stages.

Other specific characteristics are discussed briefly below.

Readiness to learn

Readiness to learn is the start of our model. The rationale for this comes from Luria's work. His first functional unit of attention/arousal is a foundation for other cognitive processes.

Readiness to learn involves the individual in focusing attention, being motivated to want to engage and showing self-regulation to restrain impulsivity. These are the foundations for the use of other cognitive skills.

Readiness to learn is the sail of the boat. Being attentive and alert puts wind in the sails and moves the boat. When learners have wind in their sails, they are then able to attend, perceive, remember, use language, reason and problem-solve. Then the learner is able to reach the destination of metacognitive awareness.

A domain structure

The Boat of Cognition model uses a domain structure, reflecting Luria's three functional units (Luria, 1976). The foundational domains in our model are Attention, Perception and Memory. Domains are used in preference to a phase model of input, elaboration and output (Feuerstein et al., 2002), which was based on his observations of adolescent structures of thinking and are not directly transferable to younger children. Deutsch (2017) points out that Feuerstein's original 'deficiency' list of cognitive functions, which was based on Piaget's fourth stage of cognitive development, does not take account what cognition might look like in early childhood. The phase model is not considered to be directly applicable to the thinking of young children (Haywood, 2003; Karmiloff-Smith, 2012a; 2012b). The idea of emerging cognitive functions in young children cannot be assumed to follow an input, elaboration and output structure. Young children start off as generalists in their neurological development. We know that the most rapid development of the brain occurs in the first five years of life. Karmiloff-Smith (2012b) suggests that the neurological pathways of the brain in a child at risk may be organising themselves, early in life, into disordered patterns of functioning. Thus, the earlier we can intervene across all areas of development, the greater the chance of lessening the impact of various risk factors which later become much harder to change. Therefore, the domain structure ensures that the model is applicable across all ages.

Within the domain structure, the Boat of Cognition separates cognitive skills into three categories: reasoning and problem-solving - basic; higher order; and executive function and metacognition. The order is not necessarily hierarchical. For example, it will be important for a learner to understand the task before, for example, deciding if they need to compare or sequence or use logical reasoning.

Language is positioned between the foundation domains and the basic and higher order cognitive skills, since it is a bridge between the two. Within the domain of language, our model draws on Bloom and Lahey's form, content and use model (Bloom and Lahey, 1978). Language *form* refers to how language is arranged and structured. We can refer to this aspect of language as grammar. This also includes syntax, which are the rules that help us to combine words to make meaningful utterances. Form also includes phonology, which is related to speech sounds and the rules that are used to make these sounds into meaningful words. Language *content* refers to vocabulary, topics and ideas of language. This might include feelings/emotions, events or actions. Language *use* (sometimes called pragmatics) refers to the functions of communication. This area includes using language in appropriate contexts.

Emotional states

The Boat of Cognition floats on the sea of emotional states. The sea keeps the boat afloat, just as our emotional states keep us afloat and thus able to think and reason. However, no matter how calm the sea, the boat itself has to be in good order with all parts ready and able to sail. So, we see the synergy between the boat and the water it sails in. Sometimes the sea is stormy, which means that the emotional states rock the boat and make it difficult to sail. When the sea is just right the boat can sail. Successful arrival at the destination depends on a bidirectional relationship between the boat and the sea; sailing is affected both by the state of the sea and of the boat. The practical applications in Part II provide the tools to navigate the Boat of Cognition.

The task

Feuerstein suggested a framework for task analysis called the 'Cognitive Map', based on Guttmann's work on facet theory (Guttman, 1954; Guttman and Levy, 1991). Feuerstein identified seven elements of the cognitive map. Others have adapted this model (for example, Haywood and Lidz, 2007; Mentis et al., 2008; Deutsch, 2020).

We propose a five-layer model of the task. The five elements of our model are:

- Content (which includes novelty and familiarity);
- Modality;
- Level of abstraction and complexity;
- Cognitive skills;
- Speed, precision and accuracy.

The five layers will be described in more detail in Chapter 5.

The mediator

The mediator is the third element of the tripartite partnership. We will begin by exploring the concept of mediation and how it relates to some current thinking, especially in support for struggling learners. The criteria of mediation will then be examined.

What is mediation and mediated learning?

The term 'mediation' comes from Vygotsky, as discussed in detail in Chapter 2. Feuerstein's work went on to specify the components of mediation, which he termed Mediated Learning Experience (MLE). Mediation is a key element of Feuerstein's theory of SCM.

The fundamental purpose of deliberate mediation is to interact with the learner in order to bring about cognitive change. Thus, mediation focuses on the processes of learning rather than the products (in school typically, the content of the curriculum). Kozulin (2024: 1) states that mediation 'helps us to explain the interaction between human beings and their environments'.

Mediation requires greater responsiveness between teacher and learner than only following a pre-planned, stripped-down curriculum. It can be challenging because individualised mediation cannot be planned in minute or forensic detail beforehand and requires a high level of attunement to the cognitive needs of learners and of the tasks they are being asked to perform, especially to the needs of those learners who are struggling.

Mediation criteria and the Boat of Cognition

In order for an interaction to be called 'mediation' a number of criteria must be present. These criteria are important and give a structure for the interaction between the learner and the mediator. Feuerstein identified three essential criteria of mediation without which an interaction is not mediational. That is not to say that other types of interactions are not valid or important. There is nothing wrong with direct instruction! Our focus is about when, where and why do we deliberately *choose* to mediate a cognitive skill, in place of or alongside other forms of interaction.

The descriptions below draw on Feuerstein's original list, with amendments to wording that draw on Lidz (2003), Haywood (2003) and Mentis et al. (2008).

The three essential criteria are:

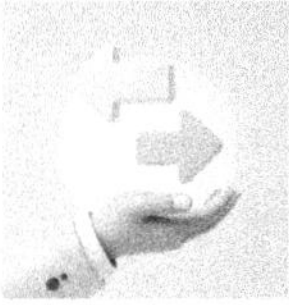

Intentionality and reciprocity. The mediator must have a clear intention to intervene with the learner in order to bring about cognitive change. Mediation cannot be left to chance; if it is, it risks being infrequent and ill thought out. Reciprocity refers to the interaction of the mediator with the learner. Mediation is responsive to the learner, it is not merely use of a script or set of instructions, delivered regardless of how the learner presents.

Meaning. Communicating the purpose of the task or activity. You might notice that throughout this book we have used the phrase: 'this is important because ...', which is our mediation of meaning in relation to the content of the book. Meaning communicates the value of the experience (Lidz, 2003). Mediation of meaning can be closely linked to motivation and engagement.

Transfer. Bridging, or teaching for transfer, is the process of making links to past and future learning. Transfer is important because it supports the learner to make connections and ensures that what is being mediated has relevance for many aspects of the learner's life. One of the essential points made by Feuerstein and others is that transcendence (transfer) does not happen by itself.

Transfer is considered the most important part of mediation (Haywood and Lidz, 2007). Teaching for transfer is a separate chapter in this book (Chapter 7) due to the important role this plays in the development of cognitive skills, executive function and ensuring that the road to metacognition is really travelled. Transfer does not apply only to cognition, as illustrated in the following example, which shows how transfer of cognitive skills was suggested as useful way forward for addressing a learner's behaviour issues.

Our work routinely involves observing pupils in class, as a key part of a holistic assessment. In England, curriculum planning is underpinned by objectives, which are often expressed to pupils in the form of the acronyms WALT (we are learning to) and WILF (what I'm looking for). Their purpose appears to be to show that the goal or objective of the lesson has been shared with the pupils. However, our observations do not always support this. In some cases, pupils spend much of the lesson copying these out and we rarely observe any direct reference to or explanation of the acronyms with pupils. This is borne out by our follow-up interactions with pupils, where we usually ask the pupil to tell us what the lesson was about and why they were doing a particular task. The most common answer is: 'don't know.' Often the pupils that respond in this way are described by staff as being disengaged from learning and having low motivation. However, our contention is that part of these problems is that the learner has little or no idea of the meaning or relevance of what they are learning; the 'why' of learning has not been shared in a meaningful way.

Liam, aged 15, was referred due to concerns about learning and behaviour. At the time of the assessment, he was attending a Pupil Referral Unit (PRU: an alternative provision for pupils who are excluded from school). In addition to challenging behaviour in school, Liam had come to the attention of the police through petty offending behaviour outside of school. He frequently 'disappeared' for hours during the evening, without telling his parents where he was going or who he was with. He spent a lot of his time with a gang of young people who were a negative influence; they frequently persuaded him to engage in inappropriate behaviour then left him to face the consequences. His peer relationships were characterised by impulsive hitting out without stopping to think or to make a considered judgement about a social situation. Assessment involved looking at Liam's cognitive skills using Dynamic Assessment (DA), with a particular focus on logical and inferential thinking. In the DA tests he was able to demonstrate some secure problem-solving skills related to cause and effect thinking, once his impulsivity had been mediated. These findings appeared to contradict the way in which he presented in and out of school, where he appeared to pay scant attention to the consequences of his behaviour. Therefore, one of the recommendations was related to transferring and generalising his successful cause and effect thinking to his behaviour choices, starting with a focus on support for reducing impulsivity.

Further to the three essential criterial defining an interaction as mediational, Feuerstein suggested additional, optional features of mediation (Feuerstein, 1986; 1990; Deutsch, 2003). Some of these optional criteria are used in other publications that use mediated learning (for example, Lidz, 2003; Deutsch, 2020; Haywood et al., 2022; Lauchlan and Daly, 2023).

A practical and manageable approach

Table 3.1 shows the mediation criteria that are used in the present publication and which are a further foundation for the practical applications in Part II. Clear wording and a manageable list are key drivers for a suggested list of criteria to be used as the basis for the

Table 3.1 Mediation criteria

Criterion	***Description***	***Rationale***
ESSENTIAL		
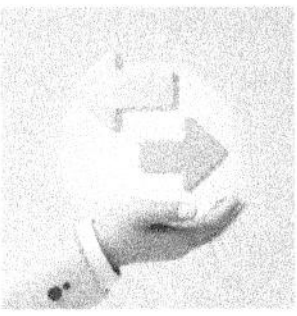 **Intentionality and reciprocity**	Mediation is intentional. The mediator adjusts their mediation according to the response of the learner.	The essential criteria of mediation are unchanged in all versions of these criteria. There is wide agreement that they are the essence of what makes an interaction 'mediational'.
 **Meaning**	Sharing the purpose: 'we are doing this because ...'; 'this is important because ...'	
 **Transfer**	Making links to past, present and future learning/problem-solving. Supporting the learner to apply and generalise theory problem-solving skills.	
ADDITIONAL (optional)		
 **Positive affirmation and empathy**	Connecting with the learner. Accepting what the learner brings to the interaction (being non-judgemental) but also expressing optimism and confidence that cognitive and affective change can happen.	This criterion is consistent with Roger's term unconditional positive regard (Rogers, 1957), which involves a non-judgemental stance. It encompasses several items in Feuerstein's original list such as individuation, optimistic alternatives and belonging. It aims to communicate a sense of worth and belief in the learner's ability to change. Empathy emphasises the importance of seeing the world through the eyes of others, which includes taking a sensitive account of culture.

(Continued)

Table 3.1 (Continued)

Criterion	*Description*	*Rationale*
 **Regulation**	Supporting the learner to reduce impulsivity or reduce trial and error behaviours so that they can focus on task requirements	Impulsivity is a significant challenge to successful problem-solving, so working toward self-regulation must be mediated.
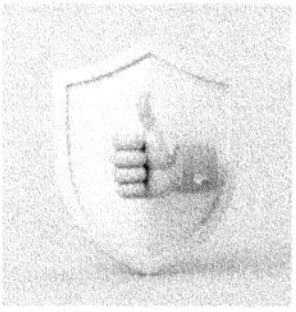 **Competence**	Offering task-related praise and encouragement. Supporting the learner to overcome blocking.	Mediating competence is important because it is part of a process that supports the learner to move from extrinsic to intrinsic motivation which is one of the key goals of Feuerstein's Instrumental Enrichment programme (Feuerstein et al. 1980). A focus on the task, not on the person, is important.
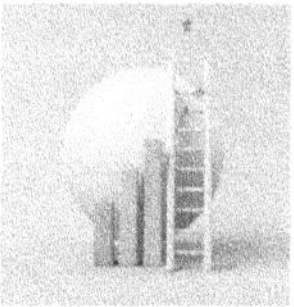 **Challenge**	Supporting the learner to tackle a more difficult aspect of the task or type of problem; stretching the learner. Working in their Zone of Proximal Development (ZPD), supporting learning just ahead of where the learner is now.	It is important to reflect the ZPD in the process of mediation. Feuerstein's approach shares the same sociocultural perspective as Vygotsky. Many education practitioners are familiar with the term ZPD, so it connects practice to their prior knowledge.
 **Goal setting and planning**	Supporting the learner to plan and work systematically. Keeping focused on the goal (attention to what is relevant). Mediating persistence and checking, so that the task or problem is seen through to the end.	Inclusion of goal setting reflects our emphasis on Luria's third functional unit which involves conscious planning.

practical work set out in Part II. In Table 3.1, the three essential criteria are unchanged and five further optional criteria have been chosen, based on Feuerstein's more extensive list.

The format of a table can tend to suggest a hierarchy, which is not the case. Mediation is a fluid, interactive process and although intentionality is likely to be the first criterion that is used at the beginning of an interaction, the remaining criteria do not follow a set order or pattern. Figure 3.3 illustrates the relationship.

The image of cogs is a way of showing the interrelatedness of the criteria. It also links to the Boat of Cognition illustration (Figure 3.2). We suggested that readiness to learn is the wind in the sails of the boat. However, wind might not always be present, so a boat might also have a motor to propel it. The cogs in Figure 3.3 can be viewed as the motor for the boat, because mediation is important in propelling the boat towards the destination of metacognition.

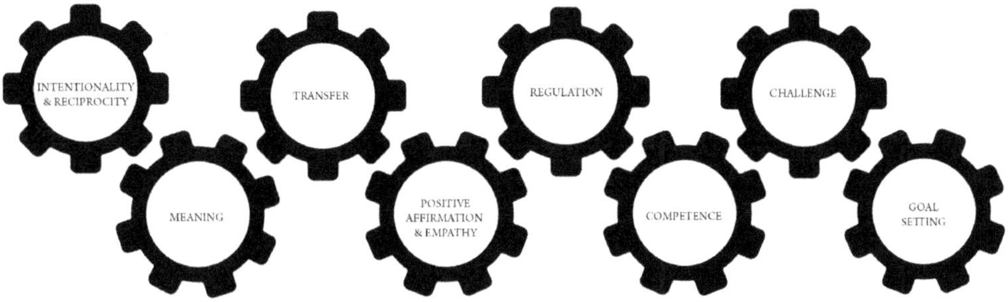

Figure 3.3 Mediation criteria

Myths about mediation

In the course of the long involvement of both authors in training practitioners in mediated learning, we have encountered some myths that tend to arise, which are important to address.

Myth one: mediation is just good teaching

It is true that teaching can be mediational, but this is not the same as the practitioner delivering deliberate, intentional mediated learning. An example from one of the authors' casework helps to illustrate this point:

> Isabel, aged three years, was referred for assessment and advice due to developmental delay. She was observed in her preschool setting during a child-initiated play session. Her key adult came alongside her during play. Some strategies used by her key worker were noted as being mediational. Some examples were: saying 'look' in an excited tone of voice to draw attention to activities or particular play materials (mediating meaning), giving positive recognition (via verbal praise and thumbs up) in response to Isabel demonstrating persistence with a task (mediating feelings of competence) and encouraging Isabel to tackle a more difficult task (mediation of challenge). However, these interactions were not noted as being examples of *mediated learning*. The reasons for this were the absence of intent and the task focus of the interactions. Isabel's key worker did not set out to intervene (that is, to mediate); it was unplanned and although there was evidence of reciprocity (since the key worker was responding to Isabel's engagement in the child-initiated play), she had not set out with the *specific* intention to intervene. The mediational interactions focused on getting the task done and not on the processes; as emphasised earlier, mediated learning is aimed at supporting and improving the processes of learning, not the products.

Mediation, therefore, is not just good teaching. The point about mediation and teaching is summarised clearly by Greenberg (2000), as shown in the following box.

Mediated learning is more than good teaching

1. Good teachers teach students what they need to know. Teacher-mediators collaborate as another learner with students to reflect on what each person already knows and to see how this knowledge connects to something new.
2. Good teachers often focus students' attention on the lesson content. Teacher-mediators also clarify and expand students' understanding beyond the immediate needs of the content and context.
3. Good teachers often isolate specific concepts for teaching. Teacher-mediators also connect concepts to students' real-world experiences.
4. Good teachers provide students with opportunities to produce right answers based on given information. Teacher-mediators more frequently provide opportunities for students to explore ideas, seek relevant information, and construct meaning independently and collaboratively.
5. Good teachers lead students through learning experiences as part of a carefully selected curriculum. Teacher-mediators also adapt activities so they are personally relevant and challenging.
6. Good teachers often model tasks, break tasks into smaller parts, and reteach when necessary. Teacher-mediators help students learn to construct their own learning strategies to solve problems.
7. Good teachers make certain to share the right answer with students. Teacher-mediators also provide extra time and assistance so every student can reflect on the process of reaching the right answer and find an approach that leads to an effective response.
8. Good teachers usually provide students with feedback related to their learning products and often reward students based on teacher standards. Teacher-mediators also encourage students to evaluate the individual process they used that led to a product and provide feedback and encouragement (rather than rewards) related to the process of learning based on mutually determined standards.
9. Good teachers often lead class discussions in which they ask questions and students respond. Teacher-mediators more frequently empower students to ask questions and to share insights with the group.
10. Good teachers establish an atmosphere in which students feel successful when they can learn easily and share what they know. Teacher-mediators establish an atmosphere that measures success by how much one is willing to accept challenges and learn how to learn.

Extract from the Cognitive Enrichment Advantage programme (Greenberg, 2000). Reproduced with permission from the author.

Myth two: mediation is a way of differentiating the curriculum

Differentiation came to the forefront of educational practice as a response to the growing emphasis on inclusion in education, reflected in SEND policy and legislation such as the Code of Practice (Department for Education and Department of Health, 2015) applicable in England or IDEA in the United States (US Department of Education, 2004). It is used as a mechanism for dealing with the wide mix of abilities in mainstream classrooms. However, neither the concept nor the practice of differentiation are defined straightforwardly. For example, Eikeland and Ohna's (2022) analysis and review of 28 papers related to differentiation led them to suggest four different views of differentiation. What does appear to be consistent in the literature is that differentiation focuses on the products and content of learning. This view is an inadequate understanding of the fundamental purpose of mediation, which is to improve the processes of learning.

Differentiation as a concept and as a pedagogical practice seems to be falling out of favour and the term 'adaptive teaching' is now more commonly used. UK government policy and legislation uses these terms in documents relating to Initial Teacher Training standards (Department for Education, 2019a) and the Early Career Framework for teachers (Department for Education, 2019b). In common with differentiation, there is little clarity about what exactly is meant by this term and how it is different from the term differentiation. Ankrum et al. (2020) cite Vygotsky's ZPD as one of the theoretical foundations of adaptive teaching, suggesting an interactional and relational approach to teaching that might point to the reciprocity criterion of mediation. However, Gallagher et al. (2022: 298) describe adaptive teaching as an 'unplanned response'. The unplanned element of adaptive teaching undermines the intentionality essential criterion of mediation. It does reflect the reciprocity criterion; however, the focus is still on content and product, not process. Passing references to Vygotsky, and mention of scaffolding as a strategy, fall woefully short of any common ground with mediation. Therefore, mediation is not simply another word for differentiation or adaptive teaching.

Myth three: mediation is only needed for struggling learners

This myth flows from myth two, because differentiation is generally thought of as an approach used for struggling learners. This is a flawed view of mediation. Feuerstein et al. (2002: 131) is clear about this point: 'the assessment of modifiability is therefore not limited to individuals with manifest levels of impairment but is a requirement for all individuals who are confronted with the need for increased adaptability'. This may explain why Feuerstein later published a list of developed cognitive functions, in order to show that his concept of mediation was not limited to those with obvious cognitive challenges. Feuerstein defines mediation as essential for all of us, as did Vygotsky. Time, place and context will vary, but without mediation we miss out on one of our unique human connections. Mediation is also important to use with gifted pupils; for example, Tannenbaum's (1991) work with gifted underachievers (see Chapter 2) and Howie's (2019) account of meeting the needs of able learners.

Myth four: mediation is subjective

This myth states that mediation is little more than a subjective approach which therefore lacks a robust evidence base. This is based on arguments that there is insufficient empirical evidence to support Feuerstein's claims that mediated learning is the proximal factor which explains and can remediate previous learning failure (Frisby and Braden, 1992; Büchel and Scharnhorst, 1993). However, other sources provide an evidence base for the impact of mediation. For example, research by Lidz (1991) and Klein's research with low birthweight children (1996) support the positive impact of mediation in relation to young children and identify *transcendence* as being the most important MLE criterion, accounting for the biggest changes in young children. Finnegan's (2024) research examined the impact of training in MLE for practitioners working with neurodiverse learners. She found that the first criterion of mediation (intentionality and reciprocity) had a positive impact on teacher self-efficacy. Finnegan links this finding to the concept of engagement and the relationship between this and student achievement. Other research also builds a picture of a robust evidence base (Romney and Samuels, 2001; White and Dinos, 2010; Keung et al. 2022; Dughi and Ianc, 2022). Additional evidence is found in the Bright Start Programme (Haywood et al., 2022) and from Cebe and Paour's (2000) research into cognitive education using mediated learning with kindergarten children ages 5-6 years, (equivalent to Year One pupils in the UK system).

Whilst all methods of evaluation are not without flaws and limitations (many of which are clearly acknowledged by the authors), there is no overwhelming evidence to support the myth of subjectivity. Overall, therefore, this is not supported if and when mediation is carried out using the essential criteria.

Myth five: the 'feel good' factor

This myth suggests that mediation is about fostering a 'feel good' factor for the learner. The consequence of this misunderstanding is that the focus on cognitive skills is reduced and that task analysis does not always clearly identify which cognitive skills are the focus for mediation. It is clearly important for the learner to be encouraged to talk about their approach to problem-solving and for the mediator to mediate feelings of competence. In our experience, in responses to questions to the mediator, 'Why are you mediating?' and 'What are you mediating?', a common response is that the mediator is trying to make the pupil 'feel good', interacting positively and helping them to arrive at the right answer. This response tends to show a focus on mediating content and not process. It also lacks the mediation of challenge criterion, which aims to support the learner to go beyond their cognitive comfort zone. Mediation of cognitive skills (as opposed to content) that involves challenge can, in many cases, result in the desired 'feel good' factor but on its own this is not enough and not mediation. Here is a case example:

Craig, aged 14, attended a special school for pupils with moderate learning difficulties. In this highly adapted learning environment with very small classes, he was struggling to access the curriculum. He was very aware that he was not keeping up with his peers. He developed a repertoire of challenging behaviours which usually resulted in him being told to leave his lesson after a very short period of time. Craig did not view this as a punishment; quite the reverse, as it was a way of him avoiding lessons and thus not risking others seeing that he couldn't cope with the lesson. Therefore, most of his school day was spent wandering around the school building or sitting in the deputy head's office.

Craig was quite a 'streetwise' young man due to the company he kept outside of school, so learning was very definitely 'uncool'. One of the present authors was asked to work with him in order to find out how to support his learning and engagement. Part of the work with Craig involved doing some DA. Referral information specifically mentioned concerns about memory, so the 16 Word Memory Test was used, which involves the pupil repeating back a list of 16 words after they have been read out. After four or five trials with no mediation (in order to look at unassisted performance and the effect of repeated exposure), mediation was given to use a categorisation strategy. In the unmediated trials he remembered two or three words but gave up very easily. He made comments such as 'I'm no good at remembering' or 'I can't do this' in between each trial. During the mediated trials, one emphasis in mediation was challenge. He was challenged to keep going and to beat his score in each successive mediated trial. He gradually began to appear more engaged, wanting to know how many he had remembered at the end of each trial. At the end of trial 10, he recalled all 16 words, at which point he became very excited about this result. He asked if he could go and show the record sheet to his teachers, so he then raced around school waving the record sheet and showing it to any member of staff he came across, saying 'look what I did'. This quite simple activity was the first time for a very long time that Craig had experienced any success in a learning activity. The follow-up to this was to talk with staff about how to support Craig's cognitive skills, including how to promote and support task-intrinsic motivation. The transfer criterion of mediation was used with Craig in a follow-up discussion, asking him to think about when else it would be helpful to keep going with a task even though it was difficult, and to think about when else it is helpful to use categories or groups to help him remember.

The goal of mediated learning in assessment and in educational practice focuses on deliberate selection of cognitive targets towards specific cognitive change. In the case example above there was a very definite 'feel good factor' at the end, but this only came about because mediation focused on challenging Craig's poor persistence and sense of worth.

Summary

This chapter has outlined the tripartite learning partnership as a framework for exploring how an individual might be supported to achieve competency of what constitutes an act of learning in terms of the cognitive skills and task analysis leading to metacognitive awareness and control. The tripartite partnership is our tool on the road to becoming an effective mediator. We have suggested a different way of conceptualising the cognitive and affective elements of learning, based on Luria's functional units model, which also reflects and draws on Feuerstein's legacy and work. Similarly, the mediation criteria and task analysis elements proposed reflect Feuerstein's work.

The three elements of the tripartite partnership provide the framework for the practical strategies and approaches which are the focus of Part II. Figure 3.4, showing the House of Metacognition, illustrates the way in which material from this and preceding chapters contributes to building metacognitive awareness.

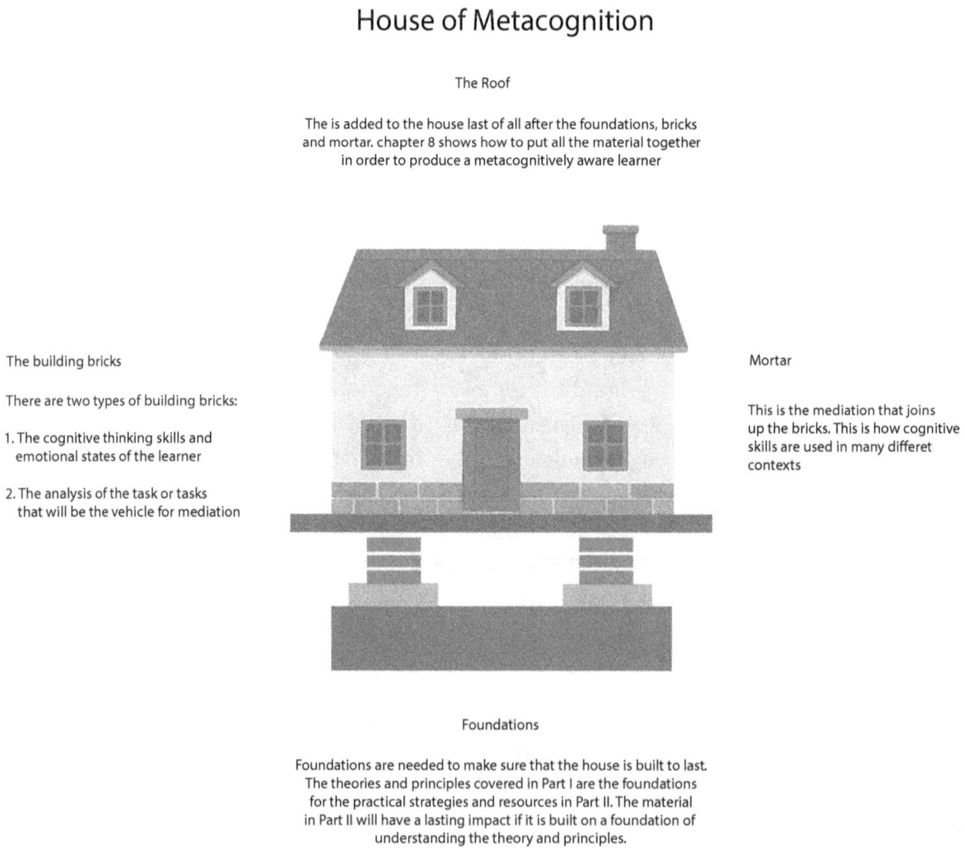

Figure 3.4 The House of Metacognition

A quote attributed to Leonardo da Vinci seems an appropriate way to conclude this chapter, and Part I as a whole: 'Those who are in love with practice without knowledge are like the sailor who gets into a ship without rudder or compass and who never can be certain where he is going.' Part I of this text has provided the rudder or compass so that practitioners can navigate the complexities of mediated learning and thus empower their learners to become metacognitively aware.

Reflection and follow-up

- What was novel for you in this chapter and which ideas either strengthened or challenged your past learning and experience?
- This chapter draws on two perspectives on cognition, Luria's and Feuerstein's. Do you consider them complementary and if so in which aspects?
- The inclusion of the sea of emotions in our Boat of Cognition model reflects Feuerstein's assertion that emotion and cognition are 'two sides of the same transparent coin'. What changes might you make to take account of the impact of the sea of emotions?

References

Ankrum, J., Morewood, A., Parsons, S., Vaughn, M., Parsons, A. and Hawkins, P. (2020). Documenting adaptive literacy instruction: the Adaptive Teaching Observation Protocol (ATOP). *Reading Psychology*, 41(2), 71–86.

Bloom, L, and Lahey, M. (1978). *Language Development and Language Disorders*. New York: Wiley.

Büchel, F.P. and Scharnhorst, U. (1993). The learning potential assessment device (LPAD): discussion of theoretical and methodological problems. In J.H. Hamers, K. Sijtma and A.J. Ruijssenaars (Eds), *Learning Potential Assessment: Theoretical, Methodological and Practical Issues*. Amsterdam: Swets and Zeitlinger.

Cebe, C. and Paour, J.L. (2000). Effects of cognitive education in kindergarten on learning to read in the primary grades. *Journal of Cognitive Education and Psychology*, 1(2), 177–200.

Department for Education (2019a). *ITT Core Content Framework*. Available at: assets.publishing.service.gov.uk/media/6061eb9cd3bf7f5cde260984/ITT_core_content_framework_.pdf. Accessed 30 July 2025.

Department for Education (2019b). *Early Career Framework*. Available at: www.gov.uk/government/publications/early-career-framework. Accessed 28 July 2025.

Department for Education and Department of Health (2015). *Special Educational Needs and Disability Code of Practice: 0 to 25 Years*. Available at: https://www.gov.uk/government/publications/send-code-of-practice-0-to-25. Accessed 27 January 2026.

Deutsch, R. (2003). Mediation from the perspective of mediated learning experience. *Journal of Cognitive Education and Psychology*, 3(1), 29–45.

Deutsch, R.M. (2017). *Reliability, Validity and Educational Use of the Cognitive Abilities Profile*, unpublished doctoral thesis, City, University of London.

Deutsch, R. (2020). *Cognitive Abilities Profile*, rev. edn. Canterbury: Real Publishing.

Dughi, T. and Ianc, F.R. (2022). Students' self efficacy and Feuerstein instrumental enrichment. *Journal Plus Education*, 30(1), 53–66.

Eikeland, I. and Ohna, S. (2022) Differentiation in education: a configurative review. *Nordic Journal of Studies in Educational Policy*, 8(3), 157–170.

Feuerstein, R. (1986). *Mediated Learning Experience.* Jerusalem: Hadassa-Wizo-Canada Research Institute.
Feuerstein, R. (1990). The theory of structural cognitive modifiability. In B. Presseisen (Ed.), *Learning and Thinking Styles: Classroom Interaction.* Washington, DC: National Education Association.
Feuerstein, R., Rand, Y., Hoffman, M.B., Hoffman, M. and Miller, R. (1980). *Instrumental Enrichment: An Intervention Program for Cognitive Modifiability.* Baltimore: University Park Press.
Feuerstein, R., Feuerstein, R., Falik, L. and Rand, Y. (2002). *The Dynamic Assessment of Cognitive Modifiability.* Jerusalem: The ICELP Press.
Feuerstein Institute (2018). *Teaching Diagrams Mediated Learning & Instrumental Enrichment.* Available at: www.feuerstein-institute.org/wp-content/uploads/2023/04/Teaching-diagrams-IE-Standard-English-2018.pdf. Accessed 11 August 2025.
Finnegan, H. (2024). *An Investigation into the Impact of Mediated Learning Strategies on the Learning Outcomes for Autistic Students*, unpublished DEdPsy thesis, University of Strathclyde.
Frisby, C.L. and Braden, J.P. (1992). Feuerstein's dynamic assessment approach: a semantic, logical, and empirical critique. *The Journal of Special Education*, 26(3), 281–301.
Gallagher, M., Parsons, S. and Vaughan, M. (2022). Adaptive teaching in mathematics: a review of the literature. *Educational Review*, 74(2), 298–320.
Greenberg, K. (2000). *The Cognitive Enrichment Advantage.* Knoxville: KCD Harris & Associates Press.
Guttman, L. (1954). Some necessary conditions for common-factor analysis. *Psychometrika*, 19, 149–161.
Guttman, L. and Levy, S. (1991). Two structural laws for intelligence tests. *Intelligence*, 15(1), 79–103.
Haywood, H.C. (2003). Mediation within a neo-Piagetian framework. *Journal of Cognitive Education and Psychology*, 3(1), 71–81.
Haywood, H.C. and Lidz, C.S. (2007). *Dynamic Assessment in Practice: Clinical and Educational Applications.* New York: Cambridge University Press.
Haywood, H.C., Brooks, P. and Burns, M.S. (2022). *Bright Start Cognitive Curriculum for Young Children*, rev. edn. Bright Start CCYC. Available at: www.brightstart-ccyc.com. Accessed 5 August 2025.
Howie, D. (2019). *Thinking about the Teaching of Thinking.* London: Routledge.
Karmiloff-Smith, A. (2012a). Rethinking the study of neurodevelopmental disorders: the importance of cross-syndrome comparisons. Paper presented at The Paediatric Neuropsychology Conference, London.
Karmiloff-Smith, A. (2012b). Perspectives on the dynamic development of cognitive capacities. Insights from Williams Syndrome. *Current Opinions in Neurology*, 25(2), 106–111.
Keung, A.Y., Ho, V.F. and Shum, K.K. (2022). Early cognitive intervention using mediated learning for preschoolers with developmental delay: a randomized controlled trial. *The British Journal of Educational Psychology*, 92(3), 1109–1132.
Klein, P. (1996). *Early Intervention: Cross-Cultural Experiences with a Mediational Approach.* New York: Garland Publishing.
Kozulin, A. (2024). *The Cultural Mind.* Cambridge: Cambridge University Press.
Lauchlan, F. and Daly, C. (2023). *Applying Dynamic Assessment in Schools.* London: Jessica Kingsley.
Lidz, C. (1991). *Practitioner's Guide to Dynamic Assessment.* New York: Guilford Press.
Lidz, C. (2003). *Early Childhood Assessment.* Hoboken: Wiley.
Luria, A.R. (1976). *The Working Brain: An Introduction to Neuropsychology.* New York: Basic Books.
McGuinness, C. (1999). *From Thinking Skills to Thinking Classrooms: A Review and Evaluation of Approaches for Developing Pupils' Thinking.* London: DfEE Research Report Number 115. DOI:10.13140/RG.2.1.4000.1129
Mentis, M., Dunn-Bernstein, M. and Mentis, M. (2008). *Mediated Learning: Teaching, Tasks, and Tools to Unlock Cognitive Potential.* Thousand Oaks: Corwin Press.
Resnick, L.B. (1987). *Education and Learning to Think.* Washington, DC: National Academy Press.
Rogers, C. (1957). The necessary and sufficient conditions of therapeutic personality change. *Journal of Consulting Psychology*, 21(2), 95–103.
Romney, D. and Samuels, M. (2001). A meta-analytic evaluation of Feuerstein's instrumental Enrichment program. *Educational and Child Psychology*, 18(4), 19–34.

Tannenbaum, A.J. (1991). Unmasking and unmaking underachievement among the gifted. In R. Feuerstein, P. Klein and A.J. Tannenbaum (Eds), *Mediated Learning Experience: Theoretical, Psychosocial and Learning Implications*. London: A.J. Freund Publishing.

US Department of Education (2004). *Individuals with Disabilities Education Improvement Act*. Available at: www.ed.gov/laws-and-policy/individuals-disabilities/idea. Accessed 27 January 2026.

White, R. and Dinos, S. (2010). Investigating the impact of mediated learning experiences on cooperative peer communication during group initiatives. *Journal of Experiential Education*, 32(3), 226-238.

Part II

Practical Applications

4

The Learner

Introduction

The goal of this chapter is that when you have finished working through it you will be able to draw up a cognitive profile of a learner that identifies their strengths and needs.

In our House of Metacognition model, the learner's cognitive skills and emotional states are represented by the first set of building bricks used to build the house. We need to gather these bricks before we can begin to put them together to build the house. Therefore, the first step of practical application is to identify the cognitive skills and emotional states of the learner.

A number of different approaches are covered in this chapter. The chapter also includes some examples of learner profiles. They are drawn from the present authors' casework but with changes made in order to ensure complete anonymity. Note that these examples are drawn from longer written summaries and are used here only to illustrate the learner profile element of the work carried out. This means that:

- What is reported under the 'information gained' heading focuses on information gained from the particular approach in order to illustrate how it was used in that case. All cases involved collecting information from multiple sources, which is good assessment practice;
- Recommendations and suggested interventions are not included. All the cases drawn on for this chapter included detailed recommendations and suggestions for intervention. However, this information is not included here, because the purpose of the case examples in this book is to illustrate how to draw up a learner profile. We do of course recognise and emphasise that assessment without intervention links is of little value.
- Where standardised scores are reported, we have not included confidence intervals,[1] because these are not relevant to these examples. However, good practice in reporting

1 A confidence interval is a way of showing that a standard score obtained from a test has a range and not just one value. If a test score is reported as having a 95 per cent confidence interval, this means that in 95 times out of 100, the score obtained by the pupil would fall within the range shown. This illustrates that test score are not always precise and are subject to some error. For example, in a test

DOI: 10.4324/9781003655329-7

test scores would always report confidence intervals so these would be included and explained.

- Examples that relate to particular assessment instruments only give brief overviews of each instrument. Therefore, it is important that you read the relevant manual before using any of the instruments that are included in this chapter.

Before you begin the process of identification and draw up a cognitive profile, there are three important points to be highlighted:

1. *First*, it is important to have some prior information about any learner or learners with whom you will be working, for example, via a referral to your service or agency, or your personal knowledge of the learner as a result of day-to-day contact. This initial information might suggest a direction for your investigations. However, it is fundamental to the concepts we are setting out here not to focus solely on one area, since cognitive processes are transactional; that is, they are interrelated and do not operate in isolation (Luria, 1976; Deutsch, 2020);
2. *Second*, it is unlikely that any one source will give you all the information that you need. Triangulation, a process which involves multiple sources of information in order to enhance reliability, is an important consideration. However, this does not mean that you should use *every* approach contained in this chapter. Choose what works for your role, work context, the time available and the reason(s) for referral;
3. *Third*, whatever approach(es) you use, information should always be obtained from practitioners involved with the learner, from parents/carers and from the learner.

Figure 4.1 shows the element of the tripartite partnership covered in this chapter.

Identifying cognitive skills

Chapter 3 introduced the Boat of Cognition model that gave an overview of cognitive skills and emotional states. In this section of the present chapter, we will look in more detail at these in order to have some more observable descriptions that will aid identification. These are in presented in Table 4.1.

The examples in Table 4.1 are not exhaustive; they are meant to give a 'flavour' of what each skill or behaviour might look like in different contexts and phases of education.

Direct approaches

Direct approaches examine and analyse cognitive skills, involving work or interaction with a learner. The most useful means of gathering direct information on the cognitive skills of a

---

a pupil might have a standard score of 54 + or - 7 at a confidence interval of 95 per cent. This means that on 95 occasions out of 100 the pupil's score would fall in the range 47 (54 - 7) to 61 (54 + 7).

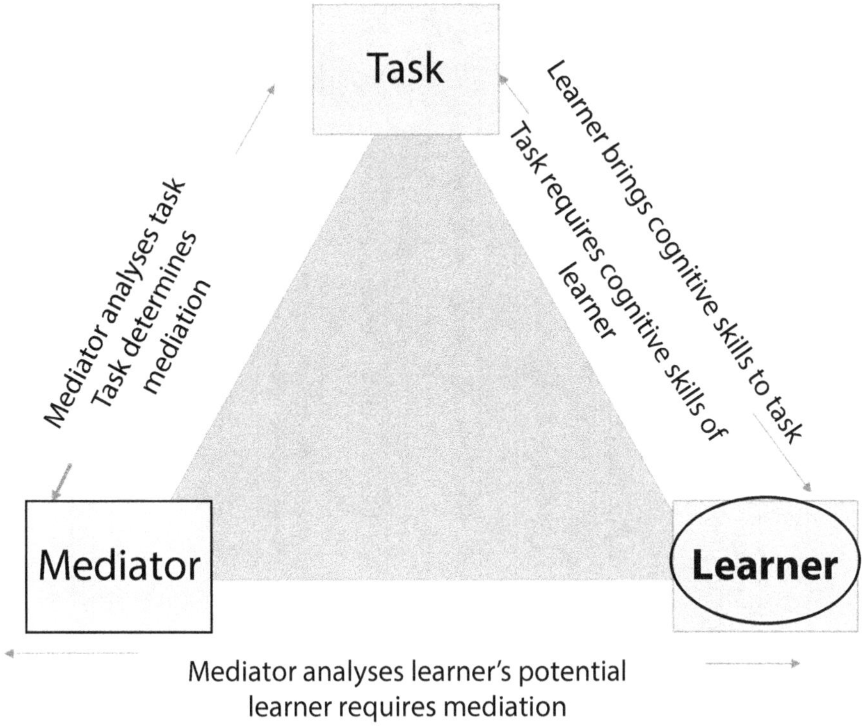

Figure 4.1 A tripartite learning partnership (learner)

learner from the perspective of planning for change, and to examine the impact of mediation provided by you, is to support them whilst problem-solving. One important method is to use Dynamic Assessment (DA). DA is an interactive method of assessment that is based on the principle that cognition is flexible and can be changed. DA was discussed briefly in Chapter 2, where the theoretical background and contribution of Feuerstein was covered. This chapter focuses on some practical applications of DA, bearing in mind the caveat in Chapter 2, that this text does not provide direct training in DA. Therefore, the content of this section is applicable to practitioners who have some background and training in DA.

There are two main ways of carrying out DA with a learner: using published tests or using materials such as games and puzzles that are appropriate for an interactive assessment focusing on cognitive skills.

There are a number of published DA tests available. Resource 4.1, downloadable from the Resource Centre, lists a range of DA tests available in English, linked to broad age and developmental suitability and cognitive skills.

Table 4.1 Descriptions of domains in the cognition model

Domain and associated skills or behaviours	***Description***	***Examples***
READINESS TO LEARN		
Alertness and self-regulation	The learner's ability to regulate their state of alertness and arousal.	The idea of an engine (from Williams and Shellenberger's Alert programme [1996]): how does your engine run? Too fast, too slow or just right? The learner is able to delay offering a solution or response until they know what the problem or task requires.
Focused attention	Focusing on the task at the outset. Paying attention to what is relevant, attending to the specific task.	'Tuning in' to the task or problem.
ATTENTION		
Staying focused	Maintaining attention over a period of time, keeping focused on what is relevant.	Being able to refocus after an interruption. Maintaining attention long enough to complete a task or solve a problem. Focusing on the specific task or problem, not on other unrelated tasks.
Shifting from one stimulus to another	Shifting between stimuli, from one stimulus to another.	Copying from the board: shifting attention between the book and the board.
Filtering out distractions	Ignoring and filtering out distractions.	Continue to attend when there are some competing stimuli such as noise outside the classroom, equipment noise.
PERCEPTION		
Systematic gathering of information, using all the senses (visual, auditory and spatial relationships)	Gathering all the information needed before beginning a task. Using senses needed to gather information, depending on the task or problem.	The learner has everything they need in order to begin and has received and processed all instructions. Depending on the task or problem, using the most appropriate/relevant sense(s) to gather information. For example, vision is needed to read a set of written instructions.
Using several sources of information	Dealing with several stimuli or pieces of information at once.	Video input for a lesson: watching and listening, then making sense of the content of the video and also referring to a written text, a diagram etc.

(Continued)

Table 4.1 (Continued)

Domain and associated skills or behaviours	***Description***	***Examples***
MEMORY		
Short-term memory (STM)	Recalling immediate information. Note modality: visual, auditory, kinaesthetic and any others.	STM is like having an in-tray on a desk, where current information is stored for a short time. V: Recalling details of a picture. A: Recalling a phone number (when it has been spoken) K: Recalling a sequence of movements in PE.
Working memory (WM)	Temporarily holding and manipulating information. Note modality: visual (V), auditory (A), kinaesthetic (K) and others. Retrieving previously used strategies.	WM is like having notes on a whiteboard or Post-It note whilst you work with some other information. Remembering a relevant strategy and applying it to the present task. V: Holding a picture in your head of a shape whilst looking for another shape to complete a pattern or puzzle. A: Recalling and retrieving after listening to instructions; holding them in your head. K: Copying actions after some time has elapsed (for example, jump, hop, skip), holding the movements in your head.
Long-term recall/long-term memory (LTM)	Recalling previously learned information or ways of solving a problem. Note modality: visual, auditory, kinaesthetic and others. Note that LTM does not mean that the stored information will necessarily be retrieved when needed. This is where WM has to tap into stored information. That is not always done.	LTM is like having a filing cabinet where information is stored which can be retrieved when needed. For example, long-term recall of how a problem was solved in the past. V: Long-term recall of a diagram of pattern or of letter patterns in spelling. A: Long-term recall of a piece of music or words of a song. K: Long-term recall of a sequence of actions such as driving a car or moves in a dance.

(Continued)

Table 4.1 (Continued)

Domain and associated skills or behaviours	***Description***	***Examples***
LANGUAGE		
Receptive and expressive (content)	Understanding (receptive) processing and using (expressive) language. Note that these two stages do not always happen. Receptive understanding may not be followed by expressive language.	***Receptive***: Following verbal instructions. To be able to label in one's mind what a task involves. Labelling the elements of a design or figure receptively. ***Expressive***: To use appropriate vocabulary when describing (for example, using a precise label for an object rather than the word 'thingy'). To be able to take a mental concept or idea and express it in words or written form.
Use (function)	Having a sense of audience, adjusting language according to the context and/or audience. Being able to express needs and feelings, to communicate information.	Taking part in a conversation where there is a back and forth of listening and responding to what has been said; keeping on topic. Using different language forms with friends and staff in school. In learning contexts, using appropriate language to explain and answer or describe how a problem was solved.
Structure (form)	Grammatical structure of language	Using sentences, nouns, verbs, pronouns, tenses, and so on.
REASONING AND PROBLEM-SOLVING: BASIC		
Comparison	Identifying similarities and differences between two or more objects, events or ideas.	In early years activities, identifying same and different shapes. Playing a game of Snap. In a history lesson, comparing the reign of two monarchs. In a citizenship lesson, comparing democracy and totalitarianism.
Conservation	Noticing what changes and when some things stay the same.	In early years water play, knowing that the amount of water stays the same when poured into different containers. Noticing that a tree has leaves in the summer and is bare in the winter, but it is still the same tree. Reversible and irreversible changes in chemistry.

(Continued)

Table 4.1 (Continued)

Domain and associated skills or behaviours	***Description***	***Examples***
Categorisation	Grouping or organising objects or ideas. Identifying relationships between objects and ideas.	Early years sorting activities (concrete). Food groups such as carbohydrates, proteins or fats (more abstract).
Sequencing	Using sequence, order and pattern in problem-solving.	Days of the week, months of the year. Number or letter patterns. Working out the steps in a task.
REASONING AND PROBLEM-SOLVING: HIGHER ORDER		
Causative thinking; inference	Using evidence to come to a conclusion; moving beyond the literal and the information that is presented. Cause and effect thinking; if … then	Make a prediction about the consequences of an action or behaviour. Using information from a text to make a prediction; reading 'between the lines', answering questions such as 'why do you think …?' (more abstract). Cause and effect toys: a concrete/perceptual example might be pressing a switch to make a toy move or light up.
Induction (including transitive thinking)	Finding a theory or a rule from the information available. A 'bottom-up' approach. Transitive thinking: a relationship between two statements is used to infer a subsequent relationship between two more statements.	In a science lesson, using observations to generate a rule. For example, what happens when we water/don't water our seeds? Can we make a rule about this? Discovery learning is an example of how inductive reasoning might be understood and used. Example of transitive thinking: ***Statement 1***: A hippo is larger than a cat. ***Statement 2***: A cat is larger than an ant. ***Conclusion***: A hippo is larger than an ant. Transitive thinking can be used to solve maths equations.

(Continued)

Table 4.1 (Continued)

Domain and associated skills or behaviours	***Description***	***Examples***
Deduction (including syllogism)	Using a rule, theory or hypothesis to identify information. A 'top-down' approach. Syllogism: where a major and minor premise are related leading to a logical conclusion.	Applying rules of grammar or spelling rules in an English/literacy lesson (for example, 'i before e except after c') An example of a syllogism: ***Statement 1***: All bears are brown. ***Statement 2***: Igor is a bear. ***Conclusion***: Igor is brown. Note that there is an important difference between ***logical validity*** which is not the same as ***veracity*** (what is true in the real world).
Analogy	Identifying and then applying a relationship (A is to B as C is to ...).	Example: dog is to puppy as cat is to ... [kitten] Applying a known relationship (a dog's young is called a puppy) to a new relationship (a cat's young is called a kitten). The analogy of an animal and its young is identified, transferred and applied in this example.
REASONING AND PROBLEM-SOLVING: METACOGNITION/EXECUTIVE FUNCTION		
Understanding the task	Knowing what the task is asking the learner to do.	The learner can say what has to be done and what the task involves. The learner can follow the task instructions.
Relevance and prioritisation, including precision and accuracy	The learner is able to identify what is relevant and not relevant for a task. For example: Knowing when it is important or necessary to be precise and accurate and when it is okay to approximate.	In maths problem-solving, identifying the relevant information about the numerical operations and disregarding the irrelevant information (for example, the names of people in the problem-solving narrative). Knowing that reading or following a set of instructions accurately is needed for successful task completion (such as building flat pack furniture or a Lego® model). In handwriting, copying the model demonstrated accurately. Knowing when precise timing is important or not (for example, in food technology).

(Continued)

Table 4.1 (Continued)

Domain and associated skills or behaviours	***Description***	***Examples***
Planning and organising materials and ideas	Working systematically, using a step by step approach.	Knowing what to do first, next and so on. Identifying the steps needed to complete a task. Following a plan once it has been drawn up. Organising workspace and materials. Organising a timeline to show the development of democracy in a particular society.
Flexibility	Finding another way to solve a problem.	When the learner is 'stuck' they can think of an alternative approach to help solve the problem.
Self-monitoring and checking	Check work; assess performance during or after finishing a task in order to ensure attainment of goal.	Proofread written work. Check maths calculations. Keep focused on the goal of the task or problem.
Justification	Explaining and defending your reasoning and your answer.	Explain how a maths problem was solved. Defend an argument in a critique.
THE SEA OF EMOTIONAL STATES		
Emotional engagement	Openness to intervention and support; engaging with the mediator. Consider also openness to working with peers in group or team work.	Verbally expressed: for example, responding to interactions and to mediation/intervention. Non-verbally expressed: eye contact, body language (leaning towards the mediator), facial expression (showing interest or boredom).
Overcoming blocking	The 'freeze' response.	The learner makes an immediate response such as: 'I can't'; 'I don't know how to ...' before even looking at the task or activity in any detail.
Persistence	Seeing a task or problem through to the end; maintaining attention. Keeping going even when the task is challenging.	Finishing a task; keeping going until a problem is solved. Being able to deal with difficulties and obstacles. Showing resilience, 'bouncing back' from setbacks. Not allowing frustration to lead to abandoning the task or problem.

(Continued)

Table 4.1 (Continued)

Domain and associated skills or behaviours	***Description***	***Examples***
Control of impulsivity	Restraining impulsivity so that problem-solving plans are followed systematically.	Following all the steps of a plan. Not jumping to conclusions. Checking work. Taking time to think and respond.
Motivation	The desire to engage. Two aspects: ***Person-related*** motivation: to work with that person in that context and in other settings. ***Task-related*** motivation: is the learner interested and motivated by the task itself?	The learner presents as 'wanting to' engage. This might be communicated verbally (one of the present author's most memorable verbal refusals from a learner was: 'I'm not working with that old witch'!) or non-verbally (for example, eye contact, posture, tone of voice). Responsiveness to adult intervention: how does the learner respond to mediation? Are they open to support?
Curiosity	The desire to find out. Showing interest.	Asking questions. Participating in an interaction. Wanting to do more of a task.

Materials that can be used with a learner that are not part of a published battery of tests

There are many kinds of games and puzzles that are useful vehicles for direct work with a learner in order to identify cognitive strengths and weaknesses. There are two challenges to consider when using these materials:

- *First*, since these materials are generally not specifically designed for an interactive assessment, they do not tend to specify the cognitive skills needed. It is obviously important to be clear about which particular cognitive skills are involved in the task or activity. Therefore, this is an essential first step when using these materials. Before using such materials, it might be advisable to look at Chapter 5, which deals with analysing tasks;
- *Second*, unlike DA tests, there are no parallel tasks or activities that enable the assessor to compare performance pre- and post-mediation (one of the defining characteristics of DA is its test-teach-test format). Generally, published materials comprise one set of tasks or activities that increase in difficulty, or are all at the same level of difficulty. This means that the mediation element of DA requires very careful thought and delivery.

Puzzles such as spot the difference, mazes or Sudoku are useful informal ways of eliciting information about cognitive skills. Stories and pictures can add to informal interactive materials that enable the assessor to intervene in ways which cannot be carried out in standardised tests of comprehension. These additions to established batteries reflect the fact that DA tests are designed to be more culture-neutral and for obvious reasons they were never included in the original DA batteries as language and comprehension is the most culturally embedded aspect of our understanding and interpretation.

Be aware that when you mediate with informal activities your interpretation can be more subjective. Therefore, do not rely on one source of information or even on one context alone. Be very careful not to generalise what you are seeing if you cannot provide evidence in other settings or contexts.

Resource 4.2, the Games Matrix, downloadable via the Resource Centre, lists a variety of games linked to particular aspects of cognition. This list is not exhaustive; there are many suppliers of these types of games.

The following box contains an example of a learner profile that was drawn up using DA as the main source of information. In addition to this example, Resource 8.1, also downloadable from the Resource Centre, is an example of a DA report.

Learner information

Philip aged 15. Referred due to concerns about the impact of Tourette's Syndrome. He demonstrated very few coping mechanisms and presented as disinterested in developing these because when the severity of his tics increased, he was allowed to leave lessons, which worked for Philip because he was not very interested in learning. Therefore, there was little incentive to manage his tics and stay in lessons. Staff and parents reported poor study skills and low motivation, despite being a high achieving pupil in relation to progress through the taught curriculum. He rarely completed homework and revision for exams was haphazard and brief. DA reported here was one element of the assessment and was carried out in order to look at how a profile of cognitive strengths and needs might be relevant for supporting study skills and for tic management (by incorporating cognitive control as part of broader support for this issue).

Information gained

Three DA tests were used:

- The 16 Word Memory Test, which involves the learner recalling 16 words read aloud. Recall can be supported by categorising the words;
- Raven's Matrices (Set B), which involves solving analogical problems using illustrations of matrix designs;
- The Representational Stencil Design Test (RSDT), which involves the learner looking at increasingly complex designs made up of differing numbers of stencils and saying which stencils are used to make the design (giving the correct order from bottom to top).

In the 16 Word Memory Test, Philip showed very little persistence in the first three trials, where spontaneous recall of words is assessed, with no specific input. The number of words recalled did not increase after the repeated exposure. He was unable to offer a memory strategy, but when the classification strategy was prompted, he immediately grouped the words and used the groups to assist recall. After three further mediated trials he recalled all 16 words.

Philip required very little mediation in order to solve the matrices problems. When asked to describe and justify his answers, he gave very vague responses, using gesture rather than words to explain his thinking, or he responded, 'don't know'.

Philip also solved the RSDT problems with minimal mediation. Again, his language was vague and unelaborated when he was asked to talk through his problem-solving. He worked out an appropriate problem-solving strategy (start with the colour in the middle) and used a process of elimination appropriately in order to work out which stencil was correct.

Profile of strengths and needs

Strengths

- Visual perception: looking carefully and working systematically;
- Using spatial relationships;
- Logical and hypothetical thinking;
- Projecting relationships;
- Identifying and then using a problem-solving rule;
- Visual transport;
- Working with several sources of information;
- Analogical thinking.

Needs

- Emotional states: persistence and motivation;
- Restraining impulsivity;
- Applying his strengths cognitive skills to a range of problem-solving contexts;
- Justifying and explaining his problem-solving.

Priority areas to include in learner profile

- Motivation; persistence in the face of ongoing challenges;
- Applying cognitive strengths in relation to two areas: managing Tourette's and application to study skills. For example, using cause and effect thinking in order to think through the consequences of some of his behaviours such as leaving lessons, (this also suggested that cognitive behaviour therapy might be a useful approach);
- Reducing impulsivity in order to support application of cognitive strengths.

Play-based assessment

A play-based assessment (PBA) approach is a helpful approach when working with pre-school or early years learners, and, in some cases, for older learners with developmental delays where play materials might be appropriate. For example, Lidz [2003] notes that PBA is potentially useful for children aged above three years. PBA is not a new approach: Montoya-Fernández et al. (2024) systematic review notes that PBA was used at the beginning of the twentieth century in psychoanalytical approaches but that its use as a cognitive assessment tool emerged during the 1970s and 1980s. Lidz (2003: 88) offers clarity about the purpose of PBA: 'what we will seek during the course of the assessment of children's play combines insights into the child's developmental status in the cognitive, affective, motor, communication and social-affective domains'.

The basic cognitive skills in the reasoning and problem-solving domain described in Table 4.1 will be a particularly useful focus, in addition to skills and behaviours in the other domains. In addition, Resource 4.3 lists early years cognitive skills.

The list below gives examples of the kind of play materials that are likely to be found in an early years setting:

- Symbolic play toys (dolls, teddies, cooking utensils, play food);
- Small world play;
- Shape sorters and shape form boards;
- Picture lotto;
- Abacus (one colour of bead per post);
- Crayons, paper, scissors;
- Sorting toys and trays;
- Nesting beakers;
- Books;
- Construction;
- Sand and water play;
- Beads and threading laces;
- Jigsaws and inset puzzles.

In choosing toys or activities, be aware of how important it is to take account of cultural familiarity. A child may perform poorly with one type of play item simply because they have never been exposed to it. In Chapter 5 we discuss the importance of considering the content (prior knowledge) of the task and its familiarity when analysing a task.

Structures for play-based assessment using interactive approaches

Sayeed and Guerin (2000) provide a structure for participatory play as part of a broader PBA approach that begins with an observation phase and is followed by an interactive phase. The participatory play phase has a three-element structure:

- Pre-play (preparation for assessment, which involves decisions about matters such as the location, and focus of the PBA);
- Play (adult-child interaction) which involves allowing the child to initiate and following on from their lead;
- Post-play (completion of assessment) which involves collating and feeding back information.

Lidz (2003) offers a structured approach to the use of toys and play materials for assessment, suggesting that the assessor chooses a familiar and unfamiliar toy to use with the child. She then suggests a sequence for proceeding (Lidz, 2003: 89):

- Familiar/independent;
- Familiar/facilitated;
- Unfamiliar/independent;

- Unfamiliar/facilitated;
- Toy set/independent;
- Toy set/facilitated.

The first four conditions use a single toy and the final two use a set of toys (Lidz suggests play dough, construction, miniatures, crayons and paper, puzzle, books, toys that can be banged or hit, and cause and effect toys).

Transdisciplinary Play Based Assessment

The Transdisciplinary Play Based Assessment approach (TPBA; Linder, 2008) emphasises assessment carried out collaboratively, using familiar toys and materials with active involvement from family members and where the assessment uses child-initiated play as a key part of the assessment. Although the transdisciplinary element might not be applicable to your context, the manual contains some very useful observation checklists related to a number of domains: sensorimotor, emotional and social, communication and cognitive. There are observation guidelines and age-related skills and behaviours and a summary form for each domain. The cognitive domain examines attention, memory, problem-solving, social cognition, complexity of play, conceptual knowledge and literacy. Problem-solving highlights specific skills and behaviours: cause and effect thinking, planning, organising and monitoring, problem analysis and generalising information, showing some overlap with the model of cognitive skills proposed in Chapter 3 and described in Table 4.1.

The following is an example of a learner profile using information from PBA. This example combines observation and PBA, which is a common approach used by the present authors when working in preschool and early years settings. In particular, observation during child-initiated play sessions can yield a great deal of useful information.

Learner information

Sofia, aged 4 years 2 months. Lack of progress across all areas. Sofia engaged in imaginative play but tended to use repetitive 'scripts'. Her language in relation to learning was delayed.

Information gained

Observation of Sofia during free play highlighted the following in relation to her cognitive skills:

- She tended to 'flit' from one activity to another and did not sustain attention to an activity for more than two or three minutes;
- She found it difficult to wait her turn (for example, waiting to use a particular tool during sand play) and dysregulated quite quickly;

- When her key worker moved alongside her during free play, she was responsive to her suggestions for expanding play and focused for longer at a particular play activity.

Three tasks carried out as part of PBA were used. These involved sorting, grouping, pattern and sequence, via three tasks:

- Copying a pattern of blocks;
- Being given a pattern to continue;
- Sorting a box of Compare Bears.

The cognitive skills needed for these tasks include:

- Looking carefully;
- Working systematically;
- Comparing;
- Categorisation;
- Being able to use order and sequences;
- Taking time to think (rather than making a trial and error impulsive response).

Sofia was able to complete the tasks with the following type of assistance:

- Breaking the task down into very small steps;
- Moving materials into her eyeline and moving away any other materials that might be a distraction;
- Modelling the desired behaviour;
- Giving prompts to focus her attention.

The assistance given suggested that in the one-to-one context of the PBA, Sofia's interest and engagement was gained with highly structured modelling; that is, very intensive mediation.

Profile of strengths and needs

Strengths

- Emotional engagement and a systematic approach were observed with a high level of support (mediation).

Needs

- Attention: filtering out distractions;
- Self-regulation;
- Comparison;
- Sequencing;
- Language content (expressive and receptive).

Priority areas to include in learner profile

Attention and self-regulation were prioritised since these are foundations for basic reasoning and problem-solving. Comparison was also included as a specific priority basic cognitive skill. The goal of supporting the priority areas was for them to be demonstrated with increasing independence.

Learner voice and views

So far, the direct approaches covered involve an adult working directly with a learner in order to identify cognitive skills and emotional states. However, the learner's own perspective on these areas is an essential part of direct approaches.

Pupil voice came to the forefront of education in the UK in the 1990s (see, for example, Bragg [2021] for an overview) and was included in key UK guidance and legislation such as Every Child Matters (Department for Education and Skills, 2003) and the Children and Families Act (2014). Pupil voice is very common in special educational needs documentation such, as a one-page profile, learning profiles and Education and Health Care Plans. We take it as a given that all practitioners will elicit the learner's views as part of any assessment. The involvement of the learner is important for the success (or otherwise!) of a cognitive intervention. This might seem an obvious point to make; however, our experience is that learners (particularly of school age) are too rarely involved in the process, despite the pupil voice emphasis mentioned above. Our concern here is not merely eliciting views but is rather about involving the learner in the process of identifying their own cognitive strengths and needs which is the prelude to their engagement with the targets for intervention.

Using a self-rating scale is one way of involving the learner in drawing up a cognitive profile. There are a number of different tools that can be used. For example, Myself As a Learner Scale (Burden, 1998) and Pupil Attitudes to Self and School (PASS; GL Assessment, 2024) are generic questionnaires about learning, whereas the CAP Short Forms (Deutsch, 2024) look more specifically at cognitive skills. You can also use the Boat of Cognition model as a 'conversation starter' or prompt sheet, asking the learner to comment and reflect on some or all of the cognitive skills and emotional states.

Indirect approaches

Indirect approaches do not involve direct contact or interaction with the learner. A number of approaches are explored below.

Observation

In some cases, it might not be possible or appropriate to work directly with the learner, so an observation is another way of gaining some information about their cognitive strengths and challenges. The choice of lesson, session or other context will be important in relation to the cognitive skills and emotional states that can be observed. However, observation is not an alternative to direct work but can add to the breadth of understanding the needs of the learner.

Observation alone might not yield all the information you need so it will be helpful to plan to collect supplementary information using some of the other sources discuss in subsequent sections of this chapter. Learner observation can give a useful perspective on a number of areas that will contribute to a cognitive profile, such as:

- *Attention*: for example, levels of distraction and how the learner copes with these;
- *Impulsivity*: for example, does the learner offer responses very quickly before taking time to think?
- *Modalities*: note what modality (or modalities) are used for presenting the task and in what modality (or modalities) the learner is expected to respond;
- *Cognitive skills*: of the task(s) and how the learner responds;
- *Emotional states*;
- *Memory*: short-, long-term and particularly working memory, where the lesson involves a recap of prior learning or use of prior strategies;
- *Language demands*: of the task and the learner's use of language for learning;
- *Level of support*: given to the learner.

Analysing tasks is covered in detail in Chapter 5. If you plan to use observation as a main tool for gaining information, it will be helpful to read Chapter 5 first.

Use of questionnaires

The use of questionnaires is a well known, widely used method of gaining information in many areas of everyday life and certainly also in psychology and education. Some questionnaires are informal and are not necessarily scored and rated, but may, for example, be used to gain background information on a potential case involvement leading to choices and planning of what to do next. Other questionnaires may have a formal structure and may be scored and compared to certain criteria.

Questionnaires do have their limitations, so it is not advisable to use them as stand-alone sources of information. For example, consider whether the questions accurately reflect the topic (validity); you cannot answer what you have not been asked. Many of us have experienced a situation where we have a questionnaire to respond to, but we notice that some of the questions themselves do not reflect our experience or thinking. This can be problematic in a multi-choice questionnaire when you feel that you cannot select any of the options offered.

The subject of questionnaire construction, including issues such as balance, bias and validity, is a topic on its own which is beyond the scope of this book. Our message here is: only use the questionnaire as a contribution to information, neither a substitute for other forms of assessment nor an adequate picture on its own. Do not be tempted by speed and ease to judge or plan on this information alone. A good assessment should use several sources of information.

This section overlaps with the use of published materials section, because you might use more structured tools in discussions with others.

Use of consultation approaches

As already emphasised, discussions with practitioners, parents/carers and the learner are an essential part of information gathering. An informal discussion with others who know the learner well (whether published materials are used or not) can yield very useful information. Whilst it might not be helpful to read from a script in these contexts, some preparation might be helpful so that you make sure you do not miss anything. If needed, begin any discussion by explaining briefly what is meant by cognitive skills and emotional states, prior to asking specific questions about these. Section B of the Cognitive Abilities Profile (CAP; Deutsch, 2020) sets out a collaborative discussion structure that can be used with key adult(s) to identify the strategies being used by the adult and the level of the learner's response.

Consultation is an example of a structured approach which preserves the collaborative element of working with others to draw up a cognitive profile. Consultation is an approach that is often used in educational psychology practice. In the context of this chapter, consultation can be one way of gathering information for a learner's cognitive profile, which adds to the breadth of information we gather from several sources in different contexts, recognising the importance of the environment around the learner. It is not only about gathering such information, it is also because those we consult with are the very people who can bring about changes in the learner's functioning on many levels. A structured consultation can involve parents and practitioners, either together or separately.

Consultation: definitions and issues

Consultation is often positioned as a joint problem-solving activity. The description most frequently used by educational psychologists is 'a voluntary, collaborative, non-supervisory approach, established to aid the functioning of a system and as inter-related systems' (Wagner, 2000: 11). Wagner was a key influence in promoting the use of consultation in educational psychology practice in the UK.

Despite this description, consultation is a rather ill-defined practice. Deutsch's (2017) overview of consultation in EP practice notes a paradox of seeing consultation as important and some even advocate replacing testing altogether with consultation (Wagner, 2000), whilst at the same time showing reluctance to move away from reliance on individual testing. Farrell and Woods (2015) point out that these two approaches (consultation and individual testing) are not mutually exclusive. Deutsch comments: 'The literature appears to indicate little evidence of specific methodologies being adopted to deliver certain kinds of consultation, making it more problematic to define client satisfaction and to evaluate outcomes' (Deutsch, 2017: 80). Overall, there is a lack of clarity about how to define and structure consultation: 'a review of relevant literature suggests contemporary definitions of consultation are sparse despite significant changes within and to the EP profession' (Royle and Atkinson, 2025: 297). Aside from the above issue about defining consultation, a core goal which research has also found is that the 'what' of consultation can often be vague and undefined (Deutsch, 2017; Royle and Atkinson, 2025), leading to questions about what we are actually consulting on and how to clarify joint goals.

Clarity is also needed about who the client is. A 'client' might mean:

- The key adults who know and work with the learner;
- The learner's parents or carers;
- The individual or organisation that commissioned (and is ultimately funding) the work;
- The learner.

We could become sidetracked by this issue; however, two important points emerge: first, that clarity of purpose is needed and explicitly shared, and, second, that whoever is involved or has commissioned the work, the learner is always at the centre of the process. However, the learner does not function in isolation. Taking Bronfenbrenner's Ecosystemic view, shown in Figure 4.2 (Bronfenbrenner, 1979), we see that the learner is surrounded by a number of interacting systems.

This brings us back to the importance of purpose. The issue is not so much about identifying the client but more about placing the learner at the centre and recognising that there are a number of key people in the systems surrounding the learner that have a stake in the outcomes. What this means in practice is to aim to address the needs and perspectives of both the learner and the systems that surround them. Therefore, in order to measure outcomes effectively we should consider both impact on the learner and on the key adults or systems.

The collaborator or expert role in consultation is an ongoing debate. One view is that one cannot be an expert, since this position interferes with authentic collaboration. Jones and Atkinson's (2022) systematic review of consultation literature highlights this point, echoed by Royle and Atkinson (2025), who comment on the tension between being collaborative and using expertise. Recognising both perspectives, it is not a question of *either*

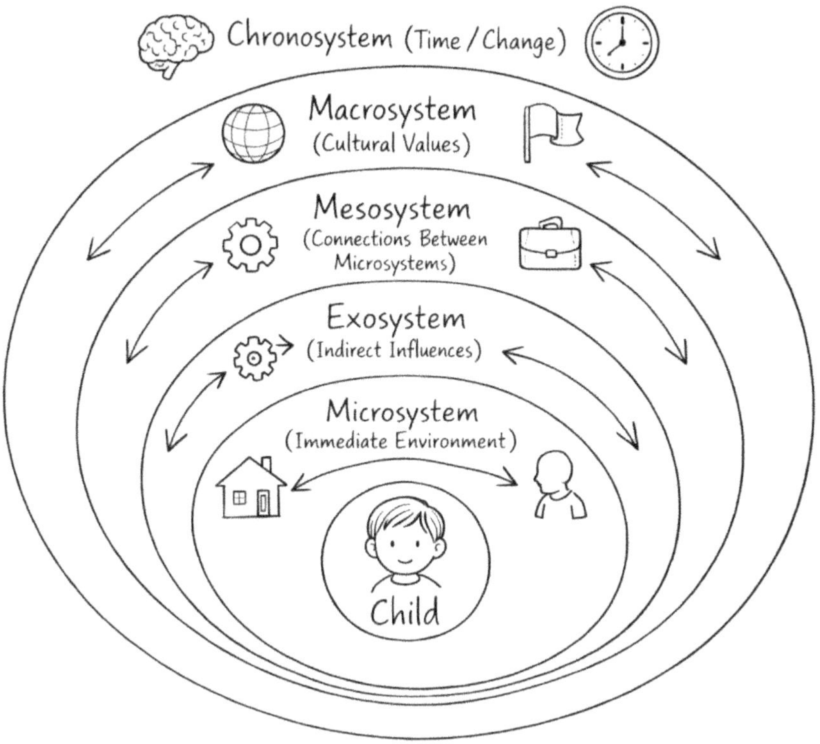

Structural Learning

Figure 4.2 Brofenbrenner's Ecosystemic Model

collaboration *or* being an expert. Both parties have 'expertise'. The teacher's expertise is related to the classroom, and the therapist or psychologist's expertise is related to understanding development and learning. Collaboration does not imply a dominant party, but it does recognise what each participant has to offer. We are really listening to each other, not imposing or dictating outcomes. It is interesting that, in contrast to the apparent distancing of educational psychologists from an expert role, the National Professional Qualification Framework for SENCos uses the term *expert* quite explicitly.

The issues of collaborator/expert and lack of clarity of roles can lead to a lack of clarity about the process or structure for consultation and results in poorly defined ways of monitoring outcomes. as noted, for example, by Leadbetter (2006) and Royle and Atkinson (2025). One of the factors for the persistent theme of lack of clarity in the research is that models used in educational psychology practice have their roots in mental health and psychotherapy models dating back to the 1960s, which is why practitioners such as Wagner (2000) saw the need to set out and adapt the concepts for educational psychology application. This leads us to suggest that a mediational approach will be helpful.

A mediational approach to consultation

The issues raised above about lack of clarity of goals and the collaborator/expert dilemma lead us to suggest that mediation characteristics and criteria might give a useful structure that helps to address these issues. Leadbetter (2006: 22) suggests three uses of the term consultation: a model of service delivery; a defined task with agreed characteristics; and a specific activity or skill. The third use is one that fits well with a mediational approach; Leadbetter describes this as follows: 'a regular occurrence whereby an EP and others meet in order to gain and share information about a problem, a specific child or some other concern. There are many ways of undertaking such an activity and of learning how to improve skills and techniques in this area. Within this type of activity, there can be information seeking or eliciting, information sharing, advice eliciting, and advice giving' (2006: 22–23). This description is useful in that it does not necessarily set up an expectation that the problem or concern that are brought to the consultation will be 'fixed'.

As has been emphasised in Chapter 3, mediation focuses on the *processes* of learning (not the products). In relation to consultation, this means that, having already received information about the concerns that have prompted referral, the consultation then aims to elicit and discuss information specifically about the learner's cognitive skills and emotional states. This reflects the consultation structure of the CAP (Deutsch, 2020), where a goal of the consultation is to further explore the pupil's learning within the context of classroom subjects or other contexts. Hymer et al (2002) point out that use of a DA model for consultation leads to a focus on process, not product. If we start with this core purpose, we can see how the criteria of mediation are reflected in the consultation process, as follows:

- *Intentionality and meaning* give clarity about purposes and goals;
- *Reciprocity* emphasises the collaborative nature of the interaction;
- *Positive affirmation* and empathy and competence reflect the active listening and sharing element of consultation;
- *Challenge* reflects how a consultation might ask what has been tried already to respond to the identified learning issues. The word *challenge* could be interpreted negatively. It needs to be clear that this is a positive discussion between those who know the learner well, not judgemental in any way. In the consultation, a question can also be about exceptions. Of course it is important to explore concerns; however, it is also important and useful to know when the concerns are less apparent. In cognitive terms, this might be to explore contexts where the learner demonstrates more secure cognitive skills, greater motivation, and so on. Knowing cognitive strengths as well as challenges helps to build a holistic picture. Therefore, consultation with a range of participants enables the consultees to hear from others and to see the wider picture. It also helps to understand transfer, because the learner might show secure cognitive skills in one context but then be unable to transfer these to other contexts;
- *Goal-setting* reflects one of the purposes of consultation, where the collaboration facilitates agreement about shared goals. Drawing on solution-focused approaches (see,

for example, Berg and de Shazer, 1993; Lutz, 2014), scaling is used in order to assist in goal-setting.

In the light of the critique of lack of clarity of definitions, we offer a working definition of mediational consultation in the following box.

Mediational consultation is a collaborative process that uses the criteria of mediation in order to:

- Gather information about the learner's current cognitive skills;
- Use scaling in order to identify the level of concern about the learner's current cognitive skills;
- Agree goals for the learner, using scaling to think about changes at, for example, half a point further up the scale;
- Prioritise the focus and type of support;
- Agree future reviews to support monitoring and evaluation.

In the context of this chapter, the main focus of a consultation is to gain information about the learner's cognitive strengths and needs and then to agree priority cognitive skills that will be the focus of mediation and support. As already noted, when discussing Leadbetter's uses of consultation, consultation is not just a way of fixing a problem or concern. It can be a starting point, the information-gathering process and the process can be revisited at a later stage as follow-up and monitoring once support has been given.

Obviously, consultation as a generic approach can relate to a wide variety of needs or concerns. The focus here is on exploring the learner's cognitive strengths and needs. Table 4.2 gives some examples of links to mediation criteria. You can use the Boat of Cognition model to assist in explaining and structuring the interaction.

Use of published materials

Published materials can be used to structure observations, gather information from others or for self-reporting. In this section we will examine five examples. They are listed in Table 4.3 below, which also shows means of data gathering for these published materials.

Each instrument is discussed in more detail below. Tables 4.4 to 4.7 show how each one maps onto cognitive skills and emotional states in the Boat of Cognition model.

Table 4.2 Mediation criteria and consultation language

Mediation criterion	***Consultation language and links***
 **Intentionality and reciprocity**	Clear statement of purpose of the meeting. Intentionality might also include using words that explain what cognition and cognitive skills are. Use active listening skills to emphasise reciprocity. Asking about 'best hopes' will help to demonstrate reciprocity.
 **Meaning**	'Cognitive skills are important because they are the foundations/ building blocks for learners to access the curriculum.' 'Our discussion is important because it will help to draw up a picture of ...'s [learner's name] cognitive skills and decide how we want to help ... move forward.'
 **Transfer**	'Tell me when/where else ... is able to ...' 'What has worked before?'
 **Positive affirmation and empathy**	Use of active listening. 'Let's keep going, we're close to having some ways to meet our goals.'
 **Regulation**	Model listening without interrupting. If necessary mention the need for only one person to talk at a time(!).
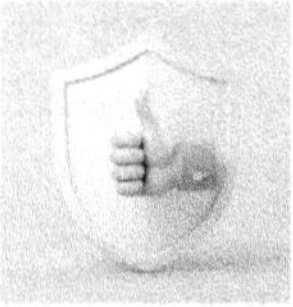 **Competence**	'That's a really interesting/useful idea.'
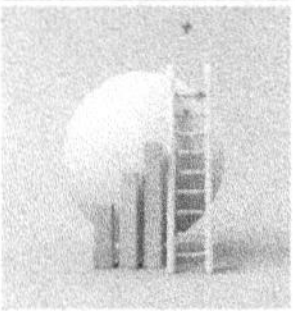 **Challenge**	'What has been tried and with what results?' 'How did X respond?' 'What has been tried which did not seem to lead to hoped-for progess?'

(Continued)

Table 4.2 (Continued)

Mediation criterion	***Consultation language and links***
 **Goal setting and planning**	'What would be a manageable goal to aim for?' 'What's best and most realistic to work on now?' Scaling: on a 0 to 10 scale: 'Where would you rate ...'s cognitive skill now?' 'Where would you like to be in half a term's time?' 'What changes would you see at half a point further up the scale?'

Table 4.3 Published materials

Instrument	**Observation**	**Information from others**	**Self report**	**Type of data**
Executive function questionnaires (Dawson and Guare, 2009)	X	√	√ self-report for parents.	1 to 5 rating scale to indicate level of agreement with statements.
BRIEF-2 (Gioia et al, 2015)	X	√	√ (age 11 upwards).	Standardised instrument, gives T scores (mean 50, standard deviation 10).
BRIEF-P (Gioia et al, 2003)	X	√	X	
Cognitive Abilities Profile (Deutsch, 2020)	√	√	√Used also in post-16 casework. The CAP Short Forms (2024) are for learner self-rating at two levels.	Uses a numerical rating scale (but not a standardised instrument).
Cognitive Assessment System Rating Scale (Naglieri et al, 2014b)	X	√	X	Standardised rating checklist gives standard scores (mean 100, standard deviation 15)

Executive Function questionnaires

These are available as downloads to accompany Dawson and Guare's publication. There are several questionnaires aimed at different age groups. The questionnaires cover a number of elements of executive function (EF).

The BRIEF-2 Executive Function and BRIEF-P checklists

The BRIEF-2 can be used with individuals aged 5 to 18. It has three versions: teacher report, parent report and self-report (from age 11 upwards). The BRIEF-P is designed for use with

Table 4.4 Dawson and Guare's EF questionnaires

Dawson and Guare's aspect of EF	***Links to cognitive skills and emotional states***
Response inhibition	Self-regulation Impulsivity
Emotional control	Self-regulation Blocking
Task initiation	Alertness
Organisation	Planning and organising materials
Goal-directed planning	Relevance Systematic gathering of information
Metacognition	Justification Expressive language
Working memory	Working memory
Sustained attention	Staying focused Filtering out distractions Persistence
Planning/prioritisation	Relevance
Time management	Planning
Flexibility	Flexibility Justification

preschool pupils aged 2–5 years and consists of one reporting scale that can be completed by parents/carers, preschool staff or daycare providers. Both scales cover similar areas of EF.

The BRIEF-2 and BRIEF-P scales consist of 63 items that are rated. The 63 items fall into nine clinical scales in the BRIEF-2 and five clinical scales in the BRIEF-P that together make up aspects of EF.

The Cognitive Assessment System second edition (CAS2) Rating Scale (Naglieri et al, 2014b)

The CAS2 Rating Scale can be used with pupils aged from 4 to 18 years. It is a norm referenced instrument. The CAS2 Rating Scale is based on PASS theory, which is drawn from Luria's functional units model (Luria, 1976). PASS and functional units were explored in detail in Chapter 2.

The CAS2 Rating Scale can be completed by an adult who knows the learner well. The rater is asked to compare the individual's behaviours with those of their peer group, so

Table 4.5 BRIEF-2 and BRIEF-P

Scale	***Description***	***Links to cognitive thinking skills and emotional states***
SCALES IN BRIEF-2 AND BRIEF-P		
Inhibit	Control impulses; appropriately stop own behaviour at the proper time	Self-regulation Impulsivity
Self-monitor	Keep track of the effect of own behaviour on others	Self-monitor, checking
Shift	Move freely from one situation, activity or aspect of a problem to another as the situation demands; transition; solve problems flexibly	Flexibility
Emotional control	Modulate emotional responses appropriately	Self-regulation Overcoming blocking
Working memory	Hold information in mind for the purpose of completing a task; stay with, or stick to, an activity	Working memory
Plan/organise	Anticipate future events; set goals; develop appropriate steps ahead of time to carry out an associated task or action; carry out tasks in a systematic manner; understand and communicate main ideas or key concepts	Systematic gathering of information Planning and organising materials Justification
SCALES IN BRIEF-2 ONLY		
Initiate	Begin a task or activity; independently generate ideas	Focused attention
Task completion	Complete school work or chores in timely fashion; finish tests within time limits; work at a satisfactory pace	Persistence
Task-monitor	Check work; assess performance during or after finishing a task in order to ensure attainment of goal	Self-monitor, checking
Organisation of materials	Keep work space, play areas and materials in an orderly manner	Planning and organising materials

they should have a good idea of what is and is not average or typical for the individual's peer group. There are ten questions for each of the PASS areas, which are rated as 'never', 'rarely', 'sometimes', 'frequently' and 'always'. The scale gives a standard score for each of the four PASS areas (mean of 100 and standard deviation of 15). Scores between 90 and 109 are described as 'average'.

The following example shows a learner profile that uses information from the BRIEF2 and the CAS2 Rating Scale.

Table 4.6 PASS areas matched with cognitive thinking skills

PASS area	***Description of PASS area (taken from CAS2 Rating Scale manual pages 2, 3 and 4)***	***Links to cognitive thinking skills and emotional states***
Planning	How well the student makes decisions about how to do things. 'The means to solve problems for which no method or solution is immediately apparent ... and may involve the retrieval of information' (page 4)	Systematic gathering of information. Planning and organising materials. Control of impulsivity. Self-monitor; checking. Flexibility. Long-term memory.
Attention	How well a student can focus attention and resist distractions, sustain attention over time and concentrate in noisy settings.	Staying focused. Shifting from one stimulus to another. Filtering out distractions.
Simultaneous	How well the student understands interrelationships among ideas and objects. The questions determine if a child can understand relationships among physical objects as well as verbal concepts. Involves 'strong visual-spatial aspects' (page 4). 'To integrate separate stimuli into a single whole or group so that a person can understand how separate elements fit together into a conceptual whole' (page 4).	Categorisation. Comparison. Induction and deduction. If ... then thinking. Visual transport. Conservation.
Successive	The student's ability to work with information that is in a specific order. 'Used to put information into a specific serial order where each element is only relayed to those that precede it' (page 4).	Sequencing. Memory.

Table 4.7 Domains of CAP Section A

CAP Section A cognitive ability domains	***Description (from CAP manual)***	***Links to cognitive thinking skills and emotional states***
Attention	The ability to regulate, filter, shift and sustain and shift attention.	Readiness to learn domain: Alertness and self-regulation; Focused attention. Attention domain: Staying focused; Shifting from one stimulus to another; Filtering out distractions.

(Continued)

Table 4.7 (Continued)

CAP Section A cognitive ability domains	***Description (from CAP manual)***	***Links to cognitive thinking skills and emotional states***
Perception	Perception is the way in which the learner makes sense of and interprets the stimuli they encounter. It relates to using the senses to gather information and whether the learner can handle more than one source of information.	Perception domain: Receiving a stimulus and giving it meaning; Systematic gathering of information using all the senses; Using several sources of information.
Memory	(i) ***Immediate recall***: (STM) Remembering of visual auditory or kinaesthetic information ii) ***Working memory***: Remembering past learning experiences/ knowledge to aid problem solving (iii) ***Long term memory***: Storing facts and information from the past LTM but not necessarily drawing on these memories for solving a current task.	Memory domain: Short-term recall; Working memory; Long-term recall; Modalities of memory. (VAK: Visual, Auditory Kinaesthetic
Language and communication	Understanding and expression. Taking account of the audience. Language structure.	Language domain: Receptive, expressive (content); Use (function); Structure (form)
Reasoning/logic	Being able to compare, classify, conserve, use logical reasoning, make predictions and infer relationships.	Reasoning and problem-solving domain: Basic; Higher order/executive function.
Strategic thinking/ metacognition	This domain involves the following specific cognitive abilities: Understanding what to do; Identifying what is relevant/irrelevant; Considering alternative strategies; Planning; Knowing when to be precise and accurate; Generalising strategies; Evaluating and adjusting performance.	
Behaviours affecting learning	Responsiveness to intervention from adults and peers, self-regulation, overcoming frustration, motivation, curiosity, response to challenge, persistence and understanding the need for task completion.	Emotional states: Emotional engagement; Overcoming blocking; Persistence; Control of impulsivity; Motivation; Curiosity.

Learner information

Susan aged 13 years 6 months. Referred due to concerns about frequent dysregulation and impulsivity, which affected curriculum access, social relationships and engagement with key adults in school.

Information gained

BRIEF-2 results

In the BRIEF-2, high T scores indicate high concerns. Specific score band descriptions from the test publisher are as follows: Scores of 70 and above indicate substantial difficulties. Scores of 65 to 69 indicate marked difficulties. Scores of 60–64 indicate some difficulties.

Scale	*T score (43–57 T score range is average)*
Inhibit	81
Self-monitor	70
Shift	77
Emotional control	Above 90
Initiate	56
Working memory	60
Plan/organise	59
Task-monitor	58
Organisation of materials	50

Composite scores:

Composite area	*T score*
Behaviour regulation	77
Emotion regulation	89
Cognitive regulation	59
Global executive composite	71

CAS2 Rating Scale results

PASS area	*Standard score (85–115 range is average)*
Planning	88
Attention	74
Simultaneous	106
Successive	88

Profile of strengths and needs

Strengths

- Planning and organising materials;
- Categorising and cause and effect thinking (related to simultaneous processing strength);
- Able to demonstrate some cognitive regulation, despite high emotional regulation.

Needs

- Restraining impulsivity (related to inhibition and emotional control in BRIEF-2). This can also affect planning and systematic working when Susan is dysregulated;
- Attention;
- Flexibility (related to shift in BRIEF-2).

Priority areas to include in learner profile

All three needs above were identified as priorities.

The Cognitive Abilities Profile

The CAP is 'a tool designed for consultation and observation of the cognitive functioning of a learner, that is, the thinking processes involved in a variety of learning and problem-solving activities' (Deutsch, 2020: 1). It is a collaborative framework for joint discussion, rating and negotiations on current practice and decisions on future targets. It can be used as a means for capturing observations of learners, as a structure for consulting with others in order to gather information about the learner which is rated by the 'team' around the learner, using a Likert type scale based on Vygotsky's concept of the Zone of Proximal Development. The CAP framework can also include the outcomes of individual DA with a learner. The CAP is divided into three sections. The sections examine the following:

- *Section A*: The cognitive abilities of the learner;
- *Section B*: The learner's response to teaching and mediation;
- *Section C*: Task analysis for classroom observation.

This is followed by a summary and cognitive learning plan with SMART targets agreed on by the 'team', which is systematically reviewed, monitored and adjusted at agreed time intervals. Learner and parental views are always sought and included.

For the purposes of this chapter, the focus is on Section A of the CAP, since this relates to identifying the cognitive skills of the learner. Specific skills and behaviours in each domain are rated. The CAP draws on the same theoretical foundations as those discussed in

Chapter 3, where the model for cognitive skills and emotional states was presented. Hence there is considerable overlap between the Section A CAP domains and the domains of the present model.

The following box is an example of a learner profile drawn up using information from the CAP.

Learner information

Kyle aged 4 years 8 months. Referred due to concerns about delayed general development, with specific concerns about speech and language, self-regulation and social skills. These were affecting access to the Early Years Foundation Stage curriculum and his peer relationships.

Information gained

Information was gathered from parents, early years setting staff, observation during child-initiated play sessions and from PBA involving sorting small world toys (favoured play materials). The CAP was completed and the graph below shows the scores obtained.

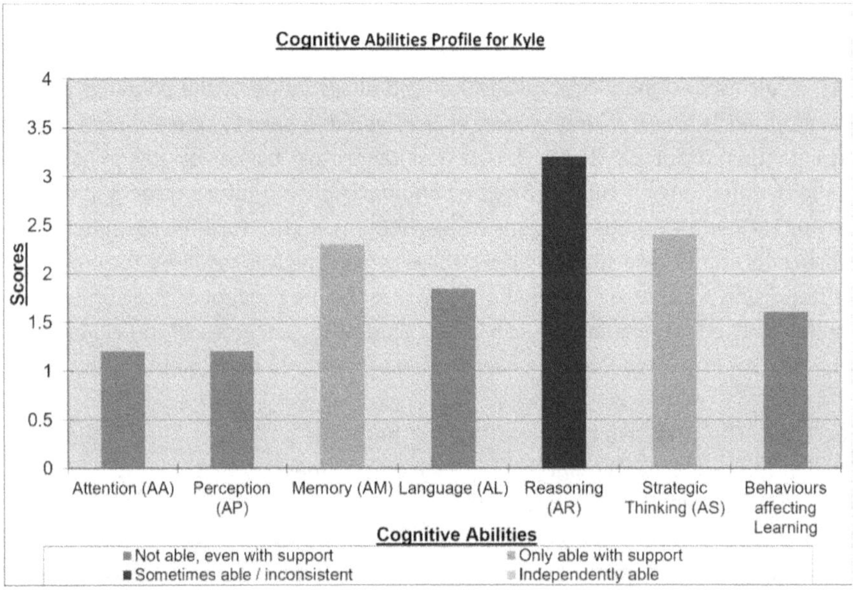

Profile of strengths and needs

Strengths

- Reasoning and logic. Kyle was independently able to classify and group objects. He spontaneously used summative behaviour to check the number of objects in each group that he sorted. He was sometimes able to establish cause and effect and to infer relationships;

- Strategic thinking. Kyle was able to understand the task and to focus on what was relevant. In a sorting activity he demonstrated some flexibility as he was able to find more than one way of grouping the objects (colour and size).

Needs

- Attention;
- Perception;
- Memory of auditory information;
- Language;
- Behaviours affecting learning (low CAP scores for self-regulation of emotions and of movement, motivation, response to challenge and persistence/task completion).

Priority areas to include in learner profile

- Self-regulation and control of impulsivity;
- Language.

The two above areas were a priority since they affected both social and academic development and progress.

Blended assessment

We have included this as a separate section because where psychometric/static tests are being used, accompanying work or follow-up might be direct or indirect. For direct approaches, this would mean that if you or someone else carries out a static assessment, you can then select and use a DA test or other interactive assessment materials to work with the learner in order to deepen insights into the learner's processing, following the use of static tests. Alternatively, you might follow up a static assessment (for example, supplied as part of background/referral information) with an indirect approach such as those already explored in the preceding section.

Introduction to blended assessment and its rationale

One of the challenges facing practitioner psychologists is how to combine standardised static psychological tests with DA. Whilst DA has been increasingly recognised in recent years as a useful, complementary way of understanding a learner's functioning, it is not always accepted by decision-making bodies, where standardised norm referenced test scores are often part of the gateway for accessing certain resources.

Despite the established use of qualitative measures and heuristics in many branches of psychology, there remains an uneasiness that 'if you can't measure and quantify it, it isn't real'. The radically different view of intelligence adopted by Vygotsky and the Russian school of psychology, in contrast to the Western psychology tradition, focusing on measurability of intelligence, predictability and permanence, as we discussed in Chapter 2, underpins the different trajectories of assessing and understanding cognitive functioning.

Stepping aside from these conceptual differences, we can recognise that each approach has different information to contribute to an overall assessment. Put simply, it all depends on why you are assessing and how you will choose the tools you will use to conduct the assessment in the best way you can. We wish to propose a blended model, drawing on useful elements of both static and dynamic approaches to address the presenting issues of a learner that are the starting point for an assessment. This section will outline methods of combining both standardised and DA assessments which we have used for many years as practising psychologists, integrating these approaches in our work. In doing so we have been able to assess children, adolescents and clients beyond the school years, leading to recommendations for how best to assist them in their further development which have been accepted by Local Authorities and other decision-making bodies with or without standardised test results.

In blended assessment we compare static performance with what we have also found out through DA. This interpretation leads onto a consideration of implications for the learner's functioning. Too often, these two different approaches are reported with no linkage between them. Bringing them together can show how the DA tests deepen our understanding of the static tests and respond to the issue of mediation within the tests themselves. We can comment on what changes have occurred and in what ways. Information from both sources is used to draw up a profile of the learner's cognitive strengths and needs.

Note that we are not suggesting that practitioners should routinely carry out static assessment and DA. One of the common contexts for a blended approach that the present authors have experienced, is where a set of static assessment results may already be provided as part of the learner's background information. These results are then used to plan interactive assessment that reflects and follows up the cognitive skills assessed via the static approach.

Differences between Dynamic Assessment and static tests

It is important to be clear about differences between dynamic, interactive assessment and static assessment before undertaking any blended assessment. The bullet points below summarises these differences.

- No DA tests are timed for scoring purposes. Performance speed is not conflated with measures of intelligence;

Table 4.8 Differences between DA and static tests

Difference	***Description***
No DA tests are timed for scoring purposes	Performance times are observed in DA and are qualitatively evaluated in relation to precision and accuracy. Performance speed is not conflated with measures of intelligence.
No overall scores are generated from DA tests	Tests selected within domains, for example, visual, spatial, auditory, higher order abstract reasoning, are compared with each other as well as a cognitive performance analysis within each subtest.
No cluster scores are generated in DA	Subtests can be selected from different batteries, for example, from the LPAD, Tzuriel, Haywood and Lidz in order to elicit and mediate different cognitive skills. Internal consistency between tests is not sought; however, patterns of cognitive skills are identified and mediated.
Age norms are not used in DA for either test selection or scoring	Tests are chosen for the cognitive skills that need exploration and mediation. There are approximate age guidelines for different batteries but these can be set aside, as the DA assessor will select tests and mediate according to the developmental needs of the learner.
Scoring of DA tests is optional	Significance of scores is not normative but qualitative. Change scores are very useful where the change scores between pre- and post-tests can reflect the impact of mediation.
Scores in DA test are not statistically significant	Cumulative information is significant if there is repeated occurrence of certain strengths or deficient cognitive patterns. Recurrence across a wide range of tests is indicative of internalised and generalised strengths or pervasive difficulty in some aspects of cognitive skills, whereas cognitive skills appearing in one test only would indicate a specific source of difficulty. We have to be very careful not to generalise from a single test, or even tests taken at one single time!
Failure on consecutive test items is not used as an exit criterion in DA	In contrast to static tests where a given number of consecutive failures indicates the termination of that test, failure on a test item becomes the point where mediation starts. The DA examiner will attempt to prevent failure by mediating before and during the test item, if necessary.
Assessing unaided performance is not the sole purpose of DA	The goal of DA is to achieve optimal performance under guided learning (mediated) conditions. Obtaining baseline information can be within the DA test or can be obtained from previous tests, including classroom or more formal tests. Baseline information obtained within a DA test or from elsewhere is helpful in order to define a starting point for test selection and then to be able to compare performance pre- and post-mediation.
DA is not designed to test school curricular achievement	DA tests are as content-neutral as possible, aiming to differentiate performance based on prior learning from underlying cognitive processes in order not to confound these with culturally specific learning experiences. We have emphasised the extent to which we recognise that nothing we do is culture-free and therefore there cannot be something that is 'pure' internal intelligence. We live within specific cultural environments, but in DA we try to separate these aspects as much as we can, recognising that some inefficiencies will be due to lack of familiarity rather than lack of intelligence.
In DA, criteria for analysis and interpretation are different	Task analysis is a key tool, where the cognitive elements of a task are analysed in order to be clear about what might affect cognitive skills and emotional states and how to mediate within the test itself. This is covered in detail in Chapter 5. Response to mediated learning and changes between phases of assessment (pre- and post-mediation, comparing independent and supported performance) are analysed.

- Scoring of DA tests is optional and no overall scores or cluster scores are generated from DA tests. Some DA tests involve pre- and post-mediation scores that are used qualitatively in order to comment on the impact of mediation;
- Scores in DA test are not statistically significant. Related to the previous point, the qualitative use of scores means that statistical analysis is not relevant;
- Age norms are not used in DA for either test selection or scoring. The only age-related element is matching the choice of test to the learner's age and developmental level;
- Failure on consecutive test items is not used as an exit criterion in DA. In DA, failure on a test item becomes the point where mediation starts. The examiner attempts to prevent failure by mediating before and during the test item, if necessary;
- Assessing unaided performance is not the sole purpose of DA. Baseline information obtained within a DA test or from elsewhere is helpful in order to define a starting point for test selection and then to be able to compare performance pre- and post-mediation;
- DA is not designed to test school curricular achievement. DA tests are as content-neutral as possible. In DA we try to separate content aspects as much as we can, recognising that some of the learner's challenges will be due to lack of familiarity rather than lack of intelligence;
- In DA, criteria for analysis and interpretation are different. Response to mediated learning and changes between phases of assessment (pre- and post-mediation, comparing independent and supported performance) are analysed.

Blended assessment procedure

Test sequence

When using both approaches, it is essential to begin with the static (norm referenced) tests. The order of testing is conceptually and practically important. Since DA is a *change* model, what one does within a DA is meant to do just that, change performance. We are thereby actively mediating to the pupil to solve the presenting tasks and in doing so we prepare them to use and reuse these strategies when given similar tasks, whether in further DA examples or in a standardised battery. In some models of DA, deliberate mediation for transfer and generalisation is built into the process. It has been shown that such intervention can impact on post-DA test performance whether on DA or on standardised tests; for example, Tzuriel's (2000) research related to the CCPAM (Children's Conceptual and Perceptual Analogical reasoning) test.

One important point about blended assessment is that the two approaches are kept separate. This might seem to contradict the term 'blended'. What we mean by blended is that the assessment uses both static and flexible approaches to assist in understanding the learner's cognitive strengths and needs. There are those who try to 'dynamise' static tests; that is, use subtests from norm referenced ability tests in an interactive way. This is *not* recommended because the purpose of the static test is to capture unaided performance, not to use it as an interactive mode of assessment. Furthermore, it invalidates any future use of that test with the client because they have received teaching and input over and above that which the test publisher recommends in the 'learning' phase of test administration. Therefore, our blended assessment model does *not* support the use of interactive approaches using materials from static tests.

Table 4.9 Blended assessment steps

Step	***Description***
Step 1: static assessment	Whether working directly or indirectly at this stage, the static assessment is the first step, either: Examining results of static tests provided; Or: Administering static tests.
Step 2: interactive assessment	Administer DA versions of static tests
Step 3: second session of interactive assessment	A second session of DA in order to follow up session 2 assessment. The specific purpose is to look at recall and transfer of problem-solving skills that were mediated in step 2.

There are three steps in a blended assessment procedure, shown in Table 4.9 (these steps are described in more detail in Resource 4.8, see information in the next section about supporting blended assessment).

Following administration of the standardised tests, one may then wish to address a different question, which the static tests are not designed to answer, which is: 'What can we learn about this person's cognitive skills and approach to problem-solving if we offer mediated learning within a test and see how they respond to problem-solving strategies and how they apply these to solve further similar problems?' This would be more in line with principles of formative assessment, leading to Step 2, interactive assessment.

In this stage, there are DA versions of some of the static tests that reflect and follow up cognitive skills sampled in the static test. Haywood and Lidz (2007) point out that a good DA test should have adequate validity and reliability when given in a static mode. An example would be comparing performance on a matrix reasoning static test, in the WISC or BAS, or similar battery and a DA version of matrix reasoning. It is the same cognitive activity but two quite different ways of using the materials. The key cognitive process being tested is analogical reasoning, which is a mental operation and requires us to understand its contributory cognitive functions and therefore how to mediate these systematically within this test and across different tests. That is, it moves the assessment focus from content (scoring right or wrong) to analysis of process.

Supporting blended assessment

In order to assist with decision-making about blended assessment, the Resource Centre contains tables that cross-reference norm referenced tests with cognitive thinking skills and DA tests. The following tests are cross-referenced:

- Resource 4.4: British Ability Scales (BAS-3; Elliott, 2011);
- Resource 4.5 Wechsler Intelligence Scale for Children (WISC-V; Wechsler, 2016) and Wechsler Pre School and Primary Intelligence Test (WPPSI-IV; Wechsler, 2012);
- Resource 4.6: Intelligence and Development Scales (IDS2; Barnett et al, 2021);
- Resource 4.7: Cognitive Assessment System (CAS2; Naglieri et al, 2014a). We have not cross-referenced to individual subtests from the CAS2 because the test authors recommend that interpretation is carried out at the composite level (see, for example, Naglieri and Otero, 2023). Cross-referencing at the composite level makes the comparisons relevant for the CAS2 Rating Scale, where scores are reported at the composite level.

Resource 4.8 in the Resource Centre contains information and guidance for implementing the three administration steps and for writing up a blended assessment report.

The following box contains an example of a learner profile drawn up using a blended approach, using the IDS2.

Learner information

Olivia aged 7 years 2 months. Referred due to concerns about slow progress in basic skills, attention and concentration.

IDS2 results

Scale	***Ability measured***	***Scaled score (8 to 12 range is average)***
Shape design	Visual processing	6
Parrots	Processing speed	2
Digit and letter span	Auditory short-term memory	2
Shape memory	Visual spatial short-term memory	3
Matrices	Abstract reasoning	6
Naming categories	Verbal reasoning	4
Story recall	Long-term memory	3

Dynamic Assessment follow-up to IDS2

During the IDS2 assessment (where assistance is strictly limited, according to the subtest instructions), some behaviours were thought to have affected the results, specifically:

- High impulsivity;

- Inability to focus on what was relevant for the task;
- Focusing attention on task instructions at the beginning of each new subtest.

These behaviours were a focus for mediation during DA. In addition, other cognitive skills related to low scoring subtests were investigated (digit and letter span, story recall and shape memory). DA tests used were:

- The **Application of Cognitive Functions auditory memory subtest** (Haywood and Lidz, 2007: 165, 174). This involves the learner hearing a short story read aloud, which they then have to re-tell. Mediation uses picture cues to aid recall. The focus cognitive skill is recall of auditory information;
- **Organisation of Dots** (Feuerstein et al, 2015). In this test, the learner is presented with 'clouds' of dots and has to join the dots to make given shapes. The focus cognitive skills are spatial perception, using rules, comparison and restraining impulsivity.

Profile of strengths and needs

Strengths

- Verbal reasoning;
- Long-term memory;
- Able to maintain attention in a short, structured lesson;
- Able to reduce impulsivity and focus on relevance during mediated learning; responded to focusing prompts prior to beginning a task, mediating feelings of competence related to attention and taking her time (restraining impulsivity).

Needs

- Focusing attention;
- Restraining impulsivity;
- Auditory memory;
- Relevance;
- Comparison;
- Inference.

Priority areas to include in learner profile

Attention and restraining impulsivity were highlighted as key 'foundation' cognitive skills. Alongside these broad domains, relevance and comparison were identified as reasoning skills to be targeted.

Creating a learner profile

The outcome of work carried out using material from this chapter is to create a learner profile. The learner profile is the first step in planning support for learners in order to support them to achieve cognitive growth and metacognitive insight. Essential information in this profile will be a summary of the learner's strengths and needs, related to your assessment of their cognitive skills and emotional states. Depending on the information you have gathered, the profile might also include some information about the impact of mediation. For example, DA will give some insights into mediation and the CAP (Deutsch, 2020) includes a specific section about the learner's response to mediational strategies.

It is possible that a long list of strengths and/or needs might emerge as a result of your assessment. In these cases, it is important to prioritise. The process of prioritisation will depend on several factors:

- Whether any of the identified needs are 'foundational'. Looking at the Boat of Cognition model (see Chapter 3, Figure 3.2), there are several domains where challenges in these will affect the learners' ability to use higher order cognitive skills. These domains are: readiness to learn, attention, perception and language. Similarly, challenges related to emotional states can also affect higher order cognitive skills. Where these foundational challenges are evident, it will be important to prioritise them;
- Relevance. Consider which cognitive skills and/or emotional states are important for the learner right now. Take account of context and relate to the concerns raised;
- Practicalities. Consider what is manageable.

Some of the above issues will be revisited when we look at target setting in Chapter 8. For now, the key outcome is to have a short list of cognitive strengths and needs. The effectiveness is in less not more.

The precise way in which the profile is used will depend on your role and how your involvement is commissioned. For example, if you are an external professional such as a visiting specialist teacher, educational psychologist or speech and language therapist, at this point you might disseminate your findings in order to make recommendations and agree strengths and needs. If you work in a specific setting having day-to-day contact with learners, develop and share the profile with key adults who will be working with the learner, and with the learner themselves.

Summary

This chapter has suggested a range of direct and indirect approaches for identifying the cognitive thinking skills and emotional states of a learner. After working through this chapter, you should be able to draw up a learner profile, which identifies the priority cognitive skills and emotional states that will be the focus of mediated learning. Therefore, you have now assembled the first set of building bricks for the House of Metacognition and are now ready to find out about the second set of bricks (analysing the task) in the next chapter.

Reflection and follow-up

- This chapter emphasises the use of multiple sources of information when constructing a cognitive profile of the learner. Consider one or two cases you have dealt with where such an approach has significantly informed your findings and your subsequent interventions.
- Reflect on which approaches are manageable and appropriate for you, based on your role and the learners with whom you work. What might you try out as a result of reading this chapter? You may want to identify a specific learner and draw up a cognitive profile.

References

Barnett, A., Stuart, N. and Vanzan, S. (2021). *The Intelligence and Development Scales*, 2nd edn. Oxford: Hogrefe.

Berg, I.K. and de Shazer, S. (1993). Making numbers talk: language in therapy. In S. Friedman (Ed.), *The New Language of Change*. New York: Guilford.

Bragg, S. (2021). Student voice in education. *Journal of the British Academy*, 8(4), 41–51.

Bronfenbrenner, U. (1979). *The Ecology of Human Development: Experiments by Nature and Design.* Cambridge, MA: Harvard University Press

Burden, R.L. (1998). Assessing children's perceptions of themselves as learners and problem-solvers: the construction of the Myself-As-A-Learner Scale (MALS), *School Psychology International*, 19(4), 291–305. [The current version of the scale is published by Imaginative Minds.]

Children and Families Act (2014). Available at: http://www.legislation.gov.uk/ukpga/2014/6/contents. Accessed 12 December 2025.

Dawson, P. and Guare, R. (2009). *Smart but Scattered.* New York: Guilford.

Department for Education and Skills (2003). *Every Child Matters: Green Paper.* Norwich: The Stationery Office.

Deutsch, R. (2017). *Reliability, Validity and Educational Use of the Cognitive Abilities Profile*, unpublished PhD thesis, School of Health Sciences, City, University of London.

Deutsch, R. (2020). *Cognitive Abilities Profile*, rev. edn. Canterbury: Real Group Limited.

Deutsch, R. (2024). *The CAP Short Form.* Canterbury: Real Group Limited

Elliott, C. (2011). *The British Ability Scales*, 3rd edn. London: GL Assessment.

Farrell, P. and Woods, K. (2015). Reflections on the role of consultation in the delivery of effective educational psychology services. *Educational Psychology Research and Practice*, 1(1), 5–9.

Feuerstein, R., Feuerstein, R., Falik, L. and Yosef, L. (2015). *Learning Potential Assessment Device LPAD Standard, Examiners Manual.* Jerusalem: The Feuerstein Institute.

Gioia, G.A., Espy, K.A. and Isquith, P.K. (2003). *Behavior Rating Inventory of Executive Function: Preschool Version.* Odessa: Psychological Assessment Resources.

Gioia, G.A., Isquith, P.K., Guy, S.C. and Kenworthy, L. (2015). *Behavior Rating Inventory of Executive Function, Second Edition (BRIEF-2).* Lutz: Psychological Assessment Resources.

GL Assessment (2024). *About PASS: Pupil Attitudes to Self and School.* Available at: https://www.gl-assessment.co.uk/products/pass/. Accessed 21 January 2026.

Haywood, H.C. and Lidz, C. (2007). *Dynamic Assessment in Practice.* New York: Cambridge University Press.

Hymer, B., Michael, D. and Todd, L. (2002). Dynamic consultation: towards process and challenge. *Educational Psychology in Practice*, 18(1), 47–62.

Jones, L. and Atkinson, C. (2022). A framework for developing educational psychologists' consultation practice. *Educational Psychology in Practice*, 7(2), 1–28.

Leadbetter, J. (2006). Investigating and conceptualising the notion of consultation to facilitate multi-agency work. *Educational Psychology in Practice*, 22(1), 19–31.

Lidz, C. (2003). *Early Childhood Assessment.* Hoboken: Wiley.

Linder, T. (2008). *Transdisciplinary Play-Based Assessment.* Baltimore: Paul H. Brooked Publishing Co.

Luria, A.R. (1976). *The Working Brain: An Introduction to Neuropsychology.* New York: Basic Books.

Lutz, C. (2014). Scaling questions: a tool for motivation and confidence to change. *Journal of Solution Focused Brief Therapy,* 1(1), 69-75.

Montoya-Fernández, C., Losada-Puente, L., Gómez-Barreto, I. and Gil-Madrona, P. (2024). Developmental play-based assessment in early childhood education: a systematic review. *European Early Childhood Education Research Journal,* 32(5), 788-813.

Naglieri, J. and Otero, T. (2023). *PASS Theory of Intelligence and the CAS2.* Available at: www .jacknaglieri.com. Accessed 10 December 2025.

Naglieri, J.A., Das, J.P. and Goldstein, S. (2014**[[a]]**) *Cognitive Assessment System-Second Edition (CAS2).* Austin: Pro-Ed.

Naglieri, J. Das, J.P. and Goldstein, S. (2014**[[b]]**). *The Cognitive Assessment System Rating Scale.* Austin: Pro-Ed.

Royle, B. and Atkinson, C. (2025). Consultation policies in UK local authority educational psychology services: a scoping review of practice. *Educational Psychology in Practice,* 41(3), 296-316.

Sayeed, Z. and Guerin, E. (2000). *Early Years Play.* London: David Fulton.

Tzuriel. T. (2000). Dynamic Assessment of young children: educational and intervention perspectives. *Educational Psychology Review,*12(4), 385-435.

Wagner, P. (2000). Consultation: developing a comprehensive approach to service delivery. *Educational Psychology in Practice,* 16(1), 9-18.

Wechsler, D. (2012). *Wechsler Preschool and Primary Scale of Intelligence, Fourth Edition (WPPSI-IV).* London: Pearson Clinical.

Wechsler, D. (2016). *Wechsler Intelligence Scale for Children, Fifth UK Edition (WISC-VUK).* London: Pearson Clinical.

Williams, M.S. and Shellenberger, S. (1996). *How Does Your Engine Run? A Leader's Guide to the Alert® Programme for Self Regulation.* Albuquerque: Therapy Works.

5

The Task

Introduction

Task analysis is the second set of bricks needed for building the house of metacognition. This chapter builds on material about the tripartite partnership that was introduced in Chapter 3. It looks at the task element of the tripartite partnership, illustrated in Figure 5.1.

This chapter is divided into two main sections. The first section will give some more detailed descriptions of the elements of the task outlined in Chapter 3. The second section will look at the process of analysing tasks from a cognitive perspective, giving some worked examples.

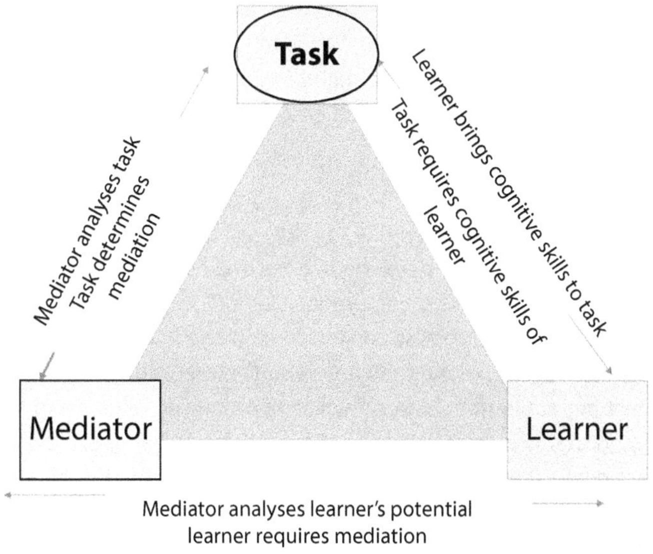

Figure 5.1 A tripartite learning partnership (task)

DOI: 10.4324/9781003655329-8

When you have completed this chapter, you will be able to analyse a task so that you know what cognitive skills need to be mediated and what other elements of a task need to be adjusted.

Analysing the task

As discussed in Chapter 3, here we go into more detail about the five elements of a task that need to be analysed. These are discussed below.

Content

Content: key questions

What subject or topic is the task about?

How familiar or novel is the content and vocabulary of the task?

It might seem counterintuitive to look at task content, since the emphasis in mediated learning is on process not product. As discussed in Chapter 1, focusing on what is learned (content, or products of learning) at the expense of how to learn (process) risks creating individuals who do not know how to be successful and independent learners. However, it would not be adequate to ignore content because this element provides the context for learning which will affect the individual's ability to use and apply their cognitive skills. The example below, based on one of the authors' casework, illustrates this point.

Daniel, aged ten years, was referred due to concerns about his progress in basic skills, particularly reading. During the assessment, the child's teacher was very concerned to highlight Daniel's poor reading comprehension skills. In order to emphasise these difficulties, during the author's assessment session she asked the author to observe her hearing Daniel read a text and then answer questions about it. Daniel read the text quite accurately but could not answer any literal or inferential questions. The teacher was very pleased that her assertion about Daniel had been supported. However, when the author examined the text that he had been asked to read, other reasons arose about his difficulty. The text he had been asked to read was about fishing. It contained words such as 'lobster pot', 'tide', 'crab' and 'bait'. Daniel lived in an inner-city area of the UK and had never been to the sea. He had no experience of some of the terms used in the book, so his inability to comprehend the text was hindered by his unfamiliarity with the content of the book. Therefore, it was impossible (and inappropriate) to come to any conclusions about Daniel's reading comprehension on the basis of this activity.

The example above emphasises the roles of novelty and familiarity in relation to task content. Novelty can affect cognitive skills in that it can be more difficult to use and apply these skills if the learner has to put effort into coping with unfamiliarity. In the example above, the difficulty with novelty was that the content of the book was completely outside of Daniel's experience. In other cases, lack of familiarity with a task might be due to the learner being at an early stage of exposure to content. This might mask the learner's cognitive skills, leading to skewed conclusions about strengths and weaknesses.

The content item of the task is a prompt for us separate out the individual's cognitive skills from context or background knowledge, in order to be clear that any weak cognitive skills are not due to inappropriate or unfamiliar content. There is a good reason why this is the first element of the task. First, we need to establish *what* is being learnt, because only then can we consider the constituent skills. This goes to the heart of Feuerstein's original observations about the impact of culture on cognition. This issue shows up often in questions which are part of standardised testing. Here is an example from one of the present authors' casework to illustrate this point.

Mariam, a nine-and-half-year-old girl, had emigrated to the UK with her family approximately one-and-a-half years before I met her. The family had fled from their native Somalia and, having spent two years in a refugee hostel in a European country, they arrived in the UK, where they were housed in a two-bedroom flat, provided by the local council. Mariam was the eldest of nine siblings. English was not spoken at home. She had been referred by her school for assessment of learning difficulties.

The question in the standardised test that was used was: 'What are the benefits of public libraries?' Mariam was not able to answer this question. After the test administration, I asked her whether she went to the school library with her class to find out whether she had some idea of the purpose of a library. Although she had been to the school library, the idea of a public library was outside her experience. She had never been to a public library because every day after school, she spent the remaining hours of the day and evening helping her mother look after her younger siblings, which explained her inability to respond: the question was simply unconnected to her experience.

One of the issues raised by the above scenario is whether we are testing and scoring comprehension as one aspect of intelligence, or whether we are confounding intelligence with culturally specific knowledge. It is tempting to say that dynamic approaches would not raise these issues, and to an extent this is true. However, we should not make the mistake of thinking that all Dynamic Assessment by contrast is culture-free. It is not! Nothing we see, teach or learn can be understood outside a specific cultural framework. We cannot think without a context to think in. Therefore, it is clear that content and prior knowledge must be considered before we can even begin to assess problem-solving skills.

Modality

Modality: key questions

In which mode(s) is the task presented?

In which mode(s) is the learner expected to respond?

Modality refers to the way in which a task is presented or the response needed. Feuerstein lists six modalities: verbal, pictorial, numerical, figural, symbolic and graphic (Feuerstein et al., 2002). In addition to these six modalities, Deutsch (2020) includes kinaesthetic as one of the three visual, auditory and kinaesthetic (VAK) modalities, being the most common in the classroom, and the Cognitive Abilities Profile (Deutsch, 2020) mentions several other possible modalities:

- Pictorial;
- Symbolic;
- Numerical;
- Verbal;
- Musical;
- Rhythmic;
- Mechanical.

Modality can impact significantly on the learner's response. The learner might not perform well in a task due to the modality, rather than to any problems with their cognitive skills. An example of the way in which modality can affect cognition is illustrated below, taken from one of the authors' casework:

Teddy, aged 6 years, was referred due to concerns about poor task completion and inattentiveness. He left his seat very frequently to show his work to his teacher, thinking that he had finished a task, only to be told that he hadn't finished and should return to his seat and complete his work. This did not lead to any further work being completed. Assessment revealed that Teddy had some significant expressive and receptive language difficulties (a subsequent speech and language therapy assessment diagnosed developmental language disorder [DLD]), together with difficulties related to processing information, especially in the auditory modality. Classroom observation indicated that multiple task instructions were always given verbally to the whole class during a carpet time session at the beginning of the lesson. Therefore, they were wholly reliant on use of the auditory (verbal) modality, which was not the most appropriate method for Teddy due to the language and processing difficulties noted. The class teacher was asked to present task instructions visually, using picture symbol cards; for example, instructions involving a list of materials for a science lesson (where the task was planting seeds) were represented by picture symbols of the container for the seeds, the seeds, soil, water and a spoon. This led to a reduction in the number of times Teddy left his seat to show partly completed work, and to an increase in task completion.

The example above demonstrates how a 'mismatch' in modalities can affect the learner's engagement and curriculum access. The auditory modality was an area of weakness and thus learning was less likely to occur when this modality was used for task instructions. There is, however, an important caveat related to this example. Although Teddy clearly did not cope well when the auditory modality was used, this does not mean that this modality had to be avoided. Support for Teddy to access the curriculum using alternative modalities to the auditory will be important but, alongside this, intervention to improve his use of the auditory modality is also likely to be beneficial.

It is important to check both the modalities of task presentation and the required response because they are often not the same. For example, a teacher verbally discusses a topic or task, but the required response modality may be written, a diagram or a picture.

Modality and learning styles

The case example above leads to a related point about modalities: learning style. VAK learning styles have been a popular means of 'pigeonholing' individuals (see, for example, Fallace [2023] for a useful historical overview). Fleming's VARK (visual, auditory, reading, kinaesthetic) model, proposed in the 1990s (Fleming, 1995), led to the publication of questionnaires designed to identify preferences. Subsequent research indicated that these questionnaires had poor reliability and validity (see, for example, Coffield et al., 2004; Fridley and Fridley, 2010; Cuevas, 2015). In the area of specific learning difficulties (SpLD), multisensory teaching is often offered as a universal panacea when in reality the evidence for this approach as being universally effective for all SpLD learners is relatively weak (for example, Snowling and Hulme, 2011; Elliott and Grigorenko, 2024). The purpose of raising this point here is to emphasise that the concept of modality, as applied to the task, is not to use it to categorise or label learners. Rather, the purpose is to look at 'best fit' between the modalities of presentation and response as part of identifying what challenges and supports the learner to use their cognitive skills. As Cuevas (2015: 330) notes: '[T]he learning styles hypothesis has been refuted by empirical research to the extent that it may be considered irresponsible for teacher education programs and public educators to apply the method in practice.' Overall, therefore, the best use of modalities is for support rather than for labelling and categorising. Here is an assessment example where adjustment of modality was an important factor in performance.

Matrix reasoning is a test frequently used to assess fluid intelligence. Matrix reasoning as set out by Raven et al. (2000) is considered relatively culture-neutral, hence it was one of the tests selected by Feuerstein which he used dynamically for his early work with refugees. An interesting historical note is that at a later date, Feuerstein discussed his use of Raven Matrices with Raven himself, who approved of this use of his testing materials.

Matrix reasoning requires several important cognitive processes and is a test of analogical reasoning. However, the modality is frequently one of visual-spatial designs which increase in visual complexity. If one of the learner's challenges is difficulty with visual perception, the visual-spatial modality of the test may be one of the contributing aspects of their difficulties. This issue might compromise the assessment. Therefore, the learner might struggle and fail this test due to the visual-spatial modality, not their reasoning skills. Bearing this in mind, we might need to consider and compare the outcome if analogies were assessed in another modality, since it is the reasoning process that is being examined. An alternative might be to offer word (verbal) analogies or pictorial analogies in order to find out whether the learner can perform and use analogical reasoning confidently in these other modalities. Use of the same cognitive task requirements, but in different modalities, might lead to the conclusion that the problem was the modality, not the underlying cognitive skills. Such alternate modalities are available in some Dynamic Assessment batteries.

Complexity and abstraction

Complexity and abstraction: key questions

How complex is the task?

How much information needs to be processed?

How abstract is the task?

Complexity

In everyday speech we sometimes use the term 'complex' in a casual way, referring to a situation or task being 'difficult'. However, as part of analysing a task, we define this term much more precisely. Based on Feuerstein's definition, complexity is a quantitative concept and refers to the number of units of information involved in a task.

Here is an example of what we mean by complexity. Compare the following: 3 + 4 = ? The learner has no problem in answering '7'. Now look at this: 3 + 4 + 1 + 5 + 2 + 7 = ? What has changed is the number of items to be dealt with. Some learners will struggle with this. Yet the learner has demonstrated that the mathematical operation of addition is within their grasp. Therefore, the problem is the level of *complexity*.

Abstraction

The meaning of abstraction refers to 'the distance between a mental act and the object or event on which it operates' (Feuerstein et al., 2002). The 'distance' being referred to here is the distance between a perceptual or concrete activity and one which requires mental representation. It is useful to think of this as a continuum. On the lower end are concrete activities and on the higher levels are more abstract tasks. The more a task or topic involves ideas and concepts and does not rely on things we can perceive and touch, the more it is a mental activity and therefore more abstract.

Essentially, looking at a task, we can analyse its level of abstraction. This involves considering how 'hands on' the task is. An abstract task is where we have to mentally visualise or work with ideas or concepts. For example, in a citizenship lesson we might talk about 'democracy'. We can define this idea and give examples of what democracy might involve, but we can't physically manipulate or draw a picture of democracy. In contrast, we can have tasks that are very hands-on or concrete. For example, maths calculations can be solved with or without concrete objects (or manipulatives as they are now called) to assist calculation. Some cognitive skills can be concrete or abstract or include elements of both. For example, comparison might be quite concrete in an early years setting (comparing two objects to find out which is larger) or abstract in a high school history lesson (comparing the notion of monarchy or kingship from different periods of history).

Abstract thinking: is it always higher order?

Abstract thinking is often associated with higher order thinking skills, leading to an assumption that these thinking skills are the sole province of abstract thinking and that a concrete element has no part to play. However, many tasks use both.

This relates to Piagetian theory, where links are made between ages and the development of children's thinking (for example, Piaget, 1964). The Formal Operations stage, where abstract thinking should be increasingly evident, is said by Piaget to start at the age of 11 or 12 years. Piaget's earlier stage, which he named Concrete Operations, was assigned to ages approximately 6 to 11 years (the elementary or primary school phase of education). Piaget described the developmental journey from early years reliance on perceptual and concrete materials as a gradual shift towards mental representation. However, he also described some mental operations which he said were in evidence in learners already in the Concrete Operations stage of development. These included seriation and categorisation. He called such thinking of a more abstract nature, albeit achieved with the use of concrete materials, *mental operations*, a term also used by Feuerstein and which we reflect in our Boat of Cognition model where we have separated out basic and higher order cognitive skills. Tzuriel's younger years tests (see Tzuriel [2000] for an overview of these tests) use concrete materials in order to assess and mediate to help the child develop higher order thinking skills (mental operations), such as inference and analogy. Therefore, concrete and abstract processes are interrelated in that use of the concrete can be a means of supporting use of higher order thinking skills. The reverse can also be applied, where a cognitive thinking skill can involve both a concrete or abstract level. Feuerstein and Lewin-Benham note: 'toddlers use concrete tasks to express the abstract idea of division' (2012: 93). A related interesting piece of evidence of the impact of mediating abstract concepts on perceptual processes was found by Tzuriel. He researched the relative changes in performance when using different parts of the Conceptual and Perceptual Pictorial Analogies test (CCPAM; Tzuriel, 2007) in a different sequence. Administering and mediating solving perceptual analogies first did not show any transfer effects to solving conceptual items, but when reversed and the conceptual analogies (which are more abstract) were administered and mediated first, followed by the perceptual items, there was a positive transfer effect on problem-solving of the perceptual items (Tzuriel, 2007).

Summarising abstraction and complexity

Summarising these two aspects of analysing a task, complexity and abstraction, we can see that complexity is about how much data we need to deal with, whereas abstraction is more qualitative. When we look at some applications of these concepts, we will see why it is important to note both. A learner may struggle with the complexity of a task, but not with abstraction or vice versa. How an individual relates to these different elements of a task gives us important information we need, to guide us as to how best to help them. However, it is important not to over-generalise. For example, the learner who struggles with complexity in a number modality may be highly efficient in dealing with complexity in a language modality. Check different tasks until you can confirm that you can see a pattern across different tasks.

Cognitive skills

Cognitive skills: key question

What cognitive skills are needed to complete this task?

This element of analysing the task refers to the cognitive skills that are needed for a task. These were illustrated in the Boat of Cognition model introduced in Chapter 3 and explored further in Chapter 4 in relation to identifying the cognitive skills of the learner. We will use the same list of cognitive skills, but now we will separate *task* demands from the *person* doing the task. As we summarise and complete all parts of the tripartite partnership, we bring the two together. We will compare task demands to the cognitive profile of the learner. From there, we can start differentiating our interventions (mediation), in order to narrow the gap between the task demands and the learner's cognitive strengths and challenges.

The Boat of Cognition model is reproduced again for ease of reference in relation to task analysis. Table 4.1 in Chapter 4 will also be helpful.

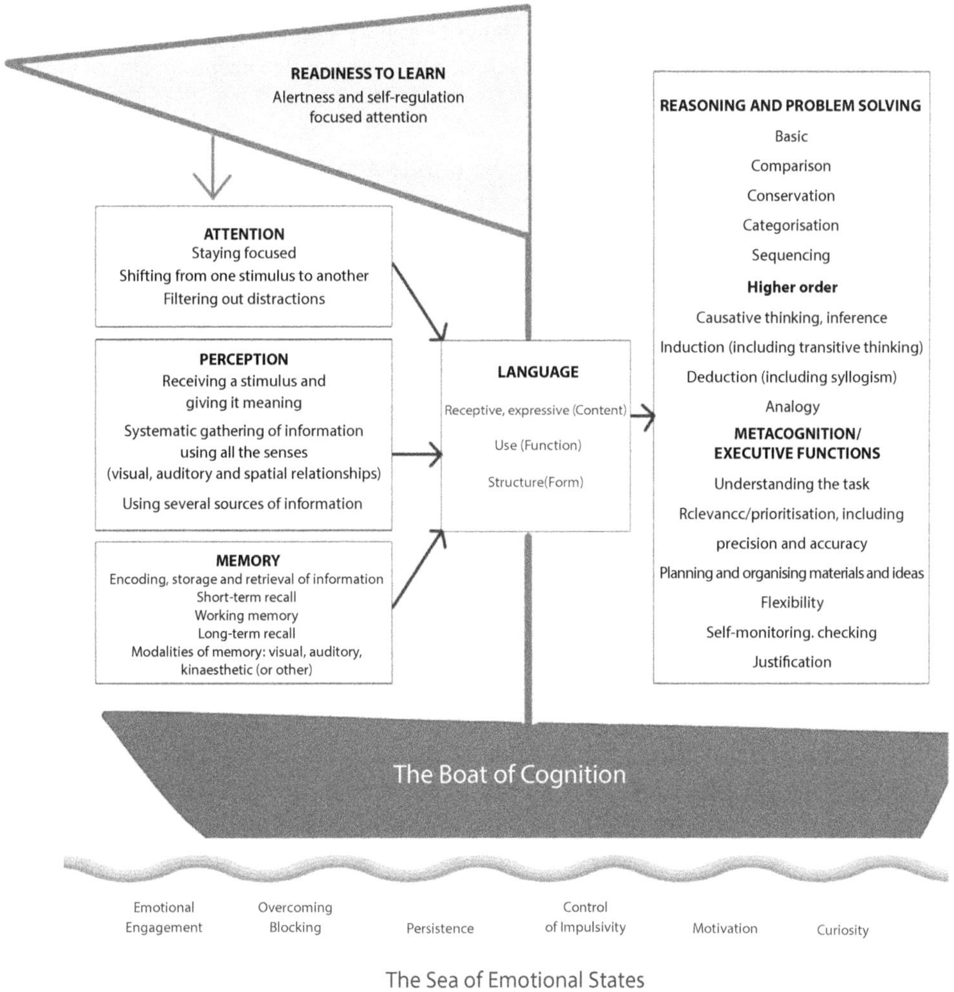

Figure 5.2 The Boat of Cognition

Speed, precision and accuracy

Speed, precision and accuracy: key questions

How quickly does the task need to be performed?

How precisely and/or accurately does the task need to be performed?

The concept of efficiency

The concept of efficiency is one of the more challenging areas to examine when analysing a task. This is because efficiency can also include the idea of effort and energy. Efficiency is one of the original parameters of Feuerstein's Cognitive Map and was defined as consisting of three aspects: speed, precision and effort. However, our five elements do not include effort. The rationale is discussed below.

We can see that it is not difficult to describe or rate a task's speed requirement. A task could require no speed, some speed or high speed. Similarly, rating or describing the precision and accuracy required by a task is also accessible to us. Some tasks need to be done absolutely precisely; for example, a pharmacist measuring and counting drugs to make up a prescription, or a maths calculation. Others do not; for example, skim reading a text to gain the main points or ideas.

In contrast, effort is much more difficult to define. Effort is about who is doing the task, not the task itself. It is not an objective measure; it is a qualitative view of what it takes to do a task. A task I find very difficult, perhaps stressful, may require a great deal of effort on my part. The same task may require no effort at all for someone else. Effort is a combination of all the elements of the task: familiarity with content, modality, complexity, abstraction, cognitive skills, speed, precision and accuracy.

If a learner is very motivated to accomplish a task they will put in considerable effort, even discomfort. If the learner is not interested, even though objectively the task might not be difficult for them, the learner will not put in the effort. It is all guided by our goals and sense of purpose, which relates to mediation of meaning. For the reasons above our five-element model when thinking about efficiency refers only to speed, precision and accuracy. Motivation is included as part of the emotional states of the learner.

Describing speed, precision and accuracy

Some tasks involve an element of speed, which can affect the learner's use of their cognitive skills; for example, writing under timed conditions. Processing speed is a common assessment domain in static tests (see the cross-referencing tables in Chapter 4) but is rarely, if ever, a feature of Dynamic Assessment tests, as Dynamic Assessment aims to separate these two aspects of task performance. However, in relation to analysing a task, it might be important to know whether speed is an issue and to examine any possible challenges that this requirement might pose for the learner. This area sometimes relates to emotional states that are also part of the learner's profile. Some learners find it very difficult to cope with timed assessment and timed work. An example of this is illustrated below, taken from one of the authors' casework:

Ava, aged 10, was referred for a dyscalculia diagnostic assessment. Results of norm referenced tests produced scores in the average range. However, when a criterion referenced assessment of fluency in maths skills was carried out under timed conditions, she fell a very long way short of the fluency criteria and made several errors, despite demonstrating secure computational skills in the norm referenced assessments and in other untimed assessments. Further investigation uncovered clinically elevated levels of anxiety, particularly related to maths. Furthermore, it transpired that previous screening and assessments that had prompted the concerns and referral were largely timed assessments. The diagnostic decision was therefore that a label of dyscalculia was not appropriate and that her difficulties were attributed to anxiety, particularly maths anxiety (it was noted that maths anxiety is not just experienced by learners who struggle with maths). Recommendations were made in relation to anxiety reduction and self-esteem. Ava's case demonstrates that the speed element of the task was a challenge to her successful task completion and prevented her from demonstrating her secure maths skills due to her elevated anxiety about timed assessments.

The next case example is one where the opposite motivation was observed.

Sandy was 14 years and came to one of the present authors for assessment and ongoing intervention. She had been diagnosed with attention deficit hyperactivity disorder several years earlier. Sandy was on and off medication according to her mood.

Sandy was cognitively able but with poor self-regulation. When a task required some speed, this actually motivated her. She could see herself doing her best and getting through it faster. Indeed, the speed element was what kept her going. When we played games or did activities needing speed, she could see how fast she was (and how the assessor struggled with speed!). The mediation that was provided was to validate her enjoyment of the speed and to build positively on her capacity for fast processing and to see whether she could combine it with also achieving a good level of accuracy. In other words, could she achieve both speed and precision? As a relationship of trust developed, we were able to discuss when speed is not always helpful. Her tendency to burst out with comments in class often resulted in her getting into trouble. We discussed when we need to pause, think and hold back, even if she might be correct. We built her awareness and insight of a strength to use it to help her modify her behaviours in other settings, combining learning activities with reflection and discussion.

The important point about precision and accuracy is knowing *when* it is necessary to be precise and accurate. Sometimes this information is not always communicated explicitly to learners; it is assumed that they can work out whether precision and accuracy is needed and to what extent. Being able to judge and decide what level is appropriate for a specific task is an important aspect of our metacognitive awareness and our executive function.

Practical applications and examples

This section moves on from the descriptions of the elements of analysing a task in order to look at some practical examples.

In order to assist analysis, there is an example record form in the Resource Centre (Resource 5.1). Section C of the Cognitive Abilities Profile (Deutsch, 2020) is another useful recording format.

There is no age limit for analysing tasks. For example, those of you working with learners in a supported work experience setting or in supported living accommodation, can use this framework to analyse activities of daily living and compare these with the learner's profile, when your goal might be to evaluate the extent of independent activities that this person can cope with or be supported in. Therefore, the framework of task analysis is flexible, enabling its use beyond the school setting and the school years.

What follows is a series of worked examples, followed by application activities for you to practise task analysis.

Early years examples

A large number of countries worldwide provide some kind of organised early years education and/or childcare. In the UK, a number of frameworks cover care and education for children from birth to five years. The EYFS (Early Years Foundation Stage) is the framework for early years providers in England. Due the large age rage covered by the EYFS and equivalent frameworks, two examples have been given below, corresponding to different age ranges.

Daycare setting: treasure basket with five- to 12-month-old babies

This example uses treasure baskets: The Treasure Basket concept was inspired by Elinor Goldschmied (see, for example, Goldschmied and Jackson, 1994) but has caught on throughout the UK and increasingly in other countries as well. 'It is a simple yet profound idea, opposing the trend to give commercial plastic toys to babies by providing them instead with a richer sensory experience' (Huleatt, 2012). Elinor Goldschmied first introduced the idea of treasure baskets, drawing on Froebel's work. Treasure baskets contain collections of natural, household and recycled objects and are used with babies and young children. The list of objects is huge, so just a small sample is given below for the purposes of illustrating task analysis. Treasure baskets are generally used with babies aged five to 12 months; usually from when they can sit unsupported.

Table 5.1 Daycare setting

Task: Exploring a treasure basket containing objects such as fir cones, shells, feathers, metal and wooden spoons, toothbrush, woollen pom-poms, paper, sponge, bells.	
Elements of analysis	***Description***
Content	This element relates to the items in the treasure basket. Familiarity will vary since the basket contains numerous items. Content is not a significant consideration for this activity because part of the purpose is for the baby to explore familiar and unfamiliar objects.
Cognitive skills	*Attention*: focusing, shifting and maintaining attention. *Perception*: using all the senses to explore objects. *Comparison*. *Memory*: not required. *Language*: not required. *Reasoning and problem-solving*: not required.
Modality	Visual (for example, shiny objects), auditory (for example, noisy objects such as bells or metal spoons banged together) and kinaesthetic (for example, fir cones or pom poms).
Abstraction and complexity	Low abstraction, all concrete objects. Low complexity (but a large number of objects to choose from).
Speed, precision and accuracy	Not required.

Nursery/reception setting

The age range targeted in this example is four to five years.

Table 5.2 Nursery/reception setting

Task: Sound bingo. The adult says a letter sound and the child has to mark the sound if it is on their bingo board	
Element of analysis	***Description***
Content	Letter sounds and shapes.
Cognitive skills	*Attention*: focusing, shifting and maintaining attention. *Perception*: auditory and visual stimuli, kinaesthetic response, systematic gathering of information (scanning the bingo sheet). *Symbol representation*: each sound represents a written letter. *Language*: receptive (understanding/following task instructions). *Reasoning and problem-solving*: comparison, if ... then.
Modality	Visual and auditory and motor output.
Complexity and abstraction	Low abstraction because the letters are printed. Low complexity; one sound at a time is said.
Speed, precision and accuracy	Not required.

School-age examples

Maths problem-solving examples

Three maths problems, suitable for different ages and stages of mathematical development, are shown in Table 5.3. These are:

- *A skittles game involving addition*. Four plastic bottles are the skittles. Each one is numbered from one to four. Roll a ball and find the score by adding up the number on each skittle that is knocked over. More skittles and different numbers can be used to match with particular maths skills (for example, six skittles numbered one to six, or numbering to produce totals above ten);
- *A money problem*. You have £2.50 to spend and have to decide how many of a particular item you can buy, the total cost of the items and how much change from £2.50;
- *A division problem*. What is the smallest number divisible by 1, 2, 3, 4, 5, 6, 7, 8, 9?

Task: reading comprehension

Two examples are shown here relating to different ages and type of reading comprehension question.

Table 5.3 Analysis example for maths problem-solving

Element of analysis	***Description***		
	Skittles game	***Money problem***	***Division problem***
Content	A skittle. Skittles game. Numbers. Addition.	Coin and note values. Four maths rules. Items that can be purchased.	Division, Prime numbers,
Cognitive skills	*Attention*: focusing, shifting and maintaining attention. *Perception*: auditory and visual stimuli, kinaesthetic response. *Language*: mathematical language (add, total). *Reasoning and problem-solving*: if ... then, deduction (applying the rule of the game). *Sequencing*: (adding numbers in order, adding each number only once).	*Attention*: focusing, shifting and maintaining attention. *Perception*: systematic information gathering. *Language*: understanding the mathematical language (add, total, divide). *Flexibility*. *Analysis and synthesis*. *Reasoning and problem-solving*: if ... then, self-monitor, checking, relevance (for example, the shop where the items are isn't relevant).	*Attention*: focusing, shifting and maintaining attention. *Perception*: systematic information gathering. *Language*: understanding the mathematical language (divide, prime factor). *Reasoning and problem-solving*: if ... then, self-monitor, checking.
Modality	Visual/numerical and kinaesthetic (eye-hand coordination)	Visual/numerical	Visual/numerical
Abstraction and complexity	Low abstraction. Some increase in complexity because the total could involve adding up to four numbers (or more if more skittles are used).	Much higher level of abstraction because the total is a value that can be subdivided. This is not a concrete task. Some complexity due to the number of items that can be bought.	Abstraction of the task is the use of a mathematical rule applied to the concept of prime numbers. High level of complexity due to the number of digits used for the calculations.
Speed, precision and accuracy	Some precision needed to knock down the skittle. Totals have to be calculated accurately.	Calculations have to be 100% accurate High level of precision.	Calculations have to be 100% accurate. High level of precision.

Table 5.4 Analysis examples for reading comprehension

Element of analysis	***Description***	
Examples	**Example 1** **Ages 5 to 7** **(Key Stage 1)**	**Example 2** **High School** **Ages 14 to 16+** **(Key Stages 3 or 4, or 16+)**
	What do you predict the troll did after the Billy Goats Gruff crossed the bridge?	In the article, is the author's political stance left-wing or right-wing? Give evidence to support your answer.
Content	Knowledge of the Three Billy Goats Gruff story.	Knowledge of left-/right-wing concepts and definitions (and of any other specific content in the article).
Cognitive skills	The need to understand what prediction means. If ... then thinking. Cause and effect thinking. Flexibility: considering more than one possibility. Justification (explain reason for answer). Relevance. Language: receptive and expressive for verbal response.	Comparison; for example, this text with other sources of understanding different political positions. Planning. Relevance/prioritisation. Deduction: using the definition of 'right-wing' and 'left-wing' to interpret the text. If ... then thinking. Considering several sources on information. Justification (reasons for your answer). Language: receptive for understanding specific vocabulary in the text such as 'right-wing', 'left-wing'. Expressive for verbal response.
Modality	Language (receptive and expressive). Visual and written presentation of materials. Response could be verbal or written depending on what is being asked for.	Visual/text presentation of materials. Response could be auditory or written depending on whether the response is spoken or written down.
Abstraction and complexity	Some abstraction because the answer cannot be gained directly from the text. Some complexity due to the number of events in the narrative (but there is a lot of repetition).	High level of abstraction because the answer cannot be gained directly from the text and the ideas involved are abstract High level of complexity as it is likely to be a long text
Speed, precision and accuracy	Accurate reading needed. Speed is not needed.	Accurate reading needed. Speed is not needed.

Using task analysis

There are two ways in which analysis of a task can be used:

- When carrying out an initial assessment in order to draw up a profile of the learner, in preparation for mediation;
- As part of the process of mediation, where the task or tasks to be used for differentiation and mediation are analysed in order to make sure that they are a suitable 'vehicle' for the specific cognitive skills being mediated.

The five elements for analysing a task are important because they are stepping stones into mediation, which is the way in which the cognitive skills are supported and promoted. Cognitive skills do not develop in isolation. The way in which learners develop these skills is by *doing*. Therefore, the tasks and activities that they are involved in are important. Cognitive skills are one element of the five elements described above. In order to make learning accessible, it is important to consider all five elements. Four areas (content; modality; abstraction and complexity; and speed, precision and accuracy) can be modified or tweaked to make sure that there are no aspects of the task that are preventing the learner from using their cognitive skills. Once changes have been made to these areas it is possible to go ahead with mediation to support the learner's cognitive skills.

Figure 5.3 illustrates that process, showing the four areas that can be adjusted as a prerequisite for mediating cognitive skills.

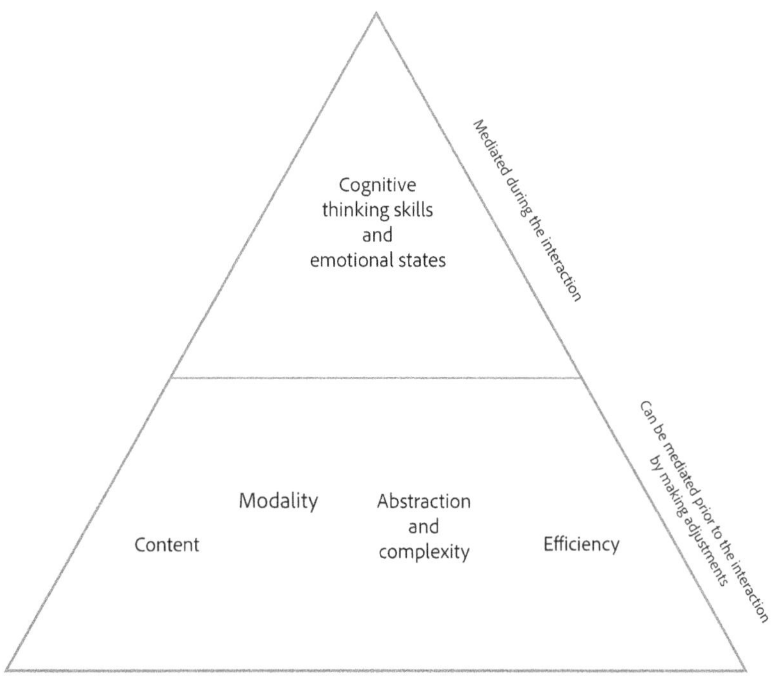

Figure 5.3 Task analysis

Summary

This chapter has taken you through the process of analysing a task, which is important for knowing what, if anything, needs to be adjusted and what needs to be mediated. Along with the cognitive profile of the learner, which was the focus of Chapter 4, you now have a complete set of bricks to build the House of Metacognition. The next chapter will look at mediation. Mediation is the mortar that turns separate piles of bricks into a coherent and robust structure.

Reflection and follow-up

- Consider three separate contexts (for example, home, school, college, social settings), in your own practice where task analysis can help shape your recommended interventions.
- Think about a particular learner with whom you work (it could be the learner that you used for the cognitive profile suggested at the end of Chapter 4). Download Resource 5.1 and practise a task analysis using a task that this learner will be given.

References

Coffield, F., Moseley, D., Hall, E. and Ecclestone, K. (2004). *Should We Be Using Learning Styles? What Research Has to Say to Practice*. London: Learning and Skills Research Centre, Learning and Skills Development Agency.

Cuevas, J. (2015). Is learning styles-based instruction effective? A comprehensive analysis of recent research on learning styles. *Theory and Research in Education*, 13(3), 308–333.

Deutsch, R. (2020). *Cognitive Abilities Profile*, rev. edn. Canterbury: Real Group Limited.

Early Years Foundation Stage (2014). *Statutory Guidance*. Available at: www.gov.uk/government/publications/early-years-foundation-stage-framework--2. Accessed 28 August 2025.

Elliott, J. and Grigorenko, E. (2024). *The Dyslexia Debate: Revisited*. Cambridge: Cambridge University Press.

Fallace, T. (2023). The long origins of the visual, auditory, and kinesthetic learning style typology, 1921-2001. *History of Psychology*, 26(4), 334–354.

Feuerstein, R., Feuerstein, R., Falik, L. and Rand, Y. (2002). *The Dynamic Assessment of Cognitive Modifiability*. Jerusalem: The ICELP Press.

Fleming, N.D. (1995). I'm different; not dumb. Modes of presentation (VARK) in the tertiary classroom. In A. Zelmer (Ed.), *Research and Development in Higher Education, Proceedings of the 1995 Annual Conference of the Higher Education and Research Development Society of Australasia (HERDSA)*, Volume 18 HERDSA, vol. 18. 308–313.

Fridley, W.L. and Fridley, C.A. (2010). Some problems & peculiarities with the learning styles rhetoric and practice. *Journal of Philosophy & History of Education*, 60, 21–27.

Goldschmied, E. and Jackson, S. (1994). *People Under Three: Young Children in Day Care*. London: Routledge.

Huleatt, H. (2012). Treasure baskets. How do babies learn and play? Available at: www.communityplaythings.co.uk/learning-library/articles. Accessed 28 August 2025.

Piaget, J. (1964). Cognitive development in children: development and learning. *Journal of Research in Science Teaching*, 2, 176–186.

Raven, J., Raven, J.C. and Court, J.H. (2000). *Manual for Raven's Progressive Matrices and Vocabulary Scales. Section 3: The Standard Progressive Matrices*. San Antonio: Harcourt Assessment.

Snowling, M.J. and Hulme, C. (2011). Evidence based interventions for reading and language difficulties; creating a virtuous circle. *British Journal of Educational Psychology*, 81(1), 1-23.
Tzuriel, D. (2000). Dynamic assessment of young children: educational and intervention perspectives. *Educational Psychology Review*, 12(4), 385-435.
Tzuriel, D. (2007). Transfer effects of conceptual and perceptual analogies. *Journal of Cognitive Education and Psychology*, 6(2), 194-217.

6

The Mediator

Introduction

Mediation is the 'beating heart' of cognitive education. It is where an adult (for example, parent, teacher, teaching assistant or therapist) intervenes in purposeful ways to help the learner make links and develop thinking skills which can then be used in different situations. We cannot take progress for granted and so we have to actively intervene to help learners make sense of their experience and so learn from it.

Figure 6.1 shows the element of the tripartite partnership covered in this chapter.

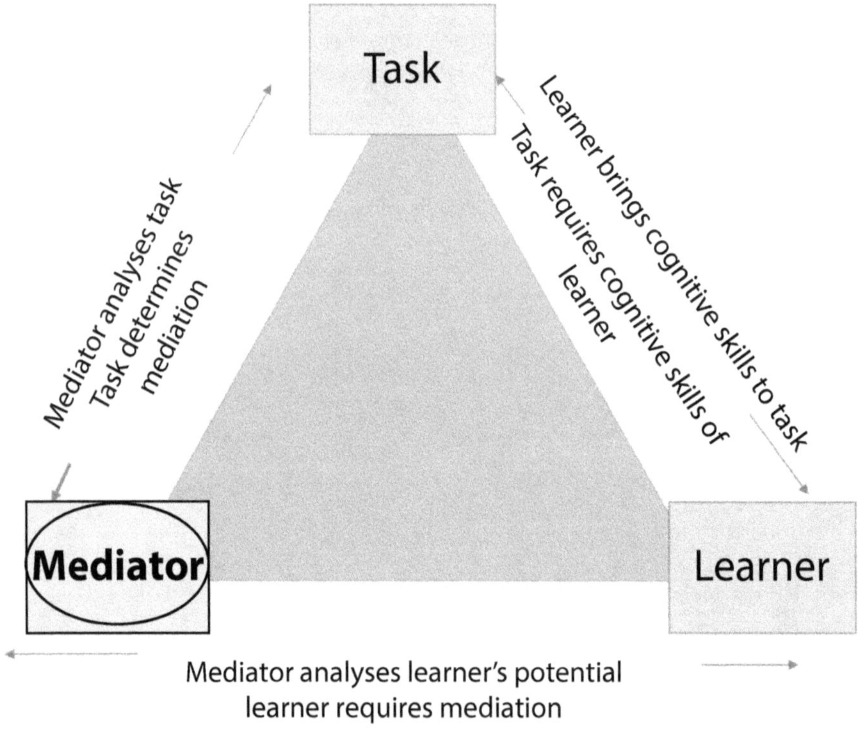

Figure 6.1 A tripartite learning partnership (mediator)

DOI: 10.4324/9781003655329-9

The deliberate interaction between learner and mediator is what brings about cognitive change and ultimately leads to the learner becoming metacognitively aware. As noted at the end of the previous chapter, mediation is the mortar of the House of Metacognition. The cognitive profile of the learner and analysis of tasks are cemented together in a coherent and robust structure so that the roof of metacognitive awareness can sit on top of firm foundations and brickwork.

This chapter presents practical applications of mediation. It is important to note that this chapter covers two of the three essential criteria of mediation as named by Feuerstein (as defined in chapter 3) and which have wide agreement (intentionality and reciprocity and mediation of meaning) in more detail. A separate chapter is devoted to the third essential criterion, transfer. This is because transfer plays a crucial role in ensuring that the cognitive skills that are mediated are generalised and applied in a range of contexts.

Why do we mediate?

Thinking about how children learn and develop helps us to understand the importance of mediation and the reasons why we might do so:

- A child learns about the world by exploring, looking, listening, copying. Therefore, *modelling* what to do and how to do it is very important. However, modelling alone is often not enough;
- A child learns by repeating experiences;
- A child learns by gradually being encouraged to do things for themselves, but with guidance from the adult;
- A child learns by connecting new experiences with previous experiences and learning from the past. This helps them to problem solve *now* and predict and plan in new situations;
- Some children have great difficulty making these connections. They do not learn easily from their experiences. They may have difficulties with language, memory and holding complex ideas in their minds. They will need more support in making connections;
- Such a child may learn how to do something well in one situation but if part of the task changes, they can no longer do it. This means learning was limited to the specific context. The child could not adapt, transfer the skills and generalise the learning to different situations.

The bullet points above emphasise the importance of mediation. Often learning cannot simply be left to chance. As already discussed in Chapter 3, mediation is an intentional act that is designed to bring about cognitive change.

What do we mediate?

As a parent or practitioner, you may choose to mediate in order to teach:

- Language, labels and concepts (vocabulary);
- Logical thinking (making sense, understanding and explaining reasons);
- Behaviours (turn taking, sharing, social rules);
- Understanding of order and sequence;
- Skills for independent learning (comparing, grouping, deciding what is relevant, prioritising, making choices and judgements, being careful and precise when needed);
- Reflection (evaluating your thinking and how you worked out your answer).

Revisiting the criteria of mediation

In this section, each criterion will be revisited in order to offer practical strategies for use. In offering these practical strategies, we have made a deliberate point of including strategies that can also be used with young and non-verbal learners. The rationale for this is that although the criteria of mediation apply across all ages, working with these learners presents some unique challenges that we feel are important to address specifically. We have already made our 'one size does not fit all' message clear in several places in this book. In our experience (one of us was a nursery and reception class teacher before her educational psychology career and we have both worked with learners who have complex and profound learning difficulties), young and non-verbal learners can sometimes be 'at the margins' of the education system.

Table 6.1 lists mediation criteria and gives examples for practice.

Golden rules of mediation

Mediation is a flexible approach; in keeping with the first essential criterion, reciprocity is responsive to the learner and is an interaction-based approach. However, there are some 'non-negotiable' elements that are important in order to be called mediation. In our experience working as external consultants with educational settings, our hearts often sink when we talk through a particular approach and then receive the response 'But I do that anyway.' The heart sinking is due to the fact that when this response is unpicked, despite the best intentions, the individual is actually not 'doing it anyway' and is often doing a trial and error, unplanned version of said approach. Mediation is not immune from this, especially as it can, on the surface, appear to be simply a conversation with the learner. Within Dynamic Assessment (DA) practice, one of us has often noticed exactly this. It is a friendly conversation with the learner, trying to make them 'feel good'. However, the cognitive skills needed for the task are not always included (see mediation myth four in Chapter 3). Mediation is a deliberate structured approach with some specific characteristics, as operationalised in the criteria which we will revisit below. Mediation is child focused but not child led. The two golden rules of mediation sit alongside the criteria and arise from our years of experience mediating learning and supporting others to mediate. They come from the two most common errors made when mediating.

Table 6.1 Mediation criteria and examples of practice

Criterion	***Description***	***Examples in practice***
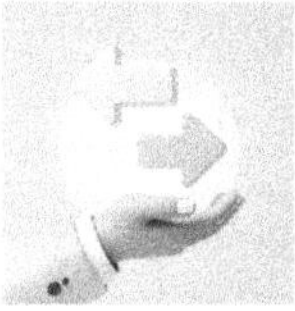 **Intentionality and reciprocity**	Mediation is intentional. The mediator consciously decides to use this specific opportunity to mediate certain cognitive processes. The mediator adjusts their mediation according to the response of the learner and makes sure that they share a joint understanding of the cognitive processes they will work on together. The focus is not on ***what*** we are doing but on the cognitive skills we will be exploring together to achieve our content goal.	Use language such as: 'We're going to ...' 'What have we got here?' 'What shall we do first?' Note the use of ***we***, showing sharing behaviour on our part. Move close to the learner so that they are aware of your presence. Some learners with more severe or complex learning difficulties benefit from use of objects of reference, for example, to indicate that it is activity time. Say the learner's name. Make eye contact. Offer specific toys, tasks or activities. Offer different toys or materials, depending on learner response.
 **Meaning**	Sharing the purpose, communicating the goals or objectives of the problem or task. Why are we doing this? Why is this relevant and important to us? This will lead directly to transfer and generalisation of the skills and strategies we are focusing on here.	Use objects of reference to cue in the learner to the activity. Use an altered tone of voice that communicates enthusiasm. Move materials close to the learner and in and out of their eyeline or grasp; only have materials at their table or workstation that will be used in mediation. Communicate the purpose: 'We're going to ...'; 'This is important because ...'; 'This is about ...'; 'Look!' Use gesture: point to materials or toys.
 **Transfer**	Making links to past, present and future learning/problem-solving. Supporting the learner to apply and generalise their problem-solving skills. Chapter 7 explores this criterion in more detail.	'When else can we ...?' 'Tell me about another time when you ...' 'When is another time we need to ...?' Offer a different activity or toy that uses the same cognitive skill(s).
 **Positive affirmation and empathy**	Connecting with the learner. Accepting what the learner brings to the interaction (being non-judgemental) but also expressing optimism and confidence that cognitive and affective change can happen.	Look at and comment on what the learner shows interest in. Make a statement to show understanding of how the learner is feeling or thinking. Non verbal cues and signals: smiling, nodding. 'Let's look at this together.' Validate the learner, emotionally and in relation to the task. 'I wonder if you're thinking that this is quite tough. You're right, this one is quite tricky, but we'll do it together.'

(Continued)

Table 6.1 (Continued)

Criterion	***Description***	***Examples in practice***
 **Regulation**	Supporting the learner to engage in the task, pay attention, reduce impulsivity or reduce blocking behaviours so that they can focus on task requirements.	'Let's stop and look carefully.' 'How can we find out?' 'Can we make a rule about this kind of problem?' 'Would it help us to have a rule here?' 'Take your time.' Soothe if the learner appears distressed; offer different materials or toys.
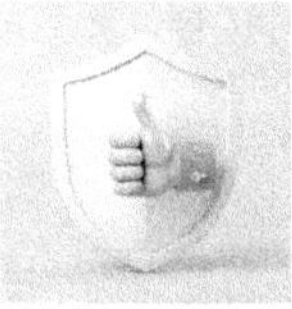 **Competence**	Offering task-related praise and encouragement. It is important to praise the task rather than the person. For example, just saying 'good boy/girl' can imply there are times when the learner is not a good boy/girl. Give feedback that is about what we do to solve a problem. Your personal regard for the learner (see above, positive regard and empathy) comes through in many other ways. Support the learner to overcome blocking.	Altered tone of voice using words of praise. Use symbol cards to express praise and encouragement (but always use language with them). Clapping, together with words 'That was well done!' Thumbs up. High five. Use form of words appropriate to the age/stage of the learner; for example: • 'Wow!' • 'I noticed that you were a bit hesitant at first but then you had a go.' • 'Well done for trying.' • 'I like the way you ...'
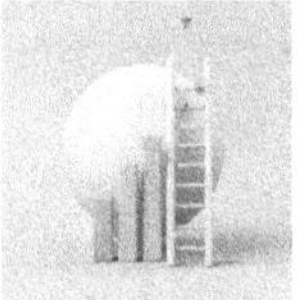 **Challenge**	Supporting the learner to tackle a more difficult aspect of the task or type of problem; stretching the learner. Working in their Zone of Proximal Development.	'Can you think of another way we can do this?' 'Yes, you are right, it could be that way. We could also look at it another way and maybe find another answer.' 'I bet you could ...' Offer toys or materials that are more complex; for example, a jigsaw puzzle or shape sorter with an increased number of pieces/shapes. 'Let's try this one. It's got more pieces, but you know a really good way to do it.'
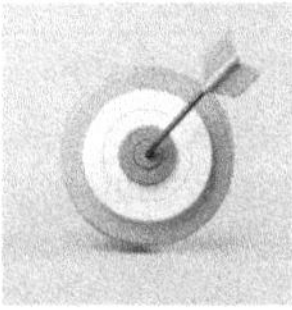 **Goal-setting**	Supporting the learner to plan and work systematically. Keeping focused on the goal (attention to what is relevant). Mediating persistence so that the task or problem is seen through to the end. Mediating checking behaviour.	'Let's make a plan so we don't miss anything.' 'Let's keep going ... that seems to be working well!' Re-present materials or toys; observe carefully so that when the pupil shows signs of discarding the toy or activity, intervene to encourage and move materials back into their eyeline or grasp. Help the child put things in order but don't do it for them! Use visuals to illustrate each step of a task; only present in order (left to right, top to bottom) if the child cannot create steps in a sequence alone. Use a finished basket.

The first golden rule is:

Always mediate cognitive skills, not content knowledge.

It can be very easy to focus on the task itself because this is the most visible part of the interaction: the materials that are in front of you and the learner. The temptation is to help the learner solve the task rather than focusing on the cognitive processes required for the task. In this way, the well-meant intervention is no different from teaching the task. Some mediators find it helpful to have a visual reminder handy which notes the cognitive skills and emotional states that need to be the focus of the interaction.

The second golden rule is:

Do not over assist.

Provide no more assistance than is necessary for successful participation.

What this means in practice is that the first thing you do when mediating is ... nothing, wait! The reason for this is that we want to find out first what the learner can do without support. It is important not to take away a learning opportunity. Then, when we begin to mediate, we can make a more informed judgement about how much and what kind of mediation to start off with. It can feel difficult to hold back at the outset because our instinct is to support the learner. It might be helpful to explain at the introductions stage of your contact with the learner that you will ask them to begin a task on their own, but there will be time to look at the task together ('Have a go first but know that I am here to help you'). Another important aspect of 'hold back and wait' is when the learner makes an error. We can be tempted to jump in and mediate to correct the error. However, if we wait, we give the learner an opportunity to self-correct. Next, we will look at levels of assistance in order to help you navigate this element of mediation.

Levels of assistance

Identifying levels of assistance is a strategy for following the second golden rule of mediation (do not over-assist). It is a way of starting mediation in a deliberately non-specific way, then gradually increasing the specificity. Using the sequence of increasing levels of assistance means that the amount and type of mediation is gradually increased, keeping in mind the essential criterion of reciprocity; that is, the gradual increase is dependent on the learner's response.

Table 6.2 Levels of mediation

Level of assistance	***Description***	***Example***
Low	Previous mediation has been taken on board and the learner can self-regulate independently (so they don't jump in and give an impulsive, ill-thought-out response).	Where have you done something like this before?
	The learner applies previous strategies and rules with increasing flexibility.	What do you need to do to begin to make this model? What will it look like when it is finished? So what do we do first?
	More direct mediation is carried out to show the learner how to choose appropriate strategies.	What would happen if you put this brick here? It might be easier to look for ... [brick] first. What should you look at to help you? (Directing attention to the instructions)
	The mediator asks for further applications of strategies used previously, referring to prior experience	Do you remember when you built ...? How did you do it? How did you make this part of the model? Can you use the same way here?
	The mediator points out general characteristics (but not specifically related to the task).	Can you notice what ... looks like (directing attention to the picture of the completed model)?
	The mediator models the task using specific examples of rules, concepts and strategies.	This part of the model uses bricks like this. Do you need this brick or this brick? (offer a choice of two types).
	The mediator models the task with initial guidance for each step, which is then gradually withdrawn.	Watch me put these together to make this part of the model (mediator demonstrates but then takes apart).
High	The mediator provides hand over hand guidance (where appropriate; depends on the type of task and whether physical contact is acceptable).	Let's pick up this one (pointing to brick). Then we need to ...

The idea of levels of assistance relates to Feuerstein's concept of 'distance' in mediation: 'the extent to which the mediator must directly interpose him or herself as a filter between the task and the subject and the ways and degrees to which this distance can be increased' (Feuerstein et al., 2002: 116).

Table 6.2 summarises levels of assistance, with an example of what this might look like in relation to building a model. As illustrated in the table, we start low, offering the smallest amount of help for the learner to go forward. We can always increase the mediation if we see that the learner needs more intensive help. back to a less intense level of mediation as soon as possible. Take the scaffolding off the building slowly when you see the learner is achieving greater independence in the activity.

Task-based mediation and person-based mediation

Here we want to share two ways of mediating which express the difference, as we see it, between two types or levels of change and what that means in the way we mediate. We have coined the terms task-based mediation (TBM) and person-based mediation (PBM). The more pre-structured the intervention, to solve a specific task, the more it is TBM. The more you focus on the individual's cognitive needs it is more like PBM. Both approaches are explored in more detail below.

Task-based mediation

The overarching principle of mediated learning is intervention to support and develop learners' problem-solving skills in activities in which they are not (yet) able to perform independently or at an adequate level of efficiency. One goal is that the intervention or mediation aims to *improve and change task performance* from pre- to post-test. This is the aim of many DA tests, which describe these changes as measures of the learning potential of the individual. We have called this TBM.

Within that general approach, we are focusing mainly on human mediation, that is person to person. We are not addressing pre-structured or scripted mediation (which can sometimes be computerised). In a pre-scripted approach how to solve the task uses a pre-prepared script and models the strategies needed to solve the post-mediation tasks. Several of the research models referred to in Chapter 2 experimented with this pre-scripted mediation, for example, Budoff (1987). Neat as it feels, this approach does not enable us to consider the non-intellective aspects of learning (what we call the emotional states), such as anxiety, fear of failure or impulsive responding. Our understanding of cognitive functioning and mediation is that mediation is equally responsive to both cognitive and emotional needs. Indeed, we know that there are learners (and certainly not only children!) for whom mediation of emotional and attitudinal aspects of their approach to learning needs to be addressed before they are even able to access their cognitive skills. TBM does not allow for this. It is certainly at one end of what we define as mediation.

TBM is a straightforward approach that will lead to some discernible change. This might be a good approach to start with if you are new to mediated learning. The opposite end is what we refer to as the most clinical, individualised type of mediation, which we call PBM.

Person-based mediation

A different goal aims to use mediation to impact more deeply on the learner's cognitive functioning, beyond changes in specific test performance. This latter approach was the stated goal of Feuerstein's Learning Propensity Assessment Device (Feuerstein et al., 2002) and is a much more ambitious aim. Feuerstein sought to modify what he termed the *Structural* Cognitive Modifiability of the learner; that is, to impact on the thinking of the learner in a more systemic way, and to mediate transfer of strategies and concepts used in the tasks presented to other applications. This intentional transfer and generalisation is carried out by explicitly mediating the principles and strategies of the task to other areas, using a metacognitive style of teaching even within the assessment itself. We call this PBM.

This is a challenging goal. It implies that:

- More time needs to be invested;
- The assessor has to master task analysis and directly relate cognitive skills taught in a specific activity, to a variety of curricular and daily life activities, in order to help the learner to transfer and generalise the concepts;
- This type of intervention puts a strong emphasis on the mediational teaching role, going beyond the typical demands on an examiner or classroom teacher, when using standardised tests or curricular materials. It requires a level of understanding on the part of the teacher in order for them to analyse, mediate and transfer specific cognitive functions from one activity to others; for example, from one area of the curriculum to others. That is, to implement cross-curricular mediation.

The boxes below give examples of both approaches, related to setting a maths problem for a class.

Task-based mediation

1. Teach facts and discuss strategies for solving the task.
2. Work on the problem.
3. Teach metacognitively. Evaluate the strategies chosen. Which strategy worked best?
4. Move on to a similar task.
5. Review strategies for the next task.

Person-based mediation

1. Teach facts and discuss strategies for solving the task.
2. Do a cognitive analysis of the task with the learner(s): Let's analyse. What are the cognitive skills needed for this type of task?

Start with content: What knowledge do we need for this type of task? For example, knowledge of number bonds, understanding the mathematical symbols. Elicit and name the cognitive skills required for this kind of task. For example:

Understanding the question: Tell me in your own words, what is it we have to do here?
Careful **comparison;**
Is **sequencing** important here? Are there several steps required?
Precision and accuracy? Or estimation only?
Taking **several sources of information** into account;
Is all the information in the question r**elevant?**
Flexibility. Is there more than one method I can use here?
Memory. What can I retrieve from my memory that may help solve the task now?
Hypothesis testing: Does my answer make sense?
Checking behaviours: Refer back to the goal of the task. Have I answered the question fully? Have I covered all the problem-solving steps?

3. Metacognitive feedback; evaluate the strategies chosen. Which strategy worked best?
4. Take these cognitive skills and *write them down* (for example, on a wall chart, in a notebook, on a whiteboard or in the maths exercise book). Now ask learners to generate other examples: Where else do we need to use these skills? Moving away from these specific maths questions, and applying to other subjects and situations, to deliberately generalise the cognitive skills much more widely.
5. After doing this a few times, the teacher can give the pupils the list of **Intelligent Action** (see Resource 6.1).
6. Teacher deliberately chooses a different area of the curriculum. For example, a text comprehension. Learners go through the task and discuss, (ask them to work in pairs or threes). 'What on our list of Intelligent Action does this task need?' 'How is this the same/different from the way we analysed the cognitive skills of a different type of task (for example, the previous maths question)?' Learners discuss and feed back their analysis in class and justify why they chose these particular cognitive skills.
7. Go a step further. 'Let's apply this cognitive analysis to non-school activities.' Examples might be friendships, family, leisure activities, or, for older learners, work experience.

Task-based mediation or person-based mediation?

It is much easier to measure change scores within a task. In the short term, one can quantify such changes. We need to think about the criteria we use to measure more pervasive changes to a person's problem-solving skills. These are conceptual as well as practical challenges, How do we measure generalisation of cognitive skills beyond the specific task or test situation and assess whether the gains made initially are sustained? We need to consider how to achieve levels of reliability and validity when aiming for *structural* cognitive changes. Whilst being aware of these challenges, our main point here is for the mediator (ourselves) to be clear about our mediational aims. We need to consider whether we are aiming for a change in task performance or more ambitious systemic change in the structure of a learner's cognitive skills. There is no 'right' or 'wrong' implied in this choice; it is simply a matter of matching mediation to your overall goals for the learner(s) and of course these aims can change over time. Here is an example taken from one of the present authors' casework.

> Oscar, aged ten, struggled to make and maintain friendships. His social skills were not well developed, leading to some inappropriate social behaviour choices and consequent isolation from peers, who were reluctant to play with him. Social skills work did not seem to have any impact. Following assessment, two weak key aspects of his cognition were identified as contributory factors: cause and effect thinking and restraining impulsivity. Support for Oscar to improve these areas was delivered via use of mediated learning. In the sessions he was able to demonstrate improvements in these areas; however, there was no change in his social behaviour. When this was unpicked, it became apparent that the mediation was purely task-focused (TBM), which meant that little systemic change had been brought about. All of the transfer activities were task-related. When a change was suggested to PBM, Oscar was supported to make links to his social behaviour in different contexts and thus began to show some improved social skills.

This example illustrates that one of the key differences between TBM and PBM is related to transfer. In TBM, the transfer and application of cognitive skills is related closely to the task itself. In the maths example above, learners would be given a similar maths task and encouraged to use the same cognitive skills for the new (related) task. In PBM, the transfer would be much broader, linking cognitive skills to contexts that are not specifically mathematical. This contrast reflects what is called near and far transfer, which will be examined in detail in Chapter 7.

Mediation strategies

Alongside the criteria for mediation, there are strategies that are generally useful for delivering mediation. The list below is taken from the Bright Start programme (Haywood et al., 2022), whose target group is learners aged approximately three to seven years. However, these points are relevant for learners of any age.

- Focus on processes rather than on responses;
- Ask questions;
- Ask process questions, that is, elicit process answers;
- Require justification, especially for correct answers;
- Communicate enthusiasm for learning;
- Use task-intrinsic incentives;
- Bridge principles to many familiar content domains;
- Relate new to past experience;
- Elicit rules;
- Elicit induction of rules;
- Elicit deduction of rules;
- Emphasise the need for order, structure and predictability;
- Create awareness and concern around imprecision, inaccuracy, and lack of logical evidence;
- Establish logical habit structures
- Accept as much as possible of children's responses, but correct inaccurate or incomplete responses.

(Haywood et al., 2022: 55)

Haywood et al. go on to suggest five 'mechanisms of mediated teaching' (2022: 59–60). These are summarised and described in Table 6.3.

Table 6.3 Haywood et al.'s (2022) five mechanisms of mediated teaching

Mechanism	***Description***
Process questions	Open-ended 'how' questions.
Bridging (we call this transfer)	Encouraging generalising and applying cognitive skills.
Challenging, or requiring justification	Asking the learner to describe how they arrived at the answer or solution: 'that's right, how did you know/work it out?' (In contrast to what can typically happen in a classroom, where a learner is only asked to describe how they solved a problem when the solution was incorrect).
Teaching about rules	This relates to transfer. If we can make a rule about something we can apply it to other problems and tasks.
Emphasising order, predictability, system, sequence and strategies.	Haywood et al. use the term 'impose logical order' (2022: 60). This mechanism relates to planning and sequence.

The above principles and strategies can be applied to any kind of task or problem. However, the reciprocal nature of mediation means that it is not always possible to make detailed advance plans or scripts. This can be very challenging! This does not mean that you have to go into an interaction with no forethought or planning. It is important to have ideas and plan a structure about what you might do or say based on your knowledge of the learner, the task you have selected, and the cognitive skills and/or emotional states that you intend to mediate.

Planning of mediation takes us back to Chapter 5, where we made a distinction between what parts of a task are adjusted and what parts are mediated. To reiterate:

- Content (including considering novelty), level of abstraction and complexity, precision and accuracy and efficiency are *adjusted*;
- Cognitive skills are *mediated.*

These strategies often need a particular way of interacting with a learner. The main emphasis is on being open so that the learner is in the 'driving seat' of learning but the learner is not alone. You, the driving instructor, are with them and guiding them.

Resources 6.2, 6.3 and 6.4 in the Resource Centre are provided to assist in planning and delivering mediation. They contain suggestions for the kind of language you might use when mediating. Resource 6.5 provides a mediation planner. Resource 6.6 is a guide to mediation with young and/or non-verbal learners.

Implementing strategies

Table 6.4 sets out some dos and don'ts for mediation that will help to support your use of mediated learning and is useful for families and caregivers at home.

Table 6.4 Mediation do and don'ts

Mediation dos	***Mediation don'ts***
Ask, don't tell: 'Where will we find ...?' 'What do we need to do next?' 'Have we finished, or is there something else we need to do? Let's check together' Yes, that's right, how do you know that's right?' 'Can you remember when we did this before?' **Explain *why*** something is going to be done or why it is important. Help the learner to find meaning in the event. For example: 'We need to write this down so we don't forget.' 'We need to plan so we don't miss anything out.' 'We need to plan our time so we can finish everything we have to do.' 'We need to think ahead and plan our writing so it fits on the line.'	Don't guess what the learner is trying to say or answer for them.

(*Continued*)

Table 6.4 (Continued)

Mediation dos	***Mediation don'ts***
Use correct language and explain your words in different ways to aid comprehension. Check that the learner understands by asking them to repeat the idea back in their own words. Use higher order, concept words to raise the level of the child's thinking - but explain. For example: 'Can you give me one the same colour/size/shape?' 'Which is larger/ largest?' 'Which has more/most?' 'Tables, chairs, beds are all kinds of ...?'	Don't rush the learner. Give them time to think.
Connect the event or activity to other times and other places (transfer). For example: 'The colour is red. Where else is it important to think about colour?' (for example, red sometimes means 'stop' or 'danger').	Don't just show the learner and expect them to copy. Developing the learner's learning is like building our House of Metacognition; first put up the 'scaffolding' to support the structure, then remove this support one piece at a time until the structure can stand on its own.
	Don't be afraid to set clear and consistent rules.

Mediation applications to language, literacy and numeracy

Language, literacy and numeracy are key foundations in learning. Language is included in our list of cognitive skills since the ability to use language for learning is a crucial foundation for the development of reasoning and problem-solving skills. Literacy and numeracy are more task-specific. In this section we will give some examples of how mediation of key cognitive skills needed for language, literacy and numeracy tasks can be mediated.

Mediating language

Language is part of the Boat of Cognition model. In Luria's view, language is a critical skill and isthe bridge that links foundational cognitive processes of attention, perception and memory to higher order thinking skills of reasoning and strategic thinking, executive function and metacognition.

The inclusion of language in our cognitive skills model emphasises how important it is as a processing skill and is a key component in Luria's framework and builds on Vygotsky's seminal work on language and thinking. The centrality of language is both as a cognitive process and as a vital element in bridging from basic cognitive processes such as attention, perception and memory to higher order thinking processes (Hasson and Joffe, 2007).

When learners struggle to solve problems or access the curriculum more generally, it is important to try to unpick the relative roles of language and cognitive skills. It may not be either or, since the two are interdependent. The identification of language issues and their relationship to learner difficulties is not an easy one for teachers to address. Research shows that more than 50 per cent of children referred by teachers for behavioural problems have a language disorder or delay (see, for example, Stringer and Lozano, 2007; Ramsay et al., 2018).

The next section explores two approaches to mediating language.

Mediating the language needed for a task

Mediating the language needed for a task is required for many reasons. One particular issue is when we are working with pupils for whom English is not their first language. Here is an example from one of the present authors' casework.

Bilal, aged 10, was referred for educational psychology input due to concerns about his overall progress. School felt that he had some cognitive challenges and asked for these to be investigated. Bilal's family had newly arrived in the UK. They were of North Indian heritage and spoke Urdu at home. The family had relocated to the UK from Germany where they had lived for some years, so Bilal's schooling had been in German. Therefore, English was his *third* language. The school had initially requested an IQ test (this was their experience and thus their expectation of educational psychology input). After discussions with the SENCo where the difficulties of using this type of test with a pupil with a very different cultural and linguistic background, it was agreed that DA would be used. One of the tests used was a Matrices test. Using the test-teach-test format of DA, Bilal was first asked to solve problems unassisted. In this phase, he struggled to solve the problems. Due to his language background, the focus of mediation was on using language for problem-solving. Initially he was asked to label elements of the problem (for example, shape labels such as square and triangle, and labels such as diagonal, horizontal, vertical, larger and smaller). He was unable to use these labels to name elements of the problem. The teach phase therefore consisted of teaching these labels. Then in the second test phase he was able to solve all the problems correctly. From this (and other data gathered in the assessment) the main recommendation was for some intensive English as an Additional Language support.

A further example of mediating language is illustrated in the following example, drawn from one of the present authors' delivery of a continuing professional development training course in DA to an educational psychology team. As part of the training, it was agreed that a child would be invited (obviously with full agreement of the child and his parents) and that the trainer would demonstrate DA procedures with him.

The background information from the school was:

'We would like to refer him to you for this demonstration, because he has very difficult behaviours, thought to be highly linked to a dysfunctional home.'

Despite some reservations about the reason for referral, the session went ahead with Wayne, aged ten. He was quiet, looked very hesitant but was very cooperative through more than one-and-a-half hours of assessment. It took less than ten minutes to find out that he had significant language issues both at the receptive and expressive levels. Put bluntly, these had been completely missed. The 'services' were so focused on his behaviours and the home situation that they decided that was the full explanation for his challenging behaviours. No one, it seemed, had considered other aspects of his functioning and learning.

We analysed the DA session together as a group. Of course, there was no way we should dismiss or discount the home situation, nor could we say to what extent this explained his behaviour challenges. However, it was clear that Wayne's language issues played a significant role in his acting out and dysregulated behaviour. He had no tools for verbal communication. He could not express his ideas or his feelings. He had no verbal negotiating skills to put forward his point of view or his wishes or negotiate with peers. He had one form of communication only: challenging behaviour.

The DA showed cognitive difficulties that could be addressed, especially when the language load of tasks was adjusted and mediated. The session was calm and unhurried, giving Wayne time to think. He was able to focus on what we were doing and was not distracted by the group of educational psychologists who were observing the session. Wayne came across as a very sensitive child, open to mediation who could show progress when we learned together. A key element of future support was on his expressive and receptive language, giving him tools to flourish academically and socially.

Two examples of mediation related to language are:

- Mediated Self Talk (MST; Feuerstein et al., 2013) is an example of mediating language needed for tasks and problem-solving. It is a way of supporting language that uses Feuerstein's mediated learning approach (Feuerstein et al., 2013). Basically, MST involves the adult in verbalising actions or feelings so that the learner is exposed to a range of aspects and elements of language. MST emphasises the three essential criteria of mediation. The way in which these are operationalised in relation to language are as follows:

Intentionality: the communication is intentional. The mediator might choose a naturally occurring or a specifically planned context but in both cases intent to mediate is paramount;

Meaning: an emphasis on the need to communicate: 'Mediation creates a need-implicitly at first-to participate in the communication, to feel a need for engagement at the receptive level' (Feuerstein et al., 2013: 20);

Transfer: interactions deal with past, present and future, encouraging generalisation of language.

- The Verbal Planning subtest from Carol Lidz's Application of Cognitive Functions Scale (Haywood and Lidz, 2007) shows how mediation can be used for a specific aspect of language. In this test, language is used in relation to order and sequence. The learner is asked to describe how to complete a task that involves a sequence of steps. The suggested task is making a sandwich; however, the test instructions note that a similar task can be substituted, based on the learner's familiarity. The task is mediated using a picture sequencing activity.

Mediating literacy

This section contains two examples: one for emergent readers that relates mainly to pre-school and early years contexts and one for reading comprehension, which is applicable across a wider age range for more fluent readers.

Mediated book sharing with an emergent reader

This activity can be carried out with an individual child or with a small group. The book sharing sequence is from research carried out by Yeomans (1998; 2003).

Materials: A selection of books (use knowledge of the child to determine what is offered, make sure that the books will engage the child). Books offered do not need to be texts that can be read independently. Be aware that some structured reading scheme books (particularly where the text is designed for the child to use decoding skills) have little or no narrative structure, so work on sequence related to the story might be more challenging. Offer books that are quite short because the activity involves reading the book through first of all and then re-reading with some comments and questions.

Note in this example the focus in this example is on letter sound recognition, which is just one element of the reading process.

Cognitive skills: Attention, self-regulation, comparison, persistence, systematic gathering of information.

Prerequisites/preparation: The child should know what 'compare' means and what putting things in order (sequence) means. Their knowledge/understanding will depend on previous input (you might have done comparing and sequencing in other contexts). Establish that comparing means looking at things and saying what is the same or different and that sequencing is about putting things in order.

Procedure:

- Sit down with the child(ren) and offer books for them to choose from. Introduce the cognitive element of the task. Mediate attention and self-regulation first of all: 'How shall we get ready to read our book together? Show me how to be ready for our book sharing.'
- Read the story;
- Go back to the beginning of the book and introduce the cognitive element of the task. Say: 'we're going to look at the book again. This time I want you to help me do some comparing.' [Check understanding of comparing. Give examples if needed. Comparing means looking at what's the same and what's different];
- Now use the story book to mediate comparing. For example:

> Comparing letters or words to identify same and different. 'Is this letter the same as or different from this one?' In a book with repeated words identify same and different words;
>
> Ask the child to find a letter or word the same as one that you point to ('Can you compare and find one that's the same');
>
> A higher level of assistance for the above might be: cover up some of the text to reduce the amount of text that has to be examined; give the target letter or word on a separate card; model running your finger under the text and say yes if the letters is the same and no if it is not the same; give just one word to find the same letter;
>
> Do a related activity (transfer) but this time focus on letter sounds. Say a letter sound and ask children to find a word containing that sound. Here you can also mediate systematic information gathering: 'How can we find the letter?' (by looking carefully at each word on the page and then at each letter in the word to compare with the sound). A higher level of assistance might be: ask children to look at just one line of text or one word; write down the letter; model looking at each letter in a word to compare whether it is the same as or different from the sound.

Table 6.5 shows links to the criteria of mediation.

Comprehension can also be mediated in a book-sharing activity via use of 'why?' questions; for example, in the story of Red Riding Hood: 'why are Grandma's ears bigger than usual?', or 'I wonder ...' questions ('I wonder how Goldilocks felt when she saw Daddy bear?').

Mediating reading comprehension with more fluent readers

This aspect of reading was chosen because it involves a range of cognitive skills and, in the authors' experience, these skills are often assumed so are not addressed directly in reading comprehension activities (what we find is that learners are simply given reading comprehension exercises with little guidance as to *how* the exercises can be completed (let al.one the different cognitive skills involved).

Table 6.5 Mediation criteria applied to book sharing

Mediation criterion	***How criteria are addressed in book sharing***
 **Intentionality and reciprocity**	***Intentionality***: a planned activity not a chance event. Identify a specific time and place. Introduce the cognitive element: 'When we look at our book, we're going to do some comparing'. ***Reciprocity***: mediation used with the child's, not the adult's, choice of book.
 **Meaning**	Convey enthusiasm about the books and that the time together is important. 'There are lots of exciting books here.' 'It's lovely to sit down and read together.'
 **Transfer**	When's another time we compare to find out what's the same and what's different? Examples: Tidy up time, when we compare the toy to the picture on the box so we know where to put it away. Sand or water play: which container has more sand/water?
 **Regulation**	Sitting still whilst story is being read. Listening without interrupting. Waiting to hear the question. Taking time to look for the answer.
 **Challenge**	Read another story: 'I wonder if you can pay attention to another story?' Find more letters or sounds: 'Let's find another one.'
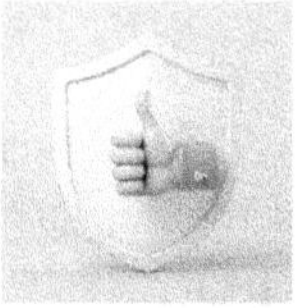 **Feelings of competence**	Give specific praise for the cognitive skills: 'You did some really good comparing to find the letter/word.'

Table 6.6 Mediation of reading comprehension

Question	***Cognitive skill***	***Examples of mediation (in ascending level of assistance)***
Based on what you have read, what do you think will happen next? How did you know?	Systematic gathering of information. Working memory. Inference. Logical justification.	How can we answer this question? Where can we find some clues? How will you remember which parts of the text to use? Try to look for clues (further assistance might be to direct attention to the title, illustrations, chapter headings, relevant part of the text). Let's say what happened so far and then we can think about what might happen next. Can you find a word or words that will help you to answer the question? What can you do to help you remember where this word is? What could you use the highlighter pen for? Give two choices of answer, choose one and say why this is better choice. Model the process.
What was this passage mostly about?	Sequencing. Precision and accuracy. Short-term recall. Summarising.	How can we find out the main idea? What can we do to help us remember? Where can we look to find out? (Further assistance might be to direct attention to the title, illustrations, chapter headings, relevant part of the text.) What happens first? And then what? What happens at the end? Model first, second, third ...
Why do you think that ...? **Can you explain why ...?**	Inference. Justification.	Identify words in text that will help to answer the question. Offer a choice of solutions/responses. Which one makes sense? Model a response. Model why ... because ...
Where/when else have you come across something like this before?	Comparison.	Mediating transfer, making links.
Can you find a word in the story that means the same as ...	Comparison. Receptive language. Relevance. Justification. Categorisation.	Elicit word meaning. Model words that are the same. Use the idea of groups, words that belong together.

Numeracy

The acquisition and development of numeracy is closely linked to and underpinned by several cognitive skills and different modalities.

Stanley-Duke et al. (2022) make a helpful distinction between rote learning (such as memorising multiplication tables or procedures) and a discovery approach, which emphasises that 'number concepts and procedures form a growing network of meaningful knowledge' (2022: 6). This latter approach lends itself more to mediation, because the learner can be supported to develop and use underlying cognitive skills that will help them to engage in the approach. Therefore, mediated learning has an important part to play in the development of mathematical understanding (in contrast to mere reliance on rote learning of facts or procedures).

The example in this section draws extensively on Hwang (2016). Hwang contrasts a non-MLE (Mediated Learning Experience) and MLE maths lesson, noting that the MLE lesson focuses on processes, monitoring learning and providing feedback (contrasting with the non-MLE lesson which focuses only on teaching concepts and then doing activities). The following box shows Hwang's example of a maths word problem with associated questions that can be used for mediation.

Megan and Ali had an equal number of stamps. After Megan gave 10 stamps away and Ali gave 20 stamps, Megan had twice as many stamps as Ali. How many stamps did they each have at first?

- What are the key words/clues/cues that we should know to understand the question?
- Tell me what you understood about the problem? Let's do it step by step.
- What do you understand by the words 'Megan had twice as many stamps as Ali'?
- How should we draw the model? Do we start with what Megan and Ali had at first? Why/Why not?
- What are the clues we need to consider at the same time when we are drawing a model for 'Megan had twice as many stamps as Ali'?
- How is Megan giving away 10 stamps and Ali giving 20 stamps connected or linked to Megan having twice as many stamps as Ali?

(Hwang, 2016: 51–52)

Summary

This chapter has given some practical applications of mediation criteria. The material here, along with the resources that are available as free downloads via the Resource Centre, should support you to begin to deliver mediation with a learner. The process can feel rather daunting if it is unfamiliar, but we would encourage you to have a go. The interactive nature of mediation and the fact that this process is not related to issues such as achievement, grades or generation of standardised data means that if things do not go exactly as you intended, the outcomes are unlikely to have major implications for the learner, especially if you make sure you end the session on a positive note; for example, mediating competence and giving positive affirmation.

Reflection and follow-up

- This is the third part of the Tripartite Learning Partnership. Consider: Would the cognitive framework, set out so far, that is cognitive skills (Chapter 4) and task analysis (Chapter 5) have been enough without this chapter on mediation?
- Reflect on situations where you have used mediation intuitively with pupils. What difference do you think it could make to your practice to become consciously aware of what and how you are mediating?
- How do you share or discuss teaching objectives with your learners? How can you use the essential criteria of intentionality and meaning to inform sharing and discussion of cognitive goals in a meaningful way?
- Download Resource 6.5 and plan some mediation with a specific learner. You could use the cognitive profile and task analysis if you completed these at the end of Chapters 4 and 5.

References

Budoff, M. (1987). Measures for assessing learning potential. In C.S. Lidz (Ed.), *Dynamic Assessment: An Interactional Approach to Evaluating Learning Potential.* New York: Guilford.

Feuerstein, R., Feuerstein, R., Falik, L. and Rand, Y. (2002). *The Dynamic Assessment of Cognitive Modifiability.* Jerusalem: The ICELP Press.

Feuerstein, R., Falik, L., Feuerstein, R. and Bohacs, K. (2013). *A Think-Aloud and Talk-Aloud Approach to Building Language.* New York: Teachers College Press.

Hasson, N. and Joffe, V. (2007). The case for dynamic assessment in speech and language therapy. *Child Language Teaching and Therapy,* 23(1), 9–21.

Haywood, H.C. and Lidz, C.S. (2007). *Dynamic Assessment in Practice: Clinical and Educational Applications.* New York: Cambridge University Press.

Haywood, H.C., Brooks, P. and Burns, M.S. (2022). Bright Start Cognitive Curriculum for Young Children, rev. edn. Bright Start CCYC. Available at: www.brightstart-ccyc.com.

Hwang, W. (2016). Applying MLE in maths. In B.L. Chua and Y.F.I. Wong (Eds), *Mediated Learning Experience: Applications in Various Contexts.* Singapore: Mediated Learning Laboratory, Psychological Studies Academic Group, National Institute of Education

Ramsay, J., Cowell, N. and Gersch, I. (2018). How school staff understand the relationship between problem behaviours and language difficulties. *Educational Psychology in Practice,* 34(1), 1-25.

Stanley-Duke, M., Wright, D., Cook, E., Reid, A., Cook, O., Reece, S., Bull-Beddows, R., Simms, L. and Graves, F. (2022). The psychological foundations of the Mediating Learning Support Assistant (MeLSA) training programme. *Educational Psychology Research and Practice,* 8(1), 1-12.

Stringer, H. and Lozano, S. (2007). Under identification of speech and language impairment in children attending a special school for children with emotional and behavioural disorders. *Educational and Child Psychology,* 24(4), 9–19.

Yeomans, J. (1998). *The Use of Antecedent Manipulation and Incidental Teaching to Promote the Early Reading Development of Nursery Aged Children,* unpublished PhD thesis, University of Birmingham.

Yeomans, J. (2003). The role of early reading behaviours in the prevention of and intervention in reading difficulties. *Support for Learning,* 14(1), 32–36.

7

Teaching for Transfer

Introduction

At the end of Chapter 6 we emphasised the importance of transfer. There is much agreement that mediation can be a powerful agent of learning and change, although there is no consensus as to which of the mediational criteria is the proximal (most closely related) factor enabling change. It may be that in different contexts one or the other criteria seems to be the most effective. However, there is wide agreement that certain criteria define an interaction as mediation or other. To recap, the three core criteria described by Feuerstein are intentionality, meaning and transcendence or transfer (Lidz, 2003), the first two of which were discussed in Chapter 6. The concept of person-based mediation, discussed in Chapter 6, involves deliberate transfer.

The mediator, as we saw in Figure 6.1, Chapter 6, takes on primary responsibility for the transfer aspect of mediation.

In this chapter, we focus on and analyse the meaning of transfer considered by some researchers to be the most critical part of mediation (see, for example, Lidz, 1991). Transfer means to be able to take an idea, concept or strategy learned in one context and apply it, adapt it and reuse it elsewhere. This leads to a number of questions:

- Why is this process considered so important?
- How does it happen?
- What are the skills needed for a learner to be able to transfer concepts and strategies from one situation to another?
- How can we teach for transfer?

This chapter will provide some answers to these questions. We will first define our terms, remembering the mantra 'description before analysis', and will then go on to give some examples that emphasise the importance of transfer, making links to learning theory. The remainder of the chapter explores the nature of change and principles of transfer, followed by a suggested four-step teaching for enabling transfer and ending with some practical examples.

DOI: 10.4324/9781003655329-10

The importance of transfer

The importance of transfer cannot be over-emphasised. Essentially, transfer relates to generalisation of learning. We are not referring to recall and application of facts and information. Of course this is important, but specifically here, we are addressing the need to actively transfer the following to a wide variety of contexts:

- Cognitive skills;
- Executive function;
- Metacognition.

The transfer element of learning is important because it helps to make sure that whatever has been taught (or mediated) becomes part of the learner's repertoire of cognitive skills and can be used in numerous situations. Using the House of Metacognition example, bricks in the previous mediated learning chapter are the general-purpose ones that are used for the overall structure of the house. The bricks used for the transfer element of mediation are what are called 'engineering bricks' in the building trade, because they are used where strength and durability of the structure is important. Using this analogy for the transfer element of mediation, lack of strength, clarity and durability in cognitive skills means that they are likely to be fragile or very limited. They may 'last' but will be context-bound, only being used if the very same context in which they were taught is repeated. Transfer is the tool enabling application to novel situations, not limited to a repeat of what has already been learned. Transfer is what helps to ensure that mediation is applied beyond the here and now interaction. The following example, from one of the present authors' teaching background, illustrates the importance of transfer of cognitive skills.

Mark was a pupil attending a special school for pupils with moderate learning difficulties where one of the present authors taught for a few years. Mark was in a colleague's Year 3 (age 8- to 9-year-olds) class. He suffered with catarrh and frequently had mucus discharge from his nose, exacerbated by the fact that he did not know how to blow his nose. At the time, task analysis was a big initiative in Special Education, and the school had invested a great deal of time in analysing the curriculum into small steps. Mark's class teacher decided that she would teach him to blow his nose. She produced a detailed task analysis of nose blowing then proceeded to give Mark short individual nose-blowing sessions every day. The task analysis included teaching Mark to recognise when he needed to blow his nose to prevent his teacher from giving constant reminders. Finally, he achieved the last step, which meant that he could blow his nose independently. His teacher was therefore very puzzled and upset when Mark failed to blow his nose independently when sitting at his desk and she had to continue to remind him to do so. On further investigation, she realised that every daily teaching session had taken place with Mark standing next to her desk. He only blew his nose when standing next to her desk as this was the only context where the skill had been learned. Therefore, further teaching steps were added that addressed generalising the skill and eventually Mark was able to recognise when he needed to blow his nose and then blow it in other locations and contexts such as other parts of the classroom or school and at home.

This may seem like an extreme example involving a learner who had some very significant challenges in all areas of his development. However, it does illustrate the importance of deliberate transfer, which is examined in the next section.

The importance of transfer of cognitive skills

Turning specifically to transfer of cognitive skills, the learner needs to recognise, or be helped to recognise, how the cognitive skill is meaningful and relevant to another context. Relevance can be a challenge where the link between the task and its cognitive skills is not obvious. Relevance is a key aspect of transfer, because a skill cannot be meaningfully transferred unless the connection between the initial context and the novel situation is recognised. This is an area of significant challenge for many learners. An example from one of the present authors' casework illustrates this issue.

Organisation of Dots is an activity used in Dynamic Assessment (DA) and in Instrumental Enrichment (IE), Feuerstein's cognitive skills teaching programme. It involves joining up what looks like a random scattering of dots to form shapes according to a model given. One of the present authors used the IE version with Lisa, aged 15. Lisa was at risk of exclusion from school and of termination of her work experience placement due to persistent rule breaking. After assessing Lisa with DA, one hypothesis was that weak logical reasoning skills and impulsivity were contributory factors in her behaviour. IE was used to address these concerns. Organisation of Dots was chosen because use of rules is an important strategy for problem-solving and because a great deal of restraint of impulsivity is needed. In addition, hypothetical thinking helps to work out what would happen: 'If I join this dot to that dot, could it form one side of a square?'

On the surface, joining dots does not appear to have any relationship to the presenting concerns. However, the transfer criterion makes the relationship clearer. Mediation focused on helping Lisa to use problem-solving rules and to work carefully and systematically, taking time to make sure she knew what the task requirements were, rather than taking a very quick glance before launching into the task and making errors. The transfer element involved discussions about when and where else rules might be important, and when else it might be helpful to stop and think about consequences (for example, what might happen if she didn't follow rules in her work placement).

Mediated learning brought about improvements in use of rules, restraining impulsivity and hypothetical thinking, and the transfer criterion meant that she applied these in school and in her work placement. The risks to her school place and work experience reduced considerably.

The key point from this example is that the crossover, or transfer, from the cognitive improvements using a mediated learning interaction to 'real life' contexts achieved transfer and application to other important areas of Lisa's life.

The nature of change

Change is an important part of transfer. Indeed, belief in the possibility of change is one of the fundamental concepts underpinning this book's elaboration of methods and strategies to transform belief into action. This section examines the nature of change to help understand the process of transfer.

We have described the essential criteria of what makes an interaction a mediated experience. There are different aspects of the mediational relationship which we choose to use and emphasise in different contexts, in accordance with the learner's needs. This is what makes mediation a flexible customised tool. However, being highly responsive to the individual's needs has led to criticisms of mediation as vague, non-specific and subjective, as we have referred to in the discussion of mediation myths in Chapter 3. It is this customised goal that is both challenging and creative and highlights the difference between process-orientated mediation and the direct teaching of facts in the curriculum. This is not an either-or choice. Of course, curriculum is essential. You cannot mediate without content in which to mediate, but as we see again and again in our learners, direct teaching is not enough. It is not about regurgitating facts from rote memory; it is about developing their cognitive skills within and beyond specific learning materials.

We need to understand why being able to transfer skills from one setting to another is so important. When we learn something new, we obviously want to remember it and reproduce it when needed. However, that kind of learning in itself is static. It places things on a shelf in our memory cupboard, and we may be able to retrieve it only if the question requires us to recall the information exactly as we learned it. When we were tested on what we learned as small children, we were mostly being tested on straight memory. As we grew older there was a gradual shift from reproducing from memory to the application of ideas, when the question is asking for more than direct recall. There is an expectation that transfer skills will just improve with age and indeed there is a developmental aspect. What happens in school subjects is that we see learners who seemed to be doing 'okay' in their primary or elementary school years, but later on are not able to transfer aspects of knowledge and strategies to a new application. A comment that one of us has not infrequently heard from secondary school pupils who work hard to revise for a test or exam is: 'It's not the same, this isn't the question and answer I revised and practised. I can't do this. We didn't learn this.'

Change and the need for flexibility might then lead to questioning whether this simply happens automatically; don't we adapt and change according to need, anyway, as we get older? However, few people can do so completely by themselves; transfer and adaptation are not givens. Therefore, if we want our learners to be able to think more laterally and to apply ideas from one area to another, we need to deliberately *teach for transfer*. This applies to most of us. If we show capacity to think and apply ideas, it is not automatic across different domains. Research (for example, Ceci, 1990; Kaniel, 2001; Barnett and Ceci, 2002) shows us that experts in one area do not necessarily apply their skills to other areas with anything like the level of sophistication they show in their expert area of activity. We are much more domain-specific creatures than we often imagine ourselves to be. If this is true of typical development, it is even more true for learners who struggle with learning. As with all mediation, we all need it, but some need it more. It is important to understand what it takes to become a thinker who can transfer cognitive skills from one domain to another. We should consider the constituent cognitive components and metacognitive skills. This is essential if we want to teach for transfer.

Principles of transfer

There are some key principles about transfer which should drive this process. Haywood has written extensively on this topic (see, for example, Haywood, 1988; 1993; Haywood and Lidz, 2007; Haywood and Tzuriel, 2002) and the principles that follow are based on his work (Haywood et al., 2022).

Transfer relates to cognitive skills

This reflects and reinforces the first golden rule of mediation. Haywood et al. (2022: 72) comment: 'the bridging of content is tempting because it is easy'. Therefore, the questions that the mediator asks should be about the cognitive skills that are the focus of the mediated learning interaction. For example, looking back at the Organisation of Dots activity described in the case example above, transfer of content would be about other activities involving joining dots, whilst transfer of cognitive skills would be about the use of rules, changing strategies when a strategy that worked up to now no longer serves our goal; the need for precision and accuracy and restraining impulsivity.

Always elicit transfer examples

Haywood et al. (2022) point out that if we simply provide examples, it means that the learner is passive. Feuerstein et al. (2006) make the point that an important subgoal of mediation is to help the learner become an active generator of thinking in place of a passive recipient of information. It is important for the learner to make the connections. Some learners might find this challenging. In 'typical' development, such insight does not tend to emerge until middle childhood (see, for example, Flavell et al., 2001). Expressive and receptive language delay might also affect the learner's insight. One of the present authors, when working with children showing developmental and/or language delay, frequently receives the response: 'I thinked it in my brain' when eliciting transfer examples. In these cases, the levels of assistance of mediation (discussed in detail in Chapter 6) can be used, where the mediator might either expand what the learner says, or suggest an example. Remember the difference between Piaget's view, which is to wait until the cognitive skill appears and then teach to it, versus Vygotsky and Feuerstein's views, to teach the skill ahead of development. This is not suggesting that we 'hothouse' youngsters, but it is especially important for a child at developmental risk, where the desired cognitive skill may not appear at 'typical age', leaving the child struggling more both cognitively and emotionally. Therefore, we mediate ahead of development to reduce any known developmental risks.

Transfer to familiar situations

Transfer examples should have meaning and relevance to the learner. For example, if working with a young adult who has not yet experienced employment, using the workplace as an example might not be helpful. Similarly, with children, we cannot assume that activities such as family holidays take place (asking for a transfer example related to planning for a holiday in this context is unhelpful).

Examples should be simple and logically straightforward

Basically, what this means is not to overcomplicate transfer! 'If the child cannot understand the connection between a principle (a main idea) and its application in a particular context, then making that connection does no good' (Haywood et al., 2022: 73). The mastery is in the simplicity.

Transfer to many and varied contexts

Haywood et al. (2022) suggest at least three different contexts: school, home and family life. We can add other relevant contexts: peer groups, recreational activities and the world of work for older pupils and those beyond the school years. These contexts are reflected by Mentis et al. (2009) who suggest home, school and community. This advice relates to the concept of near and far transfer, which is discussed later in this chapter.

The four-step process of transfer

Step 1: Retention. Begin teaching an item. We will call it item 1. As we learn it, the mediator will draw out the relevant cognitive skills, certain strategies or a main idea. Repeat, relearn and reinforce. We see if the learner has retained it, as is. We are not changing anything yet.

Step 2: Durability. Then we start to offer items which are very close to, but not identical to, item 1. We want to find out whether the learner can recognise the same strategy or principle and whether they can transfer that skill to the new item, independently or with our mediation. We are still staying very close to the original item in Step 1. It is not a big mental leap. If the learner can see that the process is the same and reuse the same strategies, *near transfer* is happening. However, this is not the end of the process; we can take this further.

Step 3: Flexibility and adaptability. We now present the learner with items that use the same strategies or principles as we taught in Step 1 and reinforced in Step 2, but now the content or context is moving further away from the original. Now we are interested in whether the learner can identify the same ideas and concepts and apply what they have learned and proceed step by step to applications which are more distant from the original activity. This is where we see the process we call *far transfer.*

Step 4: Generalisation and transformation. The learner has achieved the ability to generalise and even transform parts of the original. The strategy has become so well internalised that the learner can now manipulate and reorganise new items. This is where we often recognise creativity. Creativity does not emerge from chaos. It comes from recognising structure, enabling one to extract ideas, lift them out and above their specific content and then reorganise the reality in what appears to us to be novel ways. *There is nothing new under the sun.*

The bullet points below summarise our mediational role:

- Ask questions ('What do we have here?');
- Mediate each step; name each step;
- Point out what we are identifying: 'Let's compare this item with the next one. What changes, what stays the same?' Name the process and name each cognitive skill. What stays the same and what changes is called systematic *comparison* leading to *conservation*;
- State the rule of the change; write it down if needed;
- Now we know what is happening here, we see how we can use the same idea when we work out the next item. Each step should be made explicit. Do not just say, 'Well done.' Of course, praise is important and necessary but should then be followed up by asking: 'How did you work that out?' Ask the learner to verbally articulate the process. This helps to internalise the cognitive skills and the strategies. The importance of cognitive feedback has been shown in many studies of effective teaching (for example, Hattie, 2012; Black and Wiliam, 2009);
- Reinforce the process. The ability to think flexibly is an important executive function. If the basic structure is recognised and explicitly named, it leads to the ability to systematically transfer and reorganise. This is metacognitive teaching.

Taking the four-step approach above, Tables 7.1 and 7.2 give examples of what near and far transfer might look like for categorisation (example 1) and analogical thinking (example 2).

Table 7.1 Transfer example 1

Step	***Task/description***	***What the mediator does/says***
Retention: introduce item (task) 1, using a set of blocks of three different colours.	Learner is asked to sort the blocks into groups.	Observe the spontaneous skills first (don't tell the learner how to do the task). When the learner sorts groups by colour we say: 'Great! What made you put these together? What shall we call this group? Let's call it the blue group, and this is the ...?' Elicit the category label, colour: 'You made three groups, a blue, a red and a yellow group. So, you sorted (grouped) them by their ...?'
Durability: offer close but not identical items (near transfer)	Change colours. Instead of red, blue and yellow, prepare blocks that are different colours from the ones you have already used. This is a very small step from the first task. Ask the learner to do the same as they just did. More examples of near transfer: A small step further: use the same materials, but group using a different criterion such as **shape** or **size**. Or stay with colour and change the materials, for example, sorting toy cars or other small world play materials.	Watch if the learner can do this then say: 'Great. So, what have you done here?' Let the learner tell you that they have sorted these by their colour too. 'Well done, so was that the same as we did the first time?' Learner says 'NO!' 'Ah, what was different?' Learner: 'They aren't the same colours.' 'You are right, but what was the same? We sorted them in the same way by their colours.' Practise more if needed before moving on to step 3.
Flexibility and adaptability: moving the transfer further away from the original context (far transfer). Go step by step. Now offer a set of blocks that are different colours and shapes.	Can you sort these another way?	Wait for spontaneous performance first. If the learner succeeds, praise and ask: 'How did you sort them this time?' The learner might reply by labelling the shapes. (If they are unsure of shape names, teach these. Question further to elicit the category label shape: 'Great, so this time, you sorted them by their ...?' You hope the learner can give you the word ***shape***. At this point you are ready to emphasise the underlying principle. You say (and can write down if appropriate): First, we sorted by colour. Then we sorted by shape. We were practising ***grouping*** things. How do we do that? ***TEACH A PRINCIPLE: When we group, we put together things that are the same. Things that are different go into another group.***

(Continued)

Table 7.1 (Continued)

Step	***Task/description***	***What the mediator does/says***
Generalisation and transformation: manipulate and reorganise new items.	Tidy up time Putting books back in the school library. Play area: putting things away in the kitchen or putting items on shelves in the shop. Small world play: for example, grouping farm or zoo animals.	If appropriate elicit examples: 'When else ...?; 'Where else ...?'. Notice and comment when the learner demonstrates grouping and classification behaviours. Make sure that your comments mention the key cognitive skill; for example, 'Great job, you grouped ... together, just like we did with our blocks.'

Example 1. Early years sorting activity

Materials: A set of blocks that are at least six different colours and four different shapes.
Cognitive focus: Grouping and categorising.
Preparation: Check that the learner understands what a group is: things that go together.

Example 2: Teaching analogy and its transfer to higher order reasoning for older learners

Materials: Coloured blocks, pictures, matrix designs.

Cognitive focus: Analogical reasoning. Analogical reasoning underpins early reading, maths and spelling (see, for example, the work of Goswami, 1994). It is an important type of logical reasoning that we use a great deal, so it is really worth working on.

Preparation: Check that the learner understands the meaning of an analogy and its contributory cognitive skills. Therefore, the first additional row in the table below gives a suggested structure for preparatory work.

Table 7.2 Transfer example 2

<table>
<tr><th>Step</th><th>Task/description</th><th>What the mediator does/says</th></tr>
<tr><td>Preparation: understanding analogy.</td><td colspan="2">Here is a simple example: (A) Up is to (B) Down as (C) In is to (D) ...? What's the answer? Out.
So, we see the structure of an analogy: A is to B as C is to D. (Don't use the word analogy if it's too abstract but do make sure they grasp the process). Many learners will be able to confidently answer but cannot tell you how they arrived at the answer. However, as you know, much as we love correct answers, that is not the point of mediation. It is about the awareness of the learner to identify the cognitive skills and be able to use, consciously select and reuse them and to know when this is not the correct process to choose. Therefore, go on to ask:
'Well done, how did you work that out?' 'Well, A and B are opposites so the opposite of in is out.' 'Great. Now let's analyse this together. How do we work out this kind of thinking problem? It is called an analogy' (Only if the learner is old enough to learn the correct term). 'We start by looking at A. What is it? We then compare it to B. How are they the same or different? From here we can work out the relationship between A and B. We will then apply the same relationship for C and D. So, If B is opposite to A, then I need to find a D item that is opposite to C. You've got it! We have extracted the relationship between A and B and how to create an analogy, so now we can speak about the rule:
Whatever happens between A and B, we have to do the same for C and D.
We can write it down so you don't have to hold the rule in your head. Now we know how to look for the relationship by comparing A and B and then how to apply the rule to C and D.'</td></tr>
<tr><td>Retention: introduce item (task) 1.
Introduce the set of coloured blocks.</td><td>Put down (A) a large red circle and (B) a small red circle. Then put down (C) a large blue circle.</td><td>'What should go in the space for D? Yes! A small blue circle. What was the relationship? Size changes from big to small, but colour stays the same.'
Encourage the learner to verbalise what they have found, moving them from unconscious perceptual processes to conscious verbal abstraction. This lays the foundation for higher order logical reasoning. Remember that language is the bridge between foundation cognitive skills and higher order reasoning in the Boat of Cognition (Chapter 3).</td></tr>
</table>

(Continued)

Table 7.2 (Continued)

Step	***Task/description***	***What the mediator does/says***
Durability: offer close but not identical items (near transfer).	Change the relationship and the rules but stay with the same materials; for example: (A) blue triangle is to (B) blue square as (C) red triangle is to (D) ...?	After (and only after) a few successful near transfer items, try some error analysis. We might ask the learner: 'If you had a friend who put down a big blue circle, what is wrong with their answer?' Error analysis and especially verbalising the error, is a powerful way of confirming a correct thinking process in the mind of the learner. It's fun to point out someone else's errors (not me!) and also depersonalises the whole process.
Flexibility and adaptability: moving the context further away (far transfer).	Change materials and modalities. Instead of coloured blocks, use pictures or design. This is what Raven's Matrices or other matrix reasoning tests examine in some well known psychological test batteries. A matrix is just the format. The underpinning cognitive skill is analogical reasoning. For example: (A) aeroplane is to (B) sky as (C) ship is to (D) ... [water/sea/ocean]? Then we may go onto words (A) hungry is to (B) eat as (C) thirsty is to (D) ... [drink].	Watch for spontaneous performance first. Depending on performance, you might need to mediate by referring back to the rule/principle: 'How did we work out the answer for the blocks?'; or 'Great, so this time, how did you work out what D is?'
Generalisation and transformation: manipulate and reorganise new items.	Far transfer involves much more abstract concepts. For example, (A) Parliament is to (B) House of Lords (UK) as (C) Congress is to (D) ... [Senate (USA)].	If appropriate elicit examples: 'When else ...?'; 'Where else ...?'. Notice and comment when the learner demonstrates use of analogy. Make sure that the comment mentions the key cognitive skill; for example, 'Great job, you worked out how these items go together. What do we call it when we do this?' *Only if* the learner can manage the formal names of these skills, elicit the terms comparison, induction (discovering) a rule, deduction (applying the rule) to arrive at the analogy. Otherwise do explain the process but keep your terms simple. 'Well done you used analogy to find the missing item.'

Summary

This chapter has looked at transfer in detail, in recognition of the importance of this criterion of mediation. We have considered the nature of change, especially in relation to concepts of near and far transfer. The chapter has included examples that can help you to implement this crucial element of mediated learning.

We end this chapter with a quote that sums up the important role played by transfer which was written in the context of preschool, early years education:

> 'The goal of generalizability means that mediators are constantly on the lookout for opportunities to demonstrate the broader applicability of principles and strategies that the children might have had to use for the solving of immediate problems. In other words, they are trying to make the children more efficient at learning how to learn, by getting the children to generalise the processes they have used beyond the problems they are working on at the moment'.
>
> *(Haywood et al., 2022: 76)*

You cannot begin too soon! Mediation and metacognitive teaching begins in the nursery.

Reflection and follow-up

- Based on the ideas in this chapter, consider why generalisation and transfer cannot be left to chance.
- Think about experiences you have had, or will have, where deliberate transfer from one context to another can be introduced intentionally.
- Consider why there is an emphasis in this chapter, that the earlier this process starts, the better it is for *all* children's development.
- Parents are a child's first and most important mediators. Even if you do not work in an early years setting, consider practical ways in which transfer opportunities can be shared with parents to empower them.
- Look back at the Boat of Cognition model (Figure 3.2 in Chapter 3). Choose a cognitive skill. Then, with a particular learner in mind, identify what transfer might look like in other school/learning contexts and in contexts outside of school such as home or wider community.

References

Barnett, S.M. and Ceci, S.J. (2002). When and where do we apply what we learn? A taxonomy for far transfer. *Psychological Bulletin*, 128(4), 612-637.

Black, P. and Wiliam, D. (2009). Developing the theory of formative assessment. *Educational Assessment, Evaluation and Accountability*, 21(1), 5-31.

Ceci, S.J. (1990). *On Intelligence ... More or Less: A Bioecological Treatise on Intellectual Development.* Englewood Cliffs: Prentice Hall.

Feuerstein, R., Feuerstein, R.S., Falik, L. and Rand, Y. (2006) *The Feuerstein Instrumental Enrichment Program.* Jerusalem: ICELP Publications.

Flavell, J.H., Flavell, E.R. and Green F.L. (2001). Development of children's understanding of connections between thinking and feeling. *Psychological Science*, 12(5), 430-432

Goswami, U. (1994). Reading by analogy: theoretical and practical perspectives. In C. Hulme and M. Snowling (Eds), *Reading Development and Dyslexia.* London: Whurr Publishers.

Hattie, J. (2012). *Visible Learning for Teachers: Maximising Impact on Learning.* Abingdon: Routledge.

Haywood, H.C. (1988). Bridging: a special technique of mediation. *The Thinking Teacher*, 4(2), 4-5.

Haywood, H.C. (1993). A mediational teaching style. *International Journal of Cognitive Education and Psychology*, 3(1), 27-38.

Haywood, H.C. and Lidz, C. (2007). *Dynamic Assessment in Practice.* New York: Cambridge University Press.

Haywood, H.C. and Tzuriel, D. (2002). Applications and challenges in dynamic assessment. *Peabody Journal of Education*, 77(2), 40-63.

Haywood, H.C., Brooks, P. and Burns, M.S. (2022). Bright Start Cognitive Curriculum for Young Children, rev. edn. Bright Start CCYC. Available at: www.brightstart-ccyc.com.

Kaniel, S. (2001). Teaching for transfer from the learner's point of view. *Journal of Cognitive Education and Psychology*, 1(3), 266-293.

Lidz, C. (1991). *A Practitioner's Guide to Dynamic Assessment.* New York: Guilford Press.

Lidz, C.S. (2003). *Early Childhood Assessment.* Hoboken New Jersey: Wiley.

Mentis, M., Dunn-Bernstein, M., Mentis, M. and Skuy, M. (2009). *Bridging Learning: Unlocking Cognitive Learning Potential In and Out of the Classroom.* Thousand Oaks: Corwin (Sage Limited).

8

Putting It All Together

Delivering Metacognitive Teaching and Mediated Learning

Introduction

This chapter draws together material from previous Part II chapters in order to provide a framework for implementing mediated learning across numerous contexts, in and out of school. It sets out a six-step mediation framework, which is a structured tool to help you to plan and deliver mediated learning.

The six-step framework also aligns with the APDR (assess-plan-do-review) cycle. This cycle is a common structure used for supporting learners. It reflects the drive to emphasise the importance of high-quality universal teaching for all children and young people, aiming to support early intervention. Although it is usually related to special educational needs support, the overall idea is that high quality teaching should be available to all. This reflects our assertion that mediated learning is not just for learners with additional needs (discussed in more detail in the mediation myths section of Chapter 3). By making links to the APDR cycle, we aim to help you to have an existing context and system for applying your knowledge and practising your skills, hopefully making it easier to embed cognitive skills into your practice.

Table 8.1 shows the six-step framework, with the steps aligned to the APDR cycle. Each step will be covered in the sections of this chapter.

It is important to emphasise at the outset that this framework is not designed to be yet another document or piece of paper that has to be filled in (and in some cases, which is then filed away and not used!). It can be used flexibly. If you want to use it to make notes to assist you, by all means do so. However, you can simply use it as an *aide-mémoire* and, in time, as you use the framework, it is likely to become a quick 'mental checklist' when planning to deliver mediated learning.

The idea of 'putting it all together' can take a number of different forms, depending on your specific role and the overall purpose of your involvement with the learner or learners. In producing this text, we have assumed that our readers' practice will involve direct work with learners and work alongside others who are likely to have day to day responsibility for working with learners, or a mixture of both. For example, educational psychologists (EPs), specialist teachers and therapists might work directly with a learner and collaborate with

DOI: 10.4324/9781003655329-11

others in order to both gather and disseminate information. Special Educational Needs and Disabilities Coordinators (SENDCos) might also work with others to facilitate support for learners and work with learners directly on a more regular basis than a visiting professional.

Table 8.1 Six-step mediation framework

Step number	***Description***	***Chapter 8 content***
ASSESS		
1	Identify the cognitive skill(s) and emotional states that you will mediate.	Target setting.
PLAN		
2	Choose a task for mediating the cognitive skill(s) and emotional states.	The embedded model, where the curriculum is the context for mediated learning. A task analysis proforma to support this step.
3	Analyse the task.	
DO		
4	Offer the task.	Mediated metacognitive moments for delivering the embedded approach with classes, small groups and individuals.
5	Mediate.	
REVIEW		
6	Monitor, record, reflect and feedback. Loop back to Step 1.	Feedback and follow up, including wider dissemination.

Each section that follows corresponds to a step or steps of the framework. In order to illustrate the framework in action, we are going to follow the learning journey of Joseph, an anonymised learner (based on the present authors' casework). Note that the examples focus on the cognitive element of support for these example learners, so we have not included any detail about recommendations relating to other areas of need, or to attainment. Our educational psychology role would always involve taking a holistic view of a learner; here we are only presenting one part of this to illustrate the specific content of this chapter and to reflect the overall emphasis of this text on the processes of learning.

Here is a 'pen portrait' of Joseph.

Joseph is aged eight and is in a Year 4 primary (elementary) class in a mainstream school. His progress has been a cause for concern since he was in Year 1. He doesn't plan or organise his work, he loses things and his memory is poor. He struggled to learn to read, is still far from fluent, and with understanding basic numeracy. His work is very haphazard; often it is unfinished and he does not work systematically. His class teacher noticed that although he appears to be sitting still, he is unable to focus on his work for more than two or three minutes, either for individual seatwork (in table groups) or for plenary sessions.

Joseph had been assessed in the past by an EP. The EP carried out some ability testing and reported an IQ score for Joseph, saying that his below average scores were evidence of learning difficulties. The EP advised school to focus on differentiation of work and on playing memory games as his memory was particularly weak.

Despite following the EP advice, there has been no discernible positive change in any of the difficulties noted. Joseph's class teacher feels that many of his difficulties are due to poor attention, so she decides to focus on supporting this. As a first step, she allocates the class teaching assistant (TA) to stay close to Joseph in order to try and keep him focused. This has worked a little but as soon as the TA moves away Joseph immediately loses focus.

It must of course be emphasised that there could be a number of underlying reasons for Joseph's difficulties. For example:

- Hearing or vision difficulties;
- Language difficulties/delay;
- Tasks set are not well matched to his needs and current levels;
- Neurological issues and consequent learning delay;
- Impact of trauma/adverse childhood experiences.

In presenting this case example, there is an assumption that some or all of the above will have been considered and investigated further if needed.

Step one: identify the cognitive skill(s) and emotional states that you will mediate

This section focuses on target setting. This is important to address because it is likely to be very difficult to identify and evaluate change without any clear goals.

Target-setting context

Targets that are set for individual learners are likely to be part of some kind of individual plan or profile. This is a common context for targets, which is found globally in approaches to support for additional needs. For example, the English SEND Code of Practice (Department for Education, 2015), with similar approaches in Scotland, Wales and Northern Ireland and outside the UK (IDEA, 2004 in the USA and the European Agency for Development in Special Needs Education, 2003 documentation. The most recent UK policy document

(Department for Education, 2026) suggests Individual Support Plans for all SEND pupils. The varied nomenclature essentially refers to the same thing: some kind of written plan setting out targets and provision for an individual learner. One important role of the external consultant (such as an EP, speech and language therapist, occupational therapist or specialist teacher) is to assist with this process and not leave schools to struggle with interpretation and target setting.

SMART targets

The starting point for thinking about target setting is to look at what is currently used. Although the format for an individual plan is likely to vary, it is very likely that it will include some targets. SMART targets is a very common acronym used, standing for **S**pecific, **M**easurable, **A**chievable, **R**elevant and **T**ime-bound. SMART targets provide a structure for target setting and a means of tracking and measuring progress.

A very brief internet search for 'SMART targets for cognitive education' yields a huge number of websites that give examples of this type of target, related to aspects of cognition. There are also many SEND computer programmes that schools can purchase in order to generate targets. In addition, the increasing use of artificial intelligence makes it even easier to press a button and generate targets. However, in our experience of working with countless educational settings, we find that although the needs of the learner are the starting point for identifying suitable provision, once SMART targets are generated, they take over the driving seat from the learner and are mainly about curriculum or behavioural goals. This means that decisions about progress often fail to take account the cognitive profile of the learner and the contexts in which learning takes place because the sole focus is on the achievement target.

The following box picks up Joseph's story to illustrate target setting from an individual plan.

The class teacher and SENCo meet to talk over what to do. They agree that just having a TA next to him isn't helping Joseph to focus independently; in fact, he is becoming very uncomfortable about having a TA next to him. This feeling is fuelled by the parents' attitude that Joseph should not be different from his peers and that he ought to manage without additional support in class. Parents provided subject tutoring outside the classroom.

Joseph's class teacher and SENCo agree that a more individual approach is needed. The SENCo uses her computerised target-setting programme. This is what was generated:

Joseph will maintain attention independently for five minutes with 80 per cent accuracy (that is for four out of five minutes). This behaviour to be observed on five out of five occasions and will be evaluated as fully, partly or not achieved by the end of half term.

The target in the box is a fictitious example; however, it was written using the present authors' knowledge and experience of examples of SEND plans for individual learners, so the type of wording used is very common and is a reliable representation of the wording of an attention target (especially one that is computer generated).

Joseph's target seems deceptively clear and of course, on one level, it is. The desired behaviour is described (maintain attention) together with the conditions (independently) and there are criteria for evaluating whether the target has been met. However, there are some issues with this target:

- It presents attention as a one-dimensional concept. It also assumes that paying attention is the answer to Joseph's learning difficulties. The theoretical background in Part I and the learner profile material in Chapter 4 makes it very clear that attention is a multi-faceted concept. In the Boat of Cognition model (see Chapter 3), attention is a broad domain that is subdivided into staying focused, shifting from one stimulus to another and filtering out distractions;
- At what point does attention stop being a target? Targets need to be measured; however, the outcome criteria in the example above are unhelpful. Can we really define attention in relation to a number of occasions it is observed, or give a definitive criterion for the length of time that the learner can attend to a task in order to tick attention off a list of goals?
- It assumes readiness to learn. In our Boat of Cognition model, readiness to learn precedes attention, so the very behavioural focus does not capture the subtlety of being 'ready to learn';
- It takes no account of the learner's emotional state(s) or the contexts where the desired behaviour will be demonstrated;
- It does not address the range of difficulties that have been observed. What has been focused on is the manifest behaviour (poor attention), with no consideration of any cognitive factors that might be important.

These criticisms reflect Haywood's (Haywood, 1990; Haywood et al., 2022) distinction between behaviour management targets and cognitive targets when considering how to set targets and appropriate methods to achieve these that focus on cognitive change. Haywood maintained that these two aims are incompatible. Our position is that these important differences must be clearly understood, but at the same time it is possible to combine both in a cognitive learning plan. In the example of Joseph, more focused attention is WHAT we want to help the learner achieve (a behavioural change). However, we cannot do this without planning relevant cognitive targets. Cognitive targets focus on HOW Joseph will learn, supporting and redeveloping his repertoire of skills so that his attention can improve.

Can SMART targets be cognitive?

The criticism in the above section highlights a fundamental problem, that is, that target-setting approaches for the *products* of learning ignore the *processes* of learning. It is not possible to write targets for cognition using the same approach as that used for learning how, for example, to brush one's teeth, tie one's shoelaces or recognise grapheme-phoneme correspondences. These examples are the products of learning, whereas what we are focusing on are the processes. Therefore, the cognitive processes involved in achieving the desired product outcomes need to be addressed.

We would argue that cognitive targets can be SMART but that simply bolting a cognition target onto an achievement goal does not work. We prefer to use the term 'cognitive goal'. A cognitive goal can be SMART but not reductionist. The Cognitive Abilities Profile (CAP; Deutsch, 2020), is an example of the way in which cognitive targets can be SMART whilst maintaining a focus on process. Table 8.2 shows what each element of SMART looks like for a cognitive goal.

SMART cognitive goals in context

Goals or targets alone do not capture all that is needed to support and promote cognitive skills or emotional states, so they should be contained in a planning format that sets out provision and contexts relating to the goals. There is no prescribed format for a SEND support plan; documentation is likely to be specific to the setting. One-page profiles and pupil passports are common forms of documentation. It is not useful here to unpick the merits

Table 8.2 SMART cognitive goal descriptors

Element of SMART	***Description related to cognitive goal***
Specific	Say which cognitive skill and/or emotional state needs to be improved. These will be identified via the cognitive profile of the learner drawn up using material from Chapter 4. Use the Boat of Cognition to identify specific cognitive skills or emotional states.
Measurable	A rating scale can be used, such as the four-point scale in the CAP, which rates specific cognitive abilities and behaviours affecting learning. Scaling questions are often used in consultation approaches (see Chapter 4). A scaling question is often followed up by asking what would be different at half a point better on the scale? A more descriptive approach might be used: for example, stating what 'achieved' might look like.
Achievable	This relates to the measurable element and will be specific to the learner. Based on knowledge of the learner, is the measurable element of the target achievable? Achievable also relates to the time over which the change is to be seen.
Relevant (and realistic)	Use the strengths and needs cognitive profile, taking account of what motivates the learner, together with the contexts for support. Realistic: don't expect cognitive changes to show immediately. They take time to become internalised in the learner's way of working.
Time-bound	Set a time frame for reviewing progress; for example, over half a term, which is usually between five and eight weeks or a whole term.

or otherwise of these different formats and, from a practical perspective, it is not helpful to have a completely separate 'cognitive' plan that is additional to other planning documents. The pragmatic approach is to use existing formats for documents. Since the goals identified for cognitive skills and emotional states are cross-curricular, they can be added to an individual plan or profile as cross-curricular support.

We will pick up Joseph's story in order to look at the way in which a cognitive element might be added in order to enhance the targeted support.

The SENCo and class teacher meet to review Joseph's progress. The outcome of this review was that the target had not worked. Joseph's attention remained poor and there were no changes to his planning, organisation, completion of work or improvement in the curriculum age-related expectations. The class teacher and SENCo think that there must be reasons why he isn't making progress and wonder if he has other learning difficulties. They therefore agree that they need some further advice, so they request some input from their EP.

The EP observes Joseph and works with him individually. The focus of the EP's work is to look at Joseph's cognitive skills,(rather than his curricular achievements) using a Dynamic Assessment approach, particularly looking at the cognitive skills that have been noted as concerns: planning, memory and working systematically. The EP writes a report. You can download an abbreviated copy of the report from the Resource Centre (Resource 8.1). The report has been anonymised but draws on the present authors' casework in order to show the kind of work that can be carried out. The EP also spends time speaking to the parents to gain a fuller picture of home as well as school.

The EP has a follow up consultation with the SENCo and class teacher in order to look at how the findings of the assessment might be incorporated into Joseph's current individual plan. In the consultation, the EP talks about flexible intelligence, explaining how her assessment looked at how to change and improve thinking, rather than just taking a static view. The report is shared with the parents and a further consultation is arranged with them, together with the SENCo and class teacher. Both school and home hear from the EP how essential it is that school and home work together.

It was agreed that attention would remain as a target for Joseph, but, in addition, there will be a more specific focus on his cognitive thinking skills. Planning and organising materials was agreed as a cognitive focus.

Table 8.3 shows what Joseph's individual plan might look like when some specific information is added about supporting his cognitive skills. The plan includes two curriculum links to maths and written expression. The curriculum targets in the example are based on examples from the present authors' casework. The cognitive part of the plan uses headings from the CAP intervention plan (Deutsch, 2020).

Table 8.3 Example of an individual plan for Joseph

COGNITIVE GOALS				
Area of need	***Goal***	***Strategies, mediation, type of task, elements which led to success***		***Review***
		Adjustments to task/ context	***Mediation***	
Attention	Joseph will be able to improve focused attention. When reviewed after half a term, the goal will be noted as achieved by observing a reduction in fidgeting, looking at the person speaking, sitting on his seat and staying focused for at least five minutes of the first part of the lesson (the teacher-led demonstration) and a reduction in the number of times his TA has to prompt him to look and listen.	Environmental adjustments: minimise distractions (for example seating arrangements, monitoring and management of noise levels, use of workstation). Adults will ensure that Joseph is regulated and alert before focusing on his attention.	Competence: praise with feedback related to attention. Open-ended questions prior to starting a task ('How do we get ready to pay attention?'). Challenge: 'Let's see if you can keep going with this for a bit longer.' Meaning: 'It's important to pay attention because ...' Transfer: recall previous examples of when attention was used, related to favoured activities, where Joseph shows appropriate attention.	
Planning and organising materials and ideas	To begin to find the materials needed for a task without help. To draw up a visual plan with help, no more than 3 steps to begin with, and follow the steps independently.	Chunk tasks and information. Resources needed are stored in the same place in the classroom and labelled clearly so they are easy to find. Use backward chaining: do the first few steps of the plan with Joseph and then ask him to do the remaining step or steps to finish the task.	'What do we need?' 'Let's make a plan'. 'What's the first thing you need to do ... and the next ...' Transfer: 'When is another time you made a plan?'	

(Continued)

Table 8.3 (Continued)

COGNITIVE GOALS				
Area of need	***Goal***	***Strategies, mediation, type of task, elements which led to success***		***Review***
		Adjustments to task/ context	***Mediation***	
Written expression	To produce written work with a beginning, middle and end structure.	Use a story planner. Use mediational language to refer to planning, emphasising first, next, and so on. Open-ended questions, such as: 'What do we do first?' 'How did you do this before?' Use a mediated learning approach, involving: A focus on the process skill of planning; An intentional interaction; Mediation of meaning of a story planner: 'This might help to organise your writing.'		
Maths problem solving	To solve maths word problems with ... steps and involving ... [maths operations].	Use a mediated learning approach that focuses on the processes needed to solve maths word problems. Connect to prior learning: 'Where have you done something like this before?' 'How did you solve the problem?' Focus on relevance, identifying what information is needed/not needed. Make a plan for the problem solving, use open-ended questions: 'What's the first thing we need to do?' A higher level of mediation would be to model the process of solving the problem via a thinking aloud approach.		

It is assumed that any format of a learning plan or profile will include learner details so this section is not included in the example that follows. This example includes attention as a cognitive goal. Since attention is a cognitive skill that is needed in all learning activities, it might be important for it to be a long-term feature of the learner's support plan, with the details being amended after subsequent reviews (for example, the rating goal and/or contexts might be changed). A concurrent goal might be for the learner to transfer good attention to other contexts; for example, with friends and at home.

It must be emphasised that this step of the six-step framework focuses on target setting and thus does not (yet) address in detail *how* targets are to be achieved, monitored and then modified. These areas are addressed in subsequent sections.

There are some key points about the above learning plan which apply in all cases, not just in relation to our example. These are:

- A learning plan should not have one target only. The addition of 'planning and organising materials and ideas' supports attention via careful comparing and learning to do things in order (sequencing);
- Targets should be prioritised. Looking at Joseph's example, there are several relevant targets. In keeping with the realistic element of target setting, think about what is easiest to deliver. The more that staff are on board and feel able to implement the target using supporting strategies, the more likely it is that they will be able to follow through;
- The prioritised targets are not necessarily the most obvious ones. That seems counterintuitive. Attention is an interesting example, because there are a number of contributory causes that need to be considered in relation to attention. For example, poor understanding of language, which leads to not understanding the task and thus being unable to plan what needs to be done. This is where we look for as much evidence as we can gather to support our learning plan. In Joseph's case, he has learned to read with difficulty. He often decodes poorly without any concern that what he is reading does not make sense. We realise this is not just poor attention; there is a language issue. His comprehension of the language even in a simple story is quite poor. This leads us to suggest that Joseph might be experiencing some receptive language difficulties. When he can do a task, it is often because he has learnt it by rote (this is explored in more detail in the report, Resource 8.1).

Steps two and three: choose a task for mediating the cognitive skill(s) and emotional states; analyse the task

The introductory chapter gave a rationale for the embedded approach to delivering metacognitive teaching and mediated learning. The focus in this chapter is on applying the embedded approach. The curriculum tasks are the context but mediated learning will *always* focus on the processes of learning. This section explores the embedded model in a little more detail by looking at the curriculum context, which then sets the scene for the practical, worked examples of the embedded approach related to steps four and five of the framework.

The curriculum context

The curriculum context will vary according to national and local legislation and policy. Many countries have a prescribed curriculum that must be followed by all schools, or, like the United States, have common core curriculum guidance which is interpreted by individual states. Therefore, it is not practical to go into detail about the wide range of curriculum subjects and approaches. What we would argue is that cognitive thinking skills and emotional states can be embedded into any and all curriculum subjects or contexts.

Implementing an embedded model needs clarity about what is driving the process. Our emphasis throughout this text is on process, not product. Therefore, it might seem unexpected to give prominence to the curriculum and, to an extent, this is correct. However, the argument is more about balance. Balance means that when planning for embedding, equal weight is given to the process and the product. Both are important if embedding is to have any impact. Too much curriculum content (product) will mean that the process skills are not made sufficiently explicit and thus are less likely to be taken on board and used. Too much focus on process risks limited or poor transfer, because the process skills are not applied to other contexts (in this case, to the day-to-day curriculum content being delivered). Choo's (2000: 2) investigation of the practicalities of delivering infusion emphasises balance: 'Thus in conceptualizing a thinking model, SP [Singapore Polytechnic] has identified the following as important components of a thinking curriculum: a well-integrated knowledge base, thinking skills and processes, thinking dispositions, and strategies for life long learner.'

Overall, therefore, cognitive skills can be embedded in any curriculum context and are applicable to all subjects. The following box shows what this step might look like for Joseph.

Joseph's attention and other cognitive difficulties are not confined to one particular curriculum area. His individual plan highlights maths problem-solving and written expression because these are the two curriculum areas that he struggles with the most and where his achievements are substantially behind age-related expectations. However, staff recognise that it will be important for the cognitive target to be supported at all times.

Embedding Joseph's support for attention into the curriculum can involve all subjects and activities. For Joseph, a distinction might be made between individual and whole class support. Both might be useful.

Maths and written expression tasks are analysed to identify any adjustments to content, modality, levels of abstraction and complexity, and speed, precision and accuracy. The analysis suggested that Joseph's attention and systematic working are better when there are some visual cues or reminders and when the content is familiar.

Steps four and five: offer the task; mediate

This section focuses on how to deliver an embedded approach for supporting cognitive skills and emotional states that can be used with individuals, small groups or a whole class. It introduces the idea of what we call *mediated metacognitive moments*. This is a way of ensuring that teaching pays attention to the processes as well as the products of learning.

Mediated metacognitive moments involve identifying and supporting specific cognitive skills and emotional states that are relevant to lesson or task content. This method meets one of the key purposes of mediated learning: teaching for transfer, because the cognitive skills and emotional states are supported in a curriculum context, not taught in isolation. This makes it much easier to carry out transfer activities because the curriculum context is already present.

Mediated metacognitive moments can be used with individuals, small groups or whole classes.

Mediated metacognitive moments

The idea of this process is to expand existing lesson or individual plans in order to include some explicit teaching of cognitive skills related to the specific subject and to support and reinforce emotional states that might otherwise challenge curriculum access.

We suggest three mediated metacognitive moments in teaching sessions, at the beginning, middle and end. Before giving some examples, the three points below are important to mention that arise from the many hours spent by both authors observing classrooms:

- *First*: mediation of intentionality and reciprocity. WHAT are we learning? This is often a product or curricular goal;
- *Second*: HOW are we going to learn this topic? This relates to strategic and cognitive methods that we will use;
- *Third*: WHY are we doing this? This is what we mean by mediation of meaning. In Chapter 3 we critiqued the use of acronyms such as WALT (we are learning to) and WILF (what I'm looking for) to express lesson objectives because they are rarely explained or discussed. Meaning can be mediated via the outcomes or objectives but needs to be explicit and emphasise why.

It might seem obvious to mention readiness to learn at the beginning of a session. Some kind of attention focussing strategies are frequently used in lessons. However, the metacognitive element is sometimes missing. This element involves using explicit metacognitive language to reinforce and support readiness to learn and explaining their meaning; for example, attention, self-regulation, being alert. As Spooner and Woodcock (2013: 6) comment: 'in our work with children we have felt in many cases that the issue was not that they were unable to listen, but rather that they did not understand what good listening meant'. Many classrooms have wall displays illustrating 'good listening' but learners are not always explicitly directed to the content or importance of the display. Our observations also suggest that sometimes attention and regulation strategies are used without an explanation (or mediation of meaning) and, in some cases, the lesson begins before all learners demonstrate readiness.

Table 8.4 Generic structure for mediated metacognitive moments

Mediated metacognitive moment	***Description***	***Related mediation criteria***
Beginning of the lesson or activity	**Cognitive skills**: introduce specific cognitive skill or skills that relate to the lesson content. Link to lesson learning objectives.	**Meaning**: part of the lesson introduction. **Intentionality**, because the cognitive focus is planned and explicit. **Transfer**, where the current cognitive skill might be linked to previous learning. **Positive affirmation and empathy** (expressing confidence and our support). **Goal setting and planning**: depending on lesson content it might be appropriate to discuss how to make a plan for any set tasks. **Regulation**: if the lesson intro involves Q&A, encourage time to think before learners offer responses.
Middle: during the activity	Give specific praise with feedback that includes explicit reference to the cognitive skill(s) and emotional state(s). Depending on the content/tasks, model thinking aloud.	*Reciprocity and competence*: where the feedback is responsive to individual learners or groups of learners. *Challenge*: challenge learners to find another way to use the cognitive skill with a more complex task (an extra mile task). *Regulation*: encouraging well-thought-out responses.
End: cognitive feedback after the activity	Recap the cognitive skill(s) used and make links to other learning. Even better, ask learners to summarise what they have learned in this lesson, in what order and why? This leads to transfer to other contexts. This is you, the mediator, teaching for metacognition.	*Transfer*: explicit reference to other contexts for using the cognitive skill(s). *Regulation*: if the lesson debrief/ plenary involves Q&A, encourage time to think before learners offer responses.

Table 8.4 shows a generic structure for embedding cognitive skills into a lesson or individual/small group teaching session.

A downloadable template can be found in the Resource Centre (Resource 8.2). The template is applicable across all phases from early years up to high school and post-16. It can be used for whole class, individual or small group teaching.

We estimate that including the mediated metacognitive moments in a session will take a maximum of ten minutes session time which should be spread throughout the lesson (in a natural way, not one block of time), so we would argue that this amount of time will not significantly reduce access to content. On the contrary, these mediated metacognitive moments will *enhance* access because you are mediating transferable cognitive skills, giving the activity meaning and relevance that can be used in any curriculum subject.

Some time is needed beforehand in order to identify the key cognitive skills and emotional states needed for accessing specific content. This is the preparation stage of the learning plan, not just before the lesson takes place. Lesson planning is generally part of the duties of class teachers, so including cognition in the way suggested here should not add too significantly to planning time. As experience and familiarity is built up, it is possible to develop a 'bank' that matches cognitive skills with subject topics and tasks. Many of the emotional states will apply in all lessons, and the choice of focus here will be determined by the type of lesson and your knowledge of your learners. For example, in a PE lesson where it might be important to follow safety rules for use of equipment or apparatus, a focus on self-regulation (particularly regulation of movement) might be useful and necessary. From your knowledge of your learners, you might decide that a particular group or class should focus on persistence or blocking (for example, if learners demonstrate low self-concept related to learning and thus are reluctant to 'have a go' and/or give up easily).

For whole class, small group or as a prompt, on individual desks or as wall displays a focus on cognitive skills will be helpful. The following box shows an example of a visual step-by-step set of prompts that relates to the cognitive skill of planning. Planning was been chosen as an example here, because, as we discussed in Chapter 1, it has been shown in studies of executive function to be the most consistently commonly identified executive function skill (Goldstein et al., 2014). We have not included any suggested artwork or illustration for these prompts due to care about copyright; however, an illustration of a signpost might be useful.

How to plan accurately

- I **SAY** what I have to do
- I **NOTE** what information I have been given
- I decide what **RULES** I need to follow
- I work out my **STRATEGIES** (how I go about solving the problem)
- I decide where I am going to **START**
- I **CHECK** my answer

We have seen this simple planning sheet pinned on the wall of the classroom for all pupils to refer to.

Exactly the same beginning, middle and end process can be used with individual learners or with small groups of learners who are working on the same curriculum task and who have similar cognitive needs. The main difference is that an individual learner is likely to have a specific plan with targets based on their profile of strengths and needs. Therefore, the cognitive skills and/or emotional states infused into the session will be directly relevant to the learner. Individual support might be to expand the first metacognitive moment at the beginning of a session in order to include an introductory activity or activities that focus on targeted cognitive skills.

Resources 8.3 and 8.4, downloadable via the Online Resource Centre, give examples of specific whole class lessons and session plans for individual and small groups that include mediated metacognitive moments. In Resource 8.4, the examples that relate to literacy and numeracy will be relevant for specialist teachers supporting individuals with diagnostic labels of, for example, dyslexia and dyscalculia. Metacognition is often recommended as an important element of support for learners with these diagnostic labels (for example, Chinn, 2020; Reid, 2020; Selby, 2025).

The following box shows what steps four and five might look like for Joseph

First of all, some preparation was carried out with Joseph. This involved explaining the goals clearly to him (intentionality criterion): 'What does paying attention look like? How do we know when we are ready to learn?' 'Your feet on the floor, your back against the chair, your book open in front of you. Your hands on the table and your eyes, looking at Ms ...' [class teacher]. 'Paying attention is important because it means we will know what to do' (meaning criterion). Planning was also discussed, starting with making sure that Joseph knew what a plan is. Meaning was mediated using language such as: 'Making a plan is important because then we don't miss anything.'

Visual reminders were given as well, using symbols to show looking and listening. A visual plan was drawn up in order to illustrate being 'ready to learn'. For example, feet on the floor, empty hands, eyes towards the front (or person speaking).

Joseph was seated close to the front of the class, but to the side, to minimise distractions from other pupils. When he was moved, his teacher explained (*mediation of meaning*): 'This is to help you listen/pay attention so other children don't disturb you.' He was given a task board to help him plan his work.

Ms ... [teacher or class TA] would quietly step over to Joseph's desk and just point to something on the page and smile, or say 'Good work, keep going', giving gentle prompts without disturbing other pupils (competence criterion). The frequency of prompts was gradually reduced so that Joseph took over more of his self-regulation and attention. Challenge was mediated by familiar adults asking him: 'I think you're ready to keep going a bit longer with this task', or: 'I think you're ready to follow more steps of your plan on your own?' 'Let's have a go.'

The task board was used with support initially, where the TA and Joseph would jointly make a plan. Increasing independence was promoted by gradually reducing the TA input in making the plan and in following it. The TA would start by asking Joseph: 'What does finished look like?', then use his response to make a step by step plan. In addition, the TA ensured that he could revisit the goal and check if all parts of the plan had been carried out. This is the final step in attention: checking behaviour.

Step six: monitor, record, reflect and feedback

This final step of the framework aims to provide a means of looping back to step one, reflecting the cyclical nature of the APDR model that we have linked to the framework. This step should quite naturally lead you back to further mediation of cognitive skills and emotional states. The essential questions to be asked as part of this step are:

- What worked?
- What needs more work?
- Do I need to continue working on the same cognitive skills/emotional states, or should these be changed?
- Do I need to make changes to the way I am mediating?

Ongoing monitoring is the way in which these questions can be addressed.

As we have emphasised, the embedded approach is suitable for whole class, individual and small group teaching. The way in which learner progress related to cognitive goals is monitored will vary according to the context. In individual and small group contexts, it is much easier to track progress due to the small numbers and the fact that the cognitive goals are likely to be more 'bespoke'; that is, they have been identified via an individual learner cognitive profile. This is not such an easy task for whole class embedded cognitive goals, where the goals and focus are less likely to be specifically targeted as a result of individual assessment. The Educational Endowment Foundation (EEF; 2025a: 41) comments: 'It is widely recognised that the reliable assessment of self regulated learning and metacognition is challenging. Nevertheless, assessment is crucial to guide practice in the classroom. Alongside typical standardised test performance, there are more qualitative assessments that teachers can use.' The EEF report suggests a number of approaches useful for whole class monitoring:

- Asking learners to demonstrate specific cognitive strategies;
- Observing learners (the EEF guidance notes that this is a useful means of picking up on non-verbal behaviours, interactions with others and time on task); Noting learners' use of any visual cues and displays in the classroom;
- Self-report questionnaires;
- Asking pupils to talk through their thinking and problem-solving.

All of the above can be applied to monitoring embedded mediated learning. Specific procedures will vary according to the cognitive focus. For example, continuing with the attention goal that we have looked at in the target setting section and for Joseph, monitoring might look something like:

- Asking: 'show me how you pay attention';
- Sampling on task behaviour;
- Noticing whether learners refer to the wall display about good listening;
- Asking learners to rate their attention;
- Asking learners to tell you what they did to stay focused;
- Asking learners (if mature enough) to say how maintaining attention helped their learning and their activities.

For all contexts, learner self-monitoring can be carried out using the suggestions made in Chapter 4.

Recording

There is no set method of recording mediated learning. The way in which you capture what has happened will depend on the context for delivering mediated learning. For example:

- For whole class input, a lesson planning framework generally has a section for noting outcomes;
- For individual or small group input, tools such as tracking sheets, observation checklists or an ongoing anecdotal session by session diary can be helpful;
- For an assessment session, strategies such as contemporaneous notes or a checklist of key aspects of the assessment tools related to cognitive skills, emotional states and mediated learning can be helpful. You might find Resource 6.5 helpful. This was introduced in Chapter 6 as a tool for planning mediated learning. It also includes two sections at the end for recording and then reflecting on mediated learning.

Reflecting

Reflective practices

Reflective practice is a common feature of the standards for many professional groups. It is mentioned specifically in HCPC (Health and Care Professions Council) Professional Standards for Practitioner Psychologists and Speech and Language Therapists, in National Professional Qualifications for SENCos, in Teachers' Standards and in standards for Teaching Assistants such as the Apprenticeship route. Therefore, reflection on mediation will be relevant for the range of professionals for whom we are writing this text.

Using a rating scale to support reflective practice

Rating scales for mediated learning are a common approach for supporting reflective practice (for example, Lidz, 1991; 2003; Mentis et al., 2008; Hasson, 2018; Lauchlan and Daly, 2023). We have also drawn up a rating scale for the mediation criteria that we are using in this publication. The rating scale (Resource 8.5) can be accessed via the Online Resource Centre. It can be used in conjunction with the mediation planner and tracker (Resource 6.5).

Principles

There are three important principles related to use of a rating scale, which we feel are important in ensuring that it is a tool for self-improvement and for personal growth rather than a stick with which to beat oneself (or others!). These are:

- It should enhance practice and assist in the final step of the six-step mediation framework. It is not designed simply to be completed to 'prove' that mediated learning has taken place. We are very aware of the paperwork tsunami that is the reality of professional life (lesson plans, marking, report writing, contact records to name just a few examples) so the rating scale should not add to that burden;
- It is not designed to be part of an individual's professional appraisal; for example, where observation of practice takes place and is then fed back in managerial supervision or appraisal;
- Similar to the previous bullet point, on a more general level, the rating scale is not designed to be used to make judgements, especially where the individual being judged has no background or training in mediated learning. For example, observing a learner in their usual setting (such as home, classroom, nursery) is often part of gathering information about them. The way in which they interact with that environment can give useful insights. If the parent or practitioner being observed has no background or experience of mediated learning, it must be made clear that using a mediated learning rating scale is not about rating them but about noting the learner's response to the adult/learner interactions. The emphasis is on collaboration for joint planning, not judgement.

Practice

Some suggestions for using the rating scale are:

- For self-reflection, where practitioners complete and use the rating scale as part of ongoing professional development of practice related to mediated learning. This might lead to insights for alterations in practice, seeking further training or carrying out further reading or research. The person who facilitates this process is mediating to the key adults to support their awareness and metacognitive journey, as much as the adults are mediating to the learner (see, for example, Section B of the Cognitive Abilities Profile);
- To inform next steps for the learner. The rating scale can assist in considering the learner's response in relation to the type of mediation and the level of assistance given.

Where there is little or no response to mediation it is important to avoid situating this wholly within the learner. Therefore, a helpful way of framing the learner response is something like: '*in the time available I was not able to offer an appropriate type or level of mediation to bring about a change*'. Of course, there will also be instances of learner resistance which can challenge delivery of mediated learning. Your knowledge of the learner and professional judgement should help you to untangle this;

- For peer supervision or peer assisted learning, where a group of professionals agree to share and discuss practice, having previously completed the rating scale;
- For observation and feedback. Bearing in mind the principles above related to making judgements, observing another individual's practice must be a transparent process where the person being observed consents to the observation. As example might be where colleagues agree to observe each other and then compare notes and ratings as part of their professional development. Callicott and Limniotis' (2019) work about video feedback is very helpful. On a less formal level, it might be appropriate to comment on practice that was mediational and which was supportive of the learner, using mediation criteria as a broad guide.

Feedback

The way in which feedback is given will clearly be context-specific, depending on who is giving feedback. Mediated learning is all about feedback since it is essentially an interactive process that is a collaboration between mediator and learner. Therefore, when delivering mediated learning you will consciously be feeding back to the learner, reflecting the essential criterion of reciprocity, where mediation is adjusted according to the learner response. Other feedback contexts are where the outcomes of an assessment of cognitive skills and emotional states and/or a period of mediated learning are fed back and discussed. This might take the form of a written communication, meeting or both. For individual learners, this feedback might be linked to periodic reviews of their individual plan.

Feedback can be formative or summative. Formative feedback involves a process of using the information given and discussed to plan next steps for the learner. Summative feedback is where results are given with no indication of next steps for the learner (a little like receiving public examination results). In our experience, a summative model is often found in the work of external professionals, in the form of reports that list tests and scores for cognition but then make no reference to this aspect of the assessment in the recommendations. This links us back to Chapter 1, which discussed static and flexible approaches to assessment. A static approach, based on the notion of fixed intelligence, is much more likely to result in a summative assessment for cognition, because it is underpinned by a belief that change is unlikely. Moving from a summative to a formative approach in feedback about cognition is, in our experience, a frequent missing link in practice. Therefore, our focus here is on a formative approach (see our earlier reference to the work of Black and Wiliam [1998] who emphasised the importance of formative teaching and the positive outcomes in terms of greater achievements and learner motivation). The idea of mediational feedback, discussed in the next section, reflects this formative approach.

Mediational feedback

Mediational feedback is an approach to feedback that uses the criteria of mediation to give a structure for an interaction that focuses on the processes of learning, not the products. That said, we are not suggesting that any reference to the products of learning should not feature. The whole point of our embedded approach is that metacognitive teaching and support is delivered in a curriculum context, using the products of learning as a vehicle for the processes.

Feedback can be written or verbal. Clearly, the kind of language used in each of these contexts will vary, even though the message will be the same. Therefore, in a mediational feedback model, the criteria apply however the feedback is delivered, but the way in which they are communicated will alter. Table 8.5 suggests ways of linking mediation criteria to feedback.

Mediational feedback can be used with key staff working with the learner, with parents or carers and with the learner. Some creative approaches to engaging parents in the feedback process might be helpful; for example, a short input for all parents on parents' evening to explain the idea of a metacognitive (thinking) classroom, including ideas that parents or carers can follow up at home.

Chapter 4 discussed mediational consultation. As a reminder, our definition of this approach is: a collaborative process that uses the criteria of mediation in order to:

- Gather information about the learner's current cognitive skills;
- Use scaling in order to identify the level of concern about the learner's current cognitive skills;
- Agree goals for the learner, using scaling to think about changes at, for example, half a point further up the scale:
- Prioritise the focus and type of support;
- Agree a future review to support monitoring and evaluation.

Mediational consultation can be used to feedback and review progress and if needed, to carry out further identification of cognitive skills and priorities.

Table 8.5 Mediation criteria linked to feedback

Criterion	***Description***	***Links to feedback***
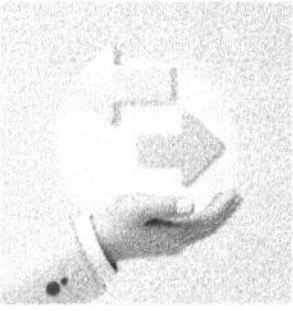 **Intentionality and reciprocity**	Mediation is intentional. The mediator adjusts their mediation.	Making sure that there is explicit reference to cognitive skills and emotional states. In verbal feedback, the course and flow of the conversation is adjusted according to the response of participants.
 **Meaning**	Sharing the purpose. Why is this relevant and important?	Our cognitive skills are important because ... Our emotional states are important because ... Emphasise the foundational nature of the above, explain why it is important to focus on these and how they relate to the content of the curriculum. Use the House of Metacognition model.
 **Transfer**	Making links to past, present and future learning.	Showing how the cognitive skills and emotional states are applied to many contexts. A key focus might be on making curriculum links, but other links might also be important. For example, where the concerns are related to social, emotional and mental health, links can be made to show how cognitive skills can be applied (such as causal thinking related to thinking through the consequences of one's actions).
 **Positive affirmation and empathy**	Accepting what others bring to the interaction (being non-judgemental) but also expressing optimism and confidence that cognitive and affective change can happen.	In verbal communication, active listening will be important. In written communication, emphasising the flexible nature of cognition, expressing confidence that the learner's thinking can change and improve. This needs care however; make sure you let your audience know you are there to support them and that supporting cognitive change and metacognition can take time.
 **Regulation**	This criterion might not be needed routinely; however, in some cases where there is an emotionally charged discussion, mediating regulation might be helpful. This might involve ensuring that you stay calm and regulated. Using other criteria such as positive affirmation and empathy might help to prevent the need to focus on regulation and sharing behaviour. We can discuss things and we can disagree and at the same time respect that we have different perspectives.	

(Continued)

Table 8.5 (Continued)

Criterion	***Description***	***Links to feedback***
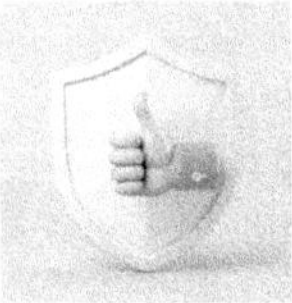 **Competence**	Positive feedback.	Focus on what is already working well for the learner. In written and verbal feedback, always feed back strengths as well as areas of need.
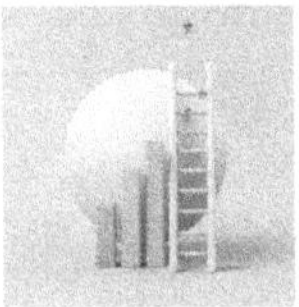 **Challenge**	Stretching: what else? What more?	Make sure that your recommendations reflect the Zone of Proximal Development, via suggestions that are just in advance of where the learner is now. The rating scale will help with this process. Say (or in a conversation, elicit) what an increase in, for example, half a point would look like.
 **Goal setting**	Planning.	Identifying broad and specific cognitive outcomes. Target setting (see previous section of this chapter). Always focus on the processes.

Learner feedback: addressing a missing link

The suggestions in the previous section are designed to be applied to a range of audiences, including the learner. However, feedback to learners can be a frequent missing link. We find that this is very much the case for external professional work, where the constraints of time often mean that feedback is confined to the key adults, or the written communication requirements are not very learner-friendly. In this section we would like to suggest ideas for learner feedback. It is interesting to note that of the four norm referenced tests discussed in the blended assessment section of Chapter 4, the CAS-2 is the only test that emphasises the importance of learner feedback. As noted, the CAS-2 is based on a flexible model of intelligence; it may be that static tests of intelligence do not emphasise feedback to the learner as important because testing is done to the learner; it is not a collaborative process. There is no joint analysis of performance or ways of improving, nor mutual discussion of ways of changing. There is no right or wrong way to provide feedback. It can be verbal, or in some written form. Obviously, the way in which is it done will depend on the learner's age and developmental level.

In addition to the suggestions above, we have often used feedback letters to learners. The idea is that the learner can read the letter independently, with a key adult in their educational setting and/or with their parent(s). There are example extracts in the Resource Centre (Resource 8.6) that you can download. We would normally add some illustrations but these are not included in the examples in order to avoid any copyright issues.

The box below shows what step six might look like for Joseph.

Cognitive feedback was given: 'Well done, Joseph, you tried hard to keep paying attention and do ... It will get easier, and I am here to help you.' Or: 'Well done, Joseph, you tried hard to follow your plan. It will get easier, and I am here to help you' (positive affirmation and empathy and competence criteria).

Joseph's TA, teacher and parents were asked to avoid saying to Joseph: 'See you did it. I knew you could!' This sounds counterintuitive; however, announcing success is often scary for a child (and an older person!) with low self-esteem. Unconsciously, they may sabotage their own performance the next day. Praise effort, always using cognitive feedback, but not achievement, especially early in the learning journey.

Feedback when things have not gone well: 'Today it was a bit more difficult for you to keep paying attention/follow your plan. Don't worry, tomorrow we will try again. Some days it is easier than other days. I'm here to help you.' This reflects the positive affirmation and empathy criterion of mediation. It is honest and, at the same time, your care and concern shows without giving long speeches telling Joseph that you believe in him. His 'team of adults' were also asked to avoid saying things like 'You can do it!'; if a learner has low self-esteem and doubts their own capacity, announcing that they will succeed can increase their feeling of fear of failure.

Recording: The class TA and class teacher made brief observational notes. At half term, the cognitive goal was reviewed in order to decide whether any adjustments were needed for the second half term.

Part of Joseph's visual support included three cards showing

☺ 😐 ☹ which were used for him to self-rate attention and whether he had followed his plan and finished his task(s).

Wider dissemination

When we introduced our embedded model, we emphasised that our goal was not to bring about any wholesale systemic change. However, this does not rule out creating, identifying and using opportunities for wider dissemination. This might form part of a setting's professional development. The content of this book will enable you to develop materials to disseminate the embedded approach to mediated learning, supporting the delivery of metacognitive teaching.

Mediated learning might be something quite new for the individuals with whom you are working and collaborating. When you feed back and discuss learners, follow-up information to leave with, for example, class teachers, early years practitioners or parents might be helpful. Resource 8.8 is an example of an information sheet about mediated learning (minus any illustrations, which you can add to suit your audience).

In addition to generic dissemination focusing on, for example, cognitive skills, executive function and metacognition. Below, we discuss two specific target audiences for wider dissemination: TAs and early years practitioners. Of course, dissemination is not limited to these two examples.

Teaching assistants

TA roles and deployment has been the topic of recent guidance (Educational Endowment Foundation, 2025b). The EEF guidance is built on a body of previous research (for example, Blatchford et al., 2012; Basford et al., 2017) about effective deployment of TAs, suggesting that their effectiveness can be very dependent on how they deliver support. Scaffolding is one area in the deployment literature which receives a great deal of attention, because there can be a tendency to over-assist learners and thus reduce the possibility of independent learning. Mediated learning is an ideal mechanism for ensuring supporting the learner towards independence. Depending on your role and the context for the dissemination, it might be helpful to have a briefing or discussion with the leadership team, including anyone who is responsible for day-to-day TA management and deployment (often this is the SENDCo).

Early years practitioners: 'readiness to learn'

The second example of a specific audience is early years practitioners. Brain development in the first five years of life is at its most rapid, but the rate of development can be affected by the child's environment and other factors. Working in the early years means that we are working with children at a stage of great brain plasticity and thus an emphasis on developing cognitive skills is very important. This section reflects a recognition of the importance of early years education, especially as large numbers of young children are accessing some kind of care and education settings from a very early age (for example, UK government statistics for 2025 indicate that 94 per cent of three- and four-year-olds accessed some form of preschool education; Explore Education Statistics, 2025).

The EYFS (Early Years Foundation Stage; Department for Education, 2024) curriculum in England is for birth to age five. The guidance and statutory framework includes 'creating and thinking critically' as one of the characteristics of effective learning. Our experience of early years settings is that this characteristic is often covered in a very incidental way and is afforded less importance than the EYFS Early Learning Goals, which are far more focussed on teaching literacy and numeracy skills (content).

Sustained shared thinking (SST; Sylva et al., 2004; Siraj-Blatchford and Sylva, 2004) is included in the creating and thinking critically section of the EYFS. It is described by Sylva et al. as: 'An episode in which two or more individuals "work together" in an intellectual way to solve a problem, clarify a concept, evaluate activities, extend a narrative, etc. Both parties must contribute to the thinking and it must develop and extend' (Sylva et al., 2004: 36). Despite the emphasis in the EYFS, SST is not very visible. However, as this description is quite abstract, it is perhaps unsurprising that it has not found its way into early years practice. This might also be due to a lack of emphasis on the importance of intentional support for cognition. 'An episode' is rather a vague description of the context for SST. The intentionality criterion of mediated learning makes support for cognitive development much more explicit and less dependent on a 'hit or miss' approach, and can be easily integrated into activities such as child-initiated free flow play sessions. This aspect of early years provision is an ideal context for disseminating an embedded approach for supporting the development of cognitive skills with young children. We would strongly recommend that all early years staff across the board should be trained in cognitive development in young children. Two published programmes can support this recommendation: the Bright Start Cognitive Curriculum for Young Children (available as a freely downloadable resource via www.brightstart-ccyc.com) or Firm Fundations (Lidz, 2015).

Summary

Now that you have completed this chapter you are ready to 'set sail' in the Boat of Cognition and support your learners to become metacognitively aware. This final chapter has introduced the six-step mediation framework, which draws together material from the previous Part II chapters into a structure that will support implementation of mediated learning and metacognitive teaching. The chapter has included guidance and resources that should help you to work through the six-step mediation framework and thus be able to deliver mediated learning with individuals, groups and whole classes. In this chapter, we followed Joseph through the six-step framework. There are two more examples that can be downloaded from the Resource Centre (Resource 8.7) which cover different ages. The chapter also addressed wider dissemination: we hope that your use of mediated learning will interest your colleagues and thus lead to opportunities to communicate and share the importance of process skills for creating successful, independent, metacognitively aware learners.

Finally, the roof is on the House of Metacognition!

Reflection and follow-up

- The previous chapters have systematically filled your toolbox. You are able to select and combine the right tools for the task. Many of the examples above are school-related, but you will have well understood that mediated learning, executive functioning and metacognitive interventions are absolutely not limited to school nor to children's learning. It is lifelong. Therefore, if you are not working directly with school-age learners, consider how you can implement this approach and these practical tools in your professional practice.
- Use the six-step framework to plan some mediation whether for your own use or in an advisory role.
- What changes you might make in your work as a result of this chapter and of the book as a whole?
- What opportunities might you have for wider dissemination? How could you follow these up?

Last words

At the beginning of this book, we spoke about how our beliefs are the basis for our actions, emphasising being committed to helping people change. Change is not limited to the learner but also to the essential supports that surround the learner: parents, carers, education systems and broader societal systems. At the systemic level, do we look at our jobs, with all their genuine constraints, time limits, policies and procedures, and ask, in the words of Feuerstein: 'Have I done everything I can to change this child?' 'Do our actions strengthen our belief in what we hold to be important and worthwhile?'

We hope that this book will be one of your tools to go beyond the here and now and help you create many Zones of Proximal Development, using mediated learning to help others reach the goal of metacognitive awareness. In doing so, you are extending your own unique humanity as a giver and facilitator to others so that many learners will have benefited and will continue to benefit from what you give them. Every day is a new opportunity to grow and learn.

References

Basford, E., Butt, G. and Newton, R. (2017). To what extent are teaching assistants really managed? 'I was thrown in the deep end, really; I just had to more or less get on with it'. *School Leadership & Management*, 37(3), 288-310.

Black, P. and Wiliam, D. (1998). *Inside the Black Box: Raising Standards Through Classroom Assessment*. London: King's College London School of Education.

Blatchford, P., Russell, A. and Webster, R. (2012). *Reassessing the Impact of Teaching Assistants*. London: Routledge Fulton.

Callicott, K. and Limniotis, M. (2019). Dynamic assessment: supporting educational psychologists' practice through the use of video during supervision. *Educational Psychology in Practice*, 36(3), 1-9.

Chinn, S. (2020). *More Trouble with Maths*. London: Routledge.

Choo, O.A. (2000). Infusing thinking into curriculum content. Paper presented at the AARE Annual Conference, Sydney.

Department for Education (2024). Early years foundation stage statutory framework for group and school-based providers. Available at: www.assets.publishing.service.gov.uk/media/65aa5e4 2ed27ca001327b2c7/EYFS_statutory_framework_for_group_and_school_based_providers.pdf. Accessed 24 November 2025.

Department for Education (2026). *Every Child Achieving and Thriving*. Available at: www.gov.uk/ government/publications/every-child-achieving-and-thriving. Accessed 24 February 2026.

Department for Education and Department of Health (2015). *Special Educational Needs and Disabilities Code of Practice*. London: Stationery Office.

Deutsch, R.M. (2020). *The Cognitive Abilities Profile*. Canterbury: Real Publishing.

Education Endowment Foundation (EEF) (2025[[a]]). *Metacognition and Self Regulated Learning*. Available at: www.educationendowmentfoundation.org.uk/education-evidence/guidance-reports /metacognition. Accessed 14 January 2026.

Education Endowment Foundation (EEF) (2025[[b]]). *Deployment of Teaching Assistants Guidance Report*. Available at: www. educationendowmentfoundation.org.uk/education-evidence/guidance -reports/teaching-assistants. Accessed 14 January 2026.

European Agency for Development in Special Needs Education (2003). *Special Needs Education in Europe. Thematic Publication*. Available at: www.european-agency.org. Accessed 1 January 2026.

Explore Education Statistics (2025). Funded early education and childcare. Available at: www .education-statistics.services.gov.uk. Accessed 4 March 2026.

Goldstein, S., Naglieri, J.A., Princiotta, D. and Otero, T.M. (2014). A history of executive functioning as a theoretical and clinical construct. In S. Goldstein and J. Naglieri (Eds), *Handbook of Executive Functioning*. New York: Springer.

Hasson, N. (2018). *The Dynamic Assessment of Language Learning*. Abingdon: Routledge.

Haywood, H. (1990). Behavior management in cognitive early education. *European Journal of Psychology of Education*, 5(2), 243-252.

Haywood, H.C., Brooks, P. and Burns, M.S. (2022). Bright Start Cognitive Curriculum for Young Children, rev. edn. Bright Start CCYC. Available at: www.brightstart-ccyc.com.

Individuals with Disabilities Education Act (USA) (2004). Available at: www.sites.ed.gov. Accessed 1 January 2026.

Lauchlan, F. and Daly, C. (2023). *Applying Dynamic Assessment in Schools*. London: Jessica Kingsley.

Lidz, C. (1991). *Practitioner's Guide to Dynamic Assessment*. New York: Guilford.

Lidz, C. (2003). *Early Childhood Assessment*. New Jersey: Wiley.

Lidz, C. (2015). *Firm Fundations Program: Parents and Teachers Working Together to Facilitate Young Children's Learning*. DOI:10.13140/RG.2.1.3813.8400

Mentis, M., Dunn-Berenstein, M. and Mentis, M. (2008). *Mediated Learning: Teaching, Tasks and Tools to Unlock Cognitive Potential*. Thousand Oaks: Corwin Press.

Naglieri, J. and Otero, T. (2017). *Essentials of CAS2 Assessment*. Hoboken New Jersey: John Wiley.

Reid, G. (2020). *Dyslexia and Inclusion: Classroom Approaches for Assessment, Teaching and Learning*. London: Routledge.

Selby, L. (2025). *All about Dyslexia*. London: Routledge.

Siraj-Blatchford, I. and Sylva, K. (2004). Researching pedagogy in early childhood education. *International Journal of Educational Research*, 41(2), 105-117.

Spooner, L. and Woodcock, J. (2013). *Teaching Children to Listen in Primary Schools*. London: Bloomsbury Featherstone.

Sylva, K., Siraj-Blatchford, I., Taggert, B., Sammons, P., Elliot, K. and Melhuish, E. (2004). *The Effective Provision of Preschool Education (EPPE) Project Technical Paper 12 - The Final Report: Effective Preschool Education*. London: DfES and Institute of Education, University of London.

Appendix 1
Further Information

In addition to the references at the end of each chapter and downloadable resources, the following might be helpful.

For more information about Catherine Hart, illustrator: www.instagram.com/imagemagicc ollection/.

Dynamic Assessment and the Cognitive Abilities Profile

www.dynamicassessment.co.uk.

Dynamic Assessment for Young Children (DAYC): tzuried@mail.biu.ac.il.

Feuerstein Institute: www.feuerstein-institute.org.

In 1990 BBC TV showed a programme about Feuerstein as part of a series called *The Transformers*. This series was about individuals whose work had transformed people's lives. The programme about Feuerstein was called 'Out of the Wilderness'. This link will take you to the whole of the programme. It is over an hour long but it is well worth watching. The link is: https://www.youtube.com/watch?v=isnmUN4IfxA.

Executive function

Peg Dawson and Richard Guare's website: www.smartbutscatteredkids.com.

The Harvard Centre for the Developing Child: www.developingchild.harvard.edu/resource -guides/guide-executivefunction.

Metacognition/thinking skills

Bright Start: Cognitive Curriculum for Young Children (CCYC) www.brightstart-ccyc.com.

Structural Learning: Paul Main's website: www.structural-learning.com.

The Education Endowment Foundation Metacognition starter kit is available via: https://d2tic4wvo1iusb.cloudfront.net/production/eef-guidance-reports/metacognition/Metacognition-A-starter-kit.pdf.

Self Regulated Strategy Development (SRSD) is an instructional approach that teaches cognitive and self regulation strategies explicitly. It has been applied to supporting written expression: see www.srsdonline.org and to supporting maths: see www.teachsrsdmath.com.

Helping Children Learn: Intervention Handouts for Use in School and at Home by Eric Pickering and Jack Naglieri is a book of handouts related to the four PASS (Planning, Attention, Simultaneous, Successive) areas assessed in the CAS2 Cognitive Assessment System test. Published by Brookes Publishing.

Index

For Product Safety Concerns and Information please contact our EU
representative GPSR@taylorandfrancis.com
Taylor & Francis Verlag GmbH, Kaufingerstraße 24, 80331 München, Germany

www.ingramcontent.com/pod-product-compliance
Lightning Source LLC
LaVergne TN
LVHW060159031026
849361LV00022B/301
* 9 7 8 1 0 4 1 1 0 4 8 9 6 *